ISBN 978-1-333-46954-2
PIBN 10508324

This book is a reproduction of an important historical work. Forgotten Books uses state-of-the-art technology to digitally reconstruct the work, preserving the original format whilst repairing imperfections present in the aged copy. In rare cases, an imperfection in the original, such as a blemish or missing page, may be replicated in our edition. We do, however, repair the vast majority of imperfections successfully; any imperfections that remain are intentionally left to preserve the state of such historical works.

English
Français
Deutsche
Italiano
Español
Português

www.forgottenbooks.com

Mythology Photography **Fiction**
Fishing Christianity **Art** Cooking
Essays Buddhism Freemasonry
Medicine **Biology** Music **Ancient
Egypt** Evolution Carpentry Physics
Dance Geology **Mathematics** Fitness
Shakespeare **Folklore** Yoga Marketing
Confidence Immortality Biographies
Poetry **Psychology** Witchcraft
Electronics Chemistry History **Law**
Accounting **Philosophy** Anthropology
Alchemy Drama Quantum Mechanics
Atheism Sexual Health **Ancient History**
Entrepreneurship Languages Sport
Paleontology Needlework Islam
Metaphysics Investment Archaeology
Parenting Statistics Criminology
Motivational

❧ ❧ ❧ and Its Celebrities

By

⊹

In Three Volumes
Volume II.

Boston ❧ ❧ ❧ ❧ ❧

❧ ❧ ❧ MDCCCCII

CONTENTS.

CHAPTER VII.

CHEAPSIDE.

CHAPTER VIII.

NEIGHBOURHOOD OF ST. PAUL'S.

CHAPTER IX.

ST. PAUL'S CATHEDRAL.

CONTENTS.

LIST OF ILLUSTRATIONS

London, Vol. II.

LONDON AND ITS CELEBRITIES.

CHAPTER I.

THE PRIORY AND CHURCH OF ST. BARTHOLOMEW.

St. Bartholomew's Priory and Church — When Built — Its Present Appearance — Refectory, Crypt, and Subterranean Passage — Bartholomew Close — Monuments in the Church — Story of Rahere, Founder of the Priory — Fracas in the Priory — St. Bartholomew's Hospital — Canonbury — Canonbury Tower — Goldsmith's Residence — Prior Bolton's Residence — Bartholomew Fair.

On the southeastern side of Smithfield stand the remains of the beautiful church and once vast and wealthy priory of St. Bartholomew, founded by Rahere, the first prior, in the reign of Henry the First. At the time of the suppression of the religious houses in the reign of Henry the Eighth, it was distinguished by its vast extent of building, its beautiful and shady gardens, its exquisite cloisters, its grand refectory, its fish-ponds, and by all the appurtenances of a great monastic establishment. Its mulberry garden, planted by Prior Bolton, was famous.

Passing under a gateway rich with carved roses and zigzag ornaments, we enter the fine old church of St. Bartholomew. As we gaze on the solidity of its massive pillars, its graceful arches, and the beauty of its architectural details, we are at once impressed with that sense of grandeur and solemnity which only such a scene can inspire. The remains of the old church are in the Norman style of architecture, and are apparently of the same date as the earlier portions of Winchester Cathedral. Some notion of its former magnificence may be conceived, when we mention that the present church is merely the chancel of the ancient edifice.

Surrounded by mean hovels and by a population of the lowest description, the exterior of the ancient priory, though degraded to strange purposes, is notwithstanding scarcely less interesting than the interior. Beauty and decay meet us at every step. In order to view the noble arches of the ancient cloisters, we must dive into a timberyard; while the old refectory, formerly one of the noblest halls in London, has long been converted into a manufactory. The fine oaken roof still remains. The exterior of the building has been sadly modernised, and the interior has been subdivided by intermediate roofs and ceilings, but still sufficient remains to recall vividly to our imaginations the days when this noble apartment was the scene of ecclesiastical hospitality, and brilliant with all the splendid paraphernalia of the Church of Rome.

The refectory stands on the south side of the church, near the end of the south transept, and is immediately connected with the beautiful eastern cloister, which, with its clustered columns and carved bosses, is now the only one which remains. Beneath the refectory is the ancient crypt, which, notwithstanding the beauty of its architecture, and its rare state of preservation, is but seldom visited and but little known. It is of great length, with a double row of finely proportioned aisles. At the extremity of this gloomy and vaulted crypt is a door, which, according to tradition, opens into a subterranean passage extending to Canonbury, formerly a rural appendage of the priors of St. Bartholomew, at Islington. Similar idle stories are not unfrequently attached to old monastic ruins, as in the cases of Malmesbury, Netley, and Glastonbury. That the door in question, however, was formerly used as a means of escape in the hour of danger, there is reason to believe. Till very recently it opened into a cellar which extended beneath a chapel, known as St. Bartholomew's Chapel, which was destroyed by fire in 1830. This chapel is known to have been secretly used by the Reformers of the fifteenth and sixteenth centuries, the passage we have referred to having afforded them a ready means of escape in the event of their being disturbed by the officers of the law.

Consequent on the accumulation of the dust

of centuries, the ground which encompasses the church of St. Bartholomew has gradually risen three or four feet, and the foundations of the nave and the entrances to the edifice are now considerably below the soil of the churchyard. As regards the eastern cloister, to such a height has the soil accumulated, that the spring of the arches is now level with the ground.

At the south side of the church was the great close of the old priory, the site of which is now occupied by modern buildings, but which still bears the name of Bartholomew Close. The lesser close, in which stood the prior's stables, the kitchens, and offices, was situated at the east end of the church, and also still preserves its designation of the Little Close. The former is especially interesting from its connection with the fortunes of Milton. At the Restoration of Charles the Second, the prominent part which the great poet had acted under the Protectorate had rendered him a proscribed man, and accordingly we find him seeking a refuge in the house of a friend in Bartholomew Close, where he remained concealed till he found himself included in the general amnesty. Doctor Johnson thinks, and with some reason, that his escape was secretly favoured by the government. That he was in the custody of the sergeant-at-arms, at least for a short time, is proved by the following curious entries in the books of the House of Commons: "Saturday, December 15, 1660, ordered that **Mr.** Milton, now in custody of the sergeant-at-arms attending this House, be forthwith released on paying his fees." And again, on Monday, the 17th: "A complaint made that the sergeant-at-arms had demanded excessive fees for the imprisonment of Mr. Milton ; ordered that it be referred to the Committee for Privileges to examine this business, and to call Mr. Milton and the sergeant before them, and to determine what is fit to be given the sergeant for his fees in this case." After his liberation, Milton took up his abode in Holborn, near Red Lion Fields.

In Bartholomew Close resided that classical artist, Hubert le Sœur, to whom we owe the beautiful statue of Charles the First at Charing Cross. He had a son, Isaac, who was buried on the 29th of November, 1630, in the neighbouring church of St. Bartholomew. Here, too, Benjamin Franklin carried on his vocation of a journeyman printer for nearly a year.

The most interesting monument in St. Bartholomew's Church is that of the founder of the Priory, Rahere. This fine specimen of the pointed style of architecture represents the effigy of the founder in his prior's dress, recumbent beneath a canopy, with an angel kneeling at his feet, and monks praying by his side. The monument is inscribed :

" Hic jacet Raherus,
Primus Canonicus, et primus Prior hujus Ecclesiæ."

no date, but from its style of architecture
have been erected many years after the
the founder.

er interesting monument in St. Bartholo-
'hurch is that of Sir Walter Mildmay,
of Emanuel College, Cambridge, who
prominent part as a courtier and a states-
ring the reigns of Henry the Eighth,
the Sixth, and Queen Elizabeth. He
of the commissioners sent to Fotheringay
o conduct the trial of Mary Queen of
nd it was to him personally that the
late queen addressed herself when she
her innocence of the crimes with which
charged, and denied the right of Elizabeth
her to trial. The monument to Sir Henry,
s finely executed in marble, and of great
sents a mixture of the Gothic and classic
f architecture, the union of which in the
h century was then for the first time
into vogue.

circumstances which led to the foundation
riory of St. Bartholomew are full of inter-
ahere, though a man of mean lineage, was
l by nature with all those graceful quali-
nind and body which help to make up for
ciencies of birth. Witty and lively in his
on, an accomplished libertine, and a fin-
usician, he was gifted with all those arts
ender their possessor welcome to the tables

of the great, and which, in the days when literature was almost entirely confined to the priesthood,
were a certain pass-key to the bower of the lady
and the revels of her lord.   His sovereign, Henry
the First, delighted in his society.   Rahere
charmed him by his songs, and fascinated him
by his wit.   According to an old monkish writer,
" He often haunted the king's palace, and among
the noiseful press of that tumultuous court con-
formed himself with polity and cardinal suavity,
by the which he drew to himself the hearts of
many a one.   There, in spectacles, in meetings,
in plays, and other courtly mockeries and trifles,
he led the business of the day.   This-wise to the
king and great men ; gentle and courteously
known, familiar and fellowly he was." [1]

Of the circumstances which impelled the courtly
Rahere to exchange a life of voluptuousness and
pleasure for one of asceticism and sanctity, but
little appears to be known.   He was still in the
full vigour of life, still in the full enjoyment of its
gratifications, when, on a sudden, he absented
himself from his accustomed haunts, and "decreed
himself to go to the court of Rome, coveting in
so great a labour to do the works of penance."
" While he tarried there," says the same old monkish writer, "he began to be vexed with grievous
sickness, and his dolours encreasing, he drew to

[1] Stow styles him " a pleasant-witted gentleman, and therefore in his time called the king's minstrel."

the extreme of life; the which, dreading within himself that he had not yet satisfied God for his sins, he supposed that God took vengeance of him for them amongst outlandish people, and deemed that the last hour of his death drew nigh. This remembering inwardly, he shed out, as water, his heart in the sight of God, and all brake out in tears. He avowed that if God would grant him health that he might return to his own country, he would make an hospital for the recreation of poor men, that they being so there gathered, he might minister necessaries to them after his power. And not long after, the benign and merciful Lord beheld this weeping man, restored him his health, and approved his vow."

Shortly after this, probably while under the influence of fever, a celestial vision — having the "majesty of a king, of great beauty and imperial authority" — is said to have appeared to the repentant voluptuary. "I am Bartholomew," he said, "the apostle of Jesus Christ, that come to succour thee in thine anguish, and to open to thee the sacred mysteries of heaven. Know me truly, by the will and commandment of the Holy Trinity, and the common favour of the celestial court and council, to have chosen a place in the suburbs of London, at Smithfield, where in my name thou shalt found a church. This spiritual house Almighty God shall inhabit, and hallow it, and glorify it. Wherefore doubt thee nought; only give thy diligence, and my part shall be to provide necessaries, direct, build, and end this work."

In due time Rahere, by his influence at court, not only obtained possession of the required site at Smithfield, but by working on the pious feelings of the rich, was enabled to perfect his great work. Moreover, the same engaging charm of manner which had rendered him the associate of courtiers and of kings, had its influence also over the ignorant and the poor, on whose better feelings he had wrought so successfully as to induce them to afford him their manual labour with little prospect of reward. When appealing to them individually, the fascination of his address is said to have been irresistible. When he exhorted them collectively, we are told that his eloquence "compelled them unto sighing and weeping."

The spot selected by Rahere for the site of his great monastic establishment was then a mere swamp; the only dry spot in the neighbourhood being at that time the ground on which stood the gallows, or " Elms." Notwithstanding every obstacle, and in spite of many powerful enmities and jealousies, Rahere lived to see his magnificent priory completed in 1113. Fortunately, Henry the First had stood his friend, and by extending to the new priory extraordinary privileges and immunities, showed how satisfied he was of the pious sincerity of his former boon companion, and what a value he set upon his pious work.

Rahere nominated himself the first prior of his own establishment, over which he presided for twenty-two years and six months, at the end of which period he "forsook the clay house of this world and entered the house everlasting." According to monkish authority, not only were numerous miracles wrought in the monastery during the lifetime of the founder, but after his death the sick who paid a pilgrimage to his tomb were restored to health, and the blind to sight.

It was about a century after the death of Rabere that an extraordinary fracas took place within the walls of the priory church, between Boniface, Archbishop of Canterbury, and his attendants, on the one side, and the superior and canons of the establishment on the other. The archbishop, it appears, had in the course of one of his visitations stopped with his suite at the priory of St. Bartholomew, where, though he was received by the holy fathers with all due honours, it was at the same time respectfully intimated to him by the sub-prior, that as the brotherhood had already another learned bishop for their visitor, they could not, out of respect for their established metropolitan, submit to the domination of any other. Indignantly the archbishop expostulated with the sub-prior on his disobedience and that of his brethren, till at length his choler rose so high as to incite him to commit a violent assault upon the former. In the words of Matthew Paris, as quoted by Stow,

the archbishop "rent in pieces the rich cope of the
sub-prior, and trod it under his feet, and thrust
him against a pillar of the chancel with such violence that he had almost killed him." The holy
brethren, seeing the danger to which their sub-
prior was exposed, hurried to his rescue, and in
the disgraceful scuffle which ensued the primate
was thrown on his back. The attendants of the
archbishop were, on their part, not wanting in
zeal. Seeing their master on the ground, — "being all strangers, and their master's countrymen,
born at Provence, — they fell upon the canons, beat
them, tore them, and trod them under feet." The
result was a general "uproar" through the city,
the citizens naturally taking part with their countrymen against the insolent foreigners. The archbishop, to avoid being torn to pieces by the mob,
flew in the first instance to his episcopal palace at
Lambeth, but even then felt himself insecure till
he found himself in the presence and under the
protection of the king.

At the dissolution of the religious houses, the
priory of St. Bartholomew was granted by Henry
the Eighth to Sir Richard Rich, in whose possession it remained till the accession of Queen Mary,
who conferred it on the Black, or Preaching Friars.
After her death it again fell into the hands of the
Rich family, who made it their residence. It was
subsequently inhabited by Sir Walter Mildmay,
whose remains lie interred in the church.

We have already mentioned the magnificent foundation of St. Bartholomew's Hospital, so called from its connection with the priory. "Alfune," writes Stow, "that had not long before built the parish church of St. Giles without Cripplegate, became the first hospitaller, or proctor, for the poor of this house, and went himself daily to the shambles and other markets, where he begged the charity of devout people for their relief." In 1352 the hospital was set apart by Edward the Third for the special relief of the poor and diseased. Four sisters were appointed to administer to their wants and to attend them in their sickness, the entire establishment being placed under the government of a master and eight priests or brethren. About the year 1423 the hospital was repaired by the executors of that munificent lord mayor, Richard Whittington. At the suppression of the monasteries in the reign of Henry the Eighth the interests of the poor were not forgotten, the hospital having been then refounded for the relief of a hundred "sore and diseased" persons.

The staircase of St. Bartholomew's Hospital, painted by Hogarth at his own expense,[1] represents the good Samaritan and the pool of Bethesda, and in another part Rabere laying the foundation-stone,

[1] It appears by the parish register that Hogarth was baptised in the neighbouring church of St. Bartholomew, on the 28th of November, 1697.

with a sick man carried on a bier attended by monks. In the handsome court-room of the hospital is a full-length portrait of Henry the Eighth, as well as portraits of Charles the Second by John Baptist Gaspars, and of Doctor Radcliffe, founder of the Radcliffe Library at Oxford, and a munificent benefactor of the hospital.

The church of St. Bartholomew the Less, though it escaped the great fire, possesses but little interest. It was originally a chapel attached to the priory, but after the dissolution of the monasteries was converted into a parish church for the convenience of those who lived within the precincts of the hospital. At the time when Stow made his survey it contained many ancient monuments and brasses, but unhappily nearly all have been swept away. The original tower still remains, but the church itself, having fallen into decay, was rebuilt by Dance in 1789, and again by the late Thomas Hardwicke in 1823. Inigo Jones was baptised in this church, and here James Heath, the author of the " Chronicle of the Late War," was interred in 1664.

Intimately associated with the priory of St. Bartholomew is its rural appendage of Canonbury, near Islington, a favourite retreat of the old priors. This interesting relic of antiquity, which was presented to the priory by Ralph de Berners in the reign of Edward the First, derives its name partly from having been the residence of the canons or priors, and partly from the word "bury," signifying a court, or dwelling-house.

"Canonbury Tower," writes Hone, "is sixty feet high and seventeen feet square. It is part of an old mansion which appears to have been erected, or much altered, about the reign of Elizabeth. The more ancient edifice was erected by the priors or the canons of St. Bartholomew, Smithfield, and hence was called Canonbury, to whom it appertained until it was surrendered with the priory to Henry the Eighth; and when the religious houses were dissolved, Henry gave the mansion to Thomas, Lord Cromwell. It afterward passed through other hands, till it was possessed by Sir John Spencer, an alderman and Lord Mayor of London, known by the name of 'Rich Spencer.' While he resided at Canonbury, a Dunkirk pirate came over in a shallop to Barking Creek and hid himself with some armed men in Islington Fields, — near the path which Sir John usually took from his house in Crosby Place to this mansion, — with the hope of making him prisoner, but as he remained in town that night, they were glad to make off for fear of detection, and returned to France disappointed of their prey and of the large ransom they calculated on for the release of his person. His sole daughter and heiress, Elizabeth, was carried off in a baker's basket from Canonbury House by William, the second Lord Compton, Lord President of Wales.

He inherited Canonbury, with the rest of Sir John Spencer's wealth, at his death, and was afterward created Earl of Northampton. In this family the manor still remains." "I ranged the old rooms," adds Hone, "and took, perhaps, a last view from the roof. The eye shrank from the wide havoc below. Where new buildings had not covered the sward, it was embowelling for bricks, and kilns emitted flickering fire and sulphurous stench." The present tower was probably built by Sir John Spencer, into whose hands the estate passed in 1570.

Canonbury Tower is rendered especially interesting from its having been frequently the hiding-place of Goldsmith, when threatened with arrest and the gaol. Here, according to tradition, he composed his "Deserted Village" and a part of the "Vicar of Wakefield." That Goldsmith resided here during the whole of the year 1763 and a portion of 1764, there can be no question; the popular authority for presuming the "Vicar of Wakefield" to have been composed in Canonbury Tower being Sir John Hawkins; while, on the other hand, Mr. Mitford, in his "Life of Goldsmith," intimates that Goldsmith composed this charming story during his residence in Wine Office Court, Fleet Street, between the years 1760 and 1762. "Canonbury," writes Washington Irving, "is an ancient brick tower, hard by 'merry Islington,' the remains of a hunting-seat of Queen Elizabeth, where she took the pleasure of the country, when the neighbourhood was all woodland. What gave it particular interest in my eyes, was the circumstance that it had been the residence of a poet. It was here Goldsmith resided when he wrote his 'Deserted Village.' I was shown the very apartment. It was a relic of the original style of the castle, with panelled wainscot and Gothic windows. I was pleased with its air of antiquity, and its having been the residence of poor Goldy."

Goldsmith's apartment is said to have been an old oak room on the first floor, in the eastern corner of which was a large press-bedstead in which he slept. The walls of this apartment present a good example of oak panelling, surpassed, however, by an upper room, which for carving and delicate tracery is hardly to be equalled.

The account given by Washington Irving of the miseries of his " Poor Devil Author" in Canonbury Tower, has probably as much truth in it as fiction. " Sunday came," he writes, " and with it the whole city world, swarming about Canonbury Castle. I could not open my window but I was stunned with shouts and noises from the cricket ground. The late quiet road beneath my windows was alive with the tread of feet and the clack of tongues, and, to complete my misery, I found that my quiet retreat was absolutely a 'show house,' being shown to strangers at sixpence a head.

There was a perpetual tramping up-stairs of citizens and their families to look about the country from the top of the tower, and to take a peep at the city through a telescope, to try if they could discern their own chimneys."

It was probably not in connection with Goldsmith alone that Washington Irving was induced to fix upon Canonbury Tower as the retreat of his "Poor Devil Author." Here, at different times, resided the unfortunate poet, Christopher Smart; David Humphreys, an indifferent poet, author of "Ulysses," an opera; and Ephraim Chambers, the author of the "Cyclopædia."

Behind Canonbury Tower stood till our time a mansion which, according to tradition, was the occasional rural retreat of Queen Elizabeth, and which bore internal evidence of having been anciently the habitation of royalty. The old drawing-room, with its fine stuccoed ceiling, its scroll-work ornaments, and its beautiful mantelpiece, must at one time have been a stately apartment. In the centre of the ceiling were the initials E. R., affording circumstantial, if not positive, evidence that the mansion was once inhabited by the virgin queen. On the ground floor was another fine apartment, known as the Stone Parlour. This apartment had also a fine decorated mantelpiece, on which were represented the cardinal virtues, as well as a stuccoed ceiling embossed and ornamented with pendants.

Adjoining this house, and standing on a rather elevated lawn, was the ancient residence of Prior Bolton, probably erected by him about the year 1520. The lawn was terminated by a raised and embowered terrace, which must at one time have commanded a fine view of the surrounding country. At each end of the wall was an octagonal garden-house, erected by Prior Bolton, in one of which was to be traced the prior's rebus, or device, —a bolt, or arrow, and a tun. The same quaint device is also to be traced in St. Bartholomew's Church and in some of the houses in the adjoining close. Ben Johnson speaks of :

" Old Prior Bolton, with his bolt and ton."

From the same source, apparently, the ancient and well-known inn in Fleet Street derived its name.

Among other relics of the past the mansion contained a carved mantelpiece of the reign of Elizabeth, and a stone passage, or corridor, in which could be seen a Tudor doorway of considerable beauty and elegance, ornamented by the rebus of Prior Bolton.

Who is there who has not felt an interest in that great Smithfield fair, which derived its name from having been for centuries held under the shadow of the neighbouring priory? The privilege of holding a fair at Smithfield during St. Bartholomew tide was originally granted to the priory by

Henry the Second. It lasted for three days being principally frequented by London drapers, as well as by country clothiers who flocked hither with their goods from all parts of England; these persons being allowed to place their booths and standings within the walls of the churchyard, the gates of which were carefully locked at night.

Such was the constitution of Bartholomew Fair till the reign of Henry the Eighth, when there sprung up those humours and saturnalia for which it continued to be celebrated even in recent times. In our own time the lord mayor still opened the fair in person; stopping his horse at Newgate in his way, to receive from the hands of the keeper of the prison a "cool tankard of wine, nutmeg, and sugar." In 1688, this custom proved fatal to Sir John Shorter, lord mayor, grandfather of the beautiful Catherine Shorter, the first wife of Sir Robert Walpole. While holding the tankard, the lid suddenly fell, when his horse, frightened at the noise, plunged and threw his rider. So severe were the injuries which he received that he died on the following day.

Bartholomew Fair was long celebrated for its theatrical entertainments. Pepys writes on the 30th of August, 1667: "I to Bartholomew Fayre to walk up and down; and there, among other things, find my Lady Castlemaine at a puppet-play,

and the street full of people expecting her coming
out. I confess I did wonder at her courage to
come abroad, thinking the people would abuse her.
But they, silly people, do not know the work she
makes, and therefore suffered her with great respect to take coach, and she away without any
trouble at all." It was in a booth at Bartholomew
Fair that Rich is said to have been so struck with
the acting of Walker, afterward the original Mac-
heath, that he engaged him for the theatre in Lincoln's Inn. Another well-known person connected
with Bartholomew Fair was the unfortunate poet,
Elkanah Settle, who was once so reduced in circumstances as to be compelled to write panto-
mimes and contrive machinery for a Smithfield
booth. Here, in fact, it was that in one of his
own wretched theatrical exhibitions, called " St.
George and the Dragon," he was reduced to per-
sonate the dragon, enclosed in a case of green
leather — a circumstance to which Doctor Young,
the author of the " Night Thoughts," alludes in his
epistles to Pope :

> " Poor Elkanah, all other changes past,
>   For bread in Smithfield-dragons hissed at last ;
>   Spit streams of fire to make the butchers gape,
>   And found his manners suited to his shape.
>   Such is the fate of talents misapplied," etc.

It was at Bartholomew Fair that the great actress,
Mrs. Pritchard, first attracted public attention.

We have the authority of Mrs. Piozzi, that Doctor Johnson's uncle, Andrew Johnson, "for a whole year kept the ring at Smithfield, where they wrestled and boxed, and never was thrown or conquered."

CHAPTER II.

THE CHARTER HOUSE.

Charter House Originally a Burial-ground — Sir Walter de Manny Founds a Carthusian Monastery There — Dreadful Punishments Inflicted on the Carthusians by Henry the Eighth — Charter House Purchased by Duke of Norfolk — Given to Earl of Suffolk — History of Sir Thomas Sutton, Founder of the Present Charter House — Scholars and Pensioners — Old Court-room — Charter House Square.

THERE is perhaps no spot in London which has witnessed so much dreary horror as the ground occupied by the Charter House. Beneath and around us lie the remains of no fewer than one hundred thousand human beings, who fell victims to the frightful plague, which devastated the metropolis in the reign of Edward the Third.[1] "No Man's Land," as it was styled by our ancestors, bore a frightful reputation. Long after the earth had closed over the vast plague-pit, it was the custom to inter there all who had either perished on

---

[1] It is to be noted, that above one hundred thousand bodies of Christian people had in that churchyard been buried; for the said knight (Sir Walter de Manny) had purchased that place for the burial of poor people, travellers, and other that were deceased, to remain for ever.

the gibbet or by their own hands. Their mutilated corpses, according to Stow, were conveyed
hither with terrifying ceremony, "usually in a close
cart, bailed over and covered with black, having a
plain white cross thwarting; and at the fore end
a St. John's cross without; and within a bell ringing by shaking of the cart, whereby the same might
be heard when it passed; and this was called the
friary cart, which belonged to St. John's, and had
the privilege of sanctuary."

At the time of the great plague in the reign of
Edward the Third, the ground on which the Charter House now stands consisted of open fields.
Then it was [1348] that, in consequence of the
ordinary London churchyards having been filled to
overflowing by the victims of the pestilence, the
ground was purchased from philanthropic motives
by Ralph Stratford, Bishop of London, who surrounded it with a wall of brick, and built a chapel
for the performance of the burial service over the
dead. This immediate spot was known by the
name of Pardon Churchyard, a name which it continued to retain in the days of Stow. The chapel
stood on the ground between the present north
wall of the Charter House and Sutton Street.

There existed at that fearful period another
beneficent philanthropist, to whom, in fact, we in-
directly owe the present magnificent establishment,
the Charter House. That person was Sir Walter
de Manny, a native of Hainault and a Knight of

the Garter, a man not only endeared to his contemporaries by his singular virtues, but whose personal gallantry shone preëminent in every battle and tournament of that chivalrous age. As compassionate as he was brave, he not only during the raging of the pestilence added thirteen acres to the ground already purchased by Bishop Stratford, but subsequently perfected his pious work by founding and endowing on the spot a religious establishment, which survived till the dissolution of the monasteries in the reign of Henry the Eighth.

In founding his new order, Sir Walter had the advice and experience of Simon Sudbury Bishop of London. It consisted of twenty-four Carthusian monks, who were formed into a branch of the Benedictines, originally established at Chartreux, in France, about the year 1080, an order principally distinguished by its austerity and self-denial. Hence the modern word, Charter House, is corrupted. Over their single undergarment, which was white, they wore a black cloak ; no other covering being permitted them, even in winter, but a single blanket. With the exception of the prior and the proctor, they were confined entirely to the walls of the monastery. Even in the most inclement weather they were compelled to attend divine service in the middle of the night. Once a week they fasted on bread, salt, and water, and on no occasion were they allowed to eat meat, nor even fish, unless it were a free gift. When Shakespeare, in his play of "Henry the Eighth," speaks of "a monk o' the Chartreux," he alludes to one of the fraternity of the ancient Charter House.

Sir Walter de Manny breathed his last in 1372, deeply and deservedly lamented. Froissart, indeed, tells us that "all the barons and knights of England were much affected at his death, on account of the loyalty and prudence they had always found in him." He was buried with great pomp in the chapel of the monastery of the Carthusians, his funeral being attended by the king in person, and by the principal nobles and prelates of the realm. By his own wish a tomb of alabaster was placed in the choir over his remains.

The Carthusians, from the time of the foundation till the extinction of their order, continued to be respected for their peaceful and exemplary lives; living entirely secluded from the vanities and temptations of the busy world around them, practising self-denial, and dispensing alms to the poor. Their virtues, however, availed them little against the grasping avarice of Henry the Eighth; and accordingly, at the dissolution of the religious houses, they received a visit from the king's commissioners, by whom they were formally required to withdraw their spiritual allegiance from the Pope, and to acknowledge the king's supremacy in the Church. In case of their submission, the prospect of honours and rewards was liberally held out to them; while, in case of obduracy, they were threatened with the gibbet and the rack. Neither, however, the fear of death, nor the hope of reward could divert these devoted men from their purpose, and accordingly their fate, as may be readily imagined, proved to be a hard one.

On the 5th of May, 1535, the venerable prior was not only hanged, drawn, and quartered at Tyburn, but one of his quarters was actually placed over the gate of his own monastery, a ghastly spectacle and a terrible forewarning to its surviving inmates. Nevertheless they continued to turn a deaf ear alike to the threats and the promises of the king's inquisitors, till at length, enraged at their obstinacy, their persecutors took the preliminary step of immuring them within the walls of the cloisters; whence, about a month after the death of their exemplary prior, many of them were dragged forth to the gibbet. Their bodies having been cut down while they were still alive, their bowels were taken out, and their heads and quarters affixed to different parts of the city. Six monks of the whole number recanted their principles and took the oath of supremacy. There now remained only ten of the unfortunate Carthusians, the fate of whom was even more pitiable than that of their deceased brethren. After a long and close confinement, such was the miserable state to which they were reduced by hunger and filth, that nine of them actually wasted away and died in their miserable cells. The only remaining one

— the last of the simple-minded and devoted Carthusians — was led forth a few years later to the
gibbet.

After the dissolution of the monasteries, the
Charter House was granted by Henry the Eighth,
in 1542, for their joint lives, to John Brydges and
Thomas Hall, the former yeoman and the latter
groom of the king's nets and tents.   Henry subsequently conferred it upon Sir Thomas Audley,
lord chancellor, who sold it in 1545 to the eminent statesman and lawyer, Sir Edward North,
afterward Lord North, who metamorphosed the
old monastery into a magnificent mansion.   He
subsequently disposed of it to the turbulent and
ambitious John Dudley, Duke of Northumberland, on whose attainder and execution, in August,
1553, it was again conferred on Lord North by
the Crown.

At the Charter House Queen Elizabeth, on her
accession to the throne in 1558, passed five days
previously to her installing herself in the royal
apartments in the Tower.

In 1565 the Charter House was purchased of
Roger, the second Lord North, by Thomas Howard, Duke of Norfolk, whose romantic attachment
to Mary Queen of Scots led him to the block.   It
was the favourite resort of this unfortunate nobleman, being at one time the scene of his revels,
at another of his desperate intrigues, and, lastly,
of his imprisonment.   The greater part of the

edifice as it now stands was rebuilt by this nobleman. In the great hall may be still seen his
heraldic bearings, with the date, 1571, the year
previous to his execution, while the pediment of
the outer gate in Charter House Square is still
supported by two lions with scrolls, his armorial
badge. It may be mentioned that the principal
evidence against the ill-fated duke was the discovery under the roofing-tiles of the Charter
House of the key to the cipher of his letters.
Whether with real or feigned reluctance, Queen
Elizabeth, notwithstanding his many virtues, his
great popularity, and their long friendship, signed
the warrant for his execution, and accordingly, on
the 2d of June, 1572, the duke perished in the
prime of life on the scaffold on Tower Hill.

The Howards being the kinsfolks of Queen
Elizabeth, she was induced to divide among them
the forfeited property of the late duke, the Charter House falling to the share of his second son,
Lord Thomas Howard, afterward Earl of Suffolk.
Here this nobleman was residing in 1603, when
James the First ascended the throne, and as it
was the policy of the Scottish monarch to show
favour to the surviving friends of his ill-fated
mother, he not only selected Lord Thomas Howard to be his host previously to his solemn entry
into London, but passed under his roof the four
days which preceded that event. Here he was
splendidly entertained by his obsequious host.

Here he showed his affection for his new subjects by dubbing no fewer than eighty knights; and here, on his departure, he displayed his gratitude to his host by creating him Earl of Suffolk, and appointing him to the high honours of Lord Treasurer of England, lord chamberlain of his household, and a Knight of the Garter.

The foundation and endowment of the Charter House by Sir Thomas Sutton is perhaps the most princely charity for which, with the exception of Guy's Hospital, England is indebted to the munificence of any single individual. Sir Thomas, who was a native of Knaith in Lincolnshire, was born in 1531; received his education at Eton and Cambridge, and subsequently entered himself as a student at Lincoln's Inn. In early life he had passed several years travelling in foreign countries, and on his return to England, in 1562, found himself, by the death of his father, in the possession of a considerable property. He now attached himself to the person and fortunes of the Duke of Norfolk, from which circumstance, probably, may have sprung that particular affection for the Charter House and its localities, which many years afterward induced him to become its purchaser.

The zeal with which he served the Duke of Norfolk induced that nobleman to introduce him to the Earl of Warwick, whose secretary he became, and by whose influence he obtained the

appointment of master-general of the ordnance
in the North.   Within a few years from this period
— in consequence of the successful result of several commercial speculations, and more especially
by the purchase of the manors of Gateshead and
Wickham, near Newcastle, the coal-mines of which
yielded him immense profits — Sir Thomas Sutton found himself one of the richest subjects in
Europe.   Wealth could scarcely have been lav-
ished on a more deserving person.   To him the
scholar never applied for assistance in vain ; neither
were the poor and needy ever sent empty-handed
from his door.   Ever on the watch for opportunities of benefiting his fellow creatures, he was in
the habit, in years of scarcity, of storing up large
quantities of grain, which he disposed of at low
prices to the poor.   More than once, while medi-
tating in his garden, he was overheard to use the
expression, " Lord, thou has given me a large
and liberal estate ; give me also a heart to make
use thereof."   Not only was he the munificent
friend of the scholar, the widow, and the orphan,
but among his papers at the Charter House are
numerous applications to him for money in the
handwriting of the noblest of the land, as well
as many bonds which to all appearance he had
allowed to remain uncancelled.   Among his debtors
are to be traced no less illustrious names than
those of the haughty Elizabeth and her ill-fated
favourite the Earl of Essex.

Notwithstanding his peaceful habits and gentle disposition, Sir Thomas Sutton was far from being the mere merchant or philanthropist. As master-general of the ordnance in the North, especial mention is made of him as having commanded in person one of the batteries raised for the reduction of Edinburgh Castle in 1573.

On the 9th of May, 1611, Sir Thomas, having completed the purchase of the Charter House from the Earl of Suffolk for the sum of £13,000, proceeded to establish his new institution on its present footing. He had proposed to nominate himself its first governor; but scarcely had his arrangements been completed, when he was seized by a fatal illness, which carried him off on the 12th of December, 1611, at the age of seventy-nine. His death took place at Hackney, exactly six weeks after he had signed the important deeds which conveyed his vast landed estates to the Charter House. His body, having been embalmed, was brought from Hackney to the house of Doctor Law, in Paternoster Row, whence it was conveyed to its temporary resting-place in Christ Church, Newgate, followed by six thousand persons. In March, 1616, it was removed to the spot where it now reposes, in the chapel of his own princely foundation.

The establishment of the Charter House, presided over by sixteen governors, consists of a master, preacher, head schoolmaster, second master, registrar, house steward or manciple, besides inferior officers and servants. The pensioners on its establishment are eighty "decayed gentlemen," and sixty scholars.

The scholars are admitted between the ages of ten and fourteen, and provided they attain a certain proficiency in learning, are transplanted in due time to the university, where, according to the will of the founder, twenty-nine exhibitions of the value of £80 a year are provided for those who were educated on his foundation. Among the most eminent persons educated at the Charter House appear to be Richard Crashaw, the poet, Addison, Sir Richard Steele, John Wesley, the founder of Methodism, and Sir William Blackstone, the lawyer and poet. Wesley, who survived till the almost patriarchal age of eighty-seven, used to attribute the health which he enjoyed through so long a life to his having kept a promise he had made to his father, never to miss a day without running a certain number of times around the Charter House playing-ground. Another eminent person educated at the Charter House was the late Lord Chief Justice of the King's Bench, Lord Ellenborough, whose strong attachment to the scenes of his youth may be assumed from the wish he expressed to be buried within its walls. A prominent object, on the south wall of the Charter House playground, is a painted crown, which is said to have been originally drawn in

chalk by the great lawyer in his boyhood, and
which has ever since been religiously preserved.
In the chapel of the Charter House is a monument to the memory of Lord Ellenborough.

The pensioners, or "decayed gentlemen," live
entirely apart from the scholars: having each
their separate apartment, and receiving an allowance of £36 a year each, besides a table being
kept for their maintenance. None but persons
who have been housekeepers are admitted, nor
any one under the age of fifty unless he has
been maimed in war. Elkanah Settle, the poet,
and John Bagford, the antiquary, were severally
"poor brethren" of the Charter House.

Although portions of the walls of the ancient
monastery are unquestionably incorporated in the
present building, the edifice as it now stands ex-
hibits but few traces of the original structure
of Sir Walter de Manny. Perhaps the only exception is the basement of the chapel turret,
which is supported on the exterior by an original
buttress, anciently forming a part of the old tower
of the Carthusian chapel. Of the monastery, however, as it existed at the more recent period of
its dissolution, the antiquary may trace some interesting remains. The chamber where the pensioners
now dine was the refectory of the old monks:
the entrances to several of their cells may still
be traced on the south side of the present playground; their ancient kitchen is still in use; and

the cloisters, which witnessed the sufferings of
the ill-fated Carthusians, still continue objects
of unfading interest.

The other objects of note in the Charter House
are the chapel, the hall, the old court-room, and
an ancient and beautiful apartment called the
evidence room, in which the records of the establishment are preserved.   The most noteworthy
object in the chapel is the large and gaudy monument of the founder, Sir Thomas Sutton, whose
recumbent effigy, in a black furred gown, with
gray hair and beard, is painted in imitation of
life.   On each side of the effigy is an upright
figure of a man in armour, and above it is a
preacher addressing a full congregation.   The
sculptor was the well-known mason and statuary,
Nicholas Stone, who was employed as master-
mason, under Inigo Jones, in building the Ban-
queting-house at Whitehall.   His bill for Sutton's
monument, which is still in existence, amounts to
£366, 15s.

The hall is said to have been built by Sir
Edward North in the reign of Henry the Eighth,
and to have been afterward used as a banqueting-
room by the ill-fated Duke of Norfolk.   The roof
is fine and massive, besides which there are in
the oriel windows some remains of painted glass
with various armorial bearings ; the mantelpiece,
too, is curious.   Above it are Sutton's arms, on
each side of which is represented a mounted piece

of cannon, supposed to have reference to his military services at the siege of Edinburgh.

The apartment known as the governor's room, in the Master's House is also well worthy a visit. Here, in curious juxtaposition, are portraits of the grave founder; of the gay and unprincipled George Villiers, Duke of Buckingham; of the pious Sheldon, Archbishop of Canterbury, and of the profligate Charles the Second; of the hero, William, Earl Craven, and the philosopher Burnet, author of the " Theory of the Earth ;" of the handsome and unfortunate Duke of Monmouth; of the eminent philosopher, Anthony, Earl of Shaftesbury, and of the celebrated statesman, Charles Talbot, Duke of Shrewsbury.

But the most interesting apartment in the Charter House is unquestionably the old court-room, with its sombre tapestry, its lofty panelled mantelpiece, and its beautiful stuccoed and gilded ceiling. Vividly it recalls to our imagination that magnificent period when Queen Elizabeth — having invited herself to pay a second visit of four days at the Charter House with her learned chancellor, Sir Edward North — proceeded thither on horseback from the Tower; her kinsman, Lord Hunsdon, carrying the sword of state before her, her ladies following close behind her on their ambling palfreys, and a magnificent procession bringing up the rear. Having passed through the principal gateway, still bearing the heraldic badge of the

Duke of Norfolk, it was in all probability to this apartment that she was conducted, and that here she held her court.

> " Girt with many a baron bold,
>   Sublime their starry fronts they rear;
>   And gorgeous dames, and statesmen old
>   In bearded majesty appear.
>   In the midst, a form divine!
>   Her eye proclaims her of the Briton-line;
>   Her lion-port, her awe-commanding face,
>   Attempered sweet to virgin-grace;
>   What strings symphonious tremble in the air!"

Charter House Square stands on the site of the burial-place of the ancient monastery. At the northeast corner formerly stood the residence of the Rutland family, and afterward, on its site, the well-known theatre opened by Sir William Davenant in 1656.

In Charter House Square died, on the 8th of December, 1691, Richard Baxter, the eminent non-conformist divine.

Pardon Passage, in the immediate vicinity of Charter House Square, forms a curious link between the days of Edward the Third and our own time. Pardon Churchyard, it may be remembered, was the designation given to the ground purchased by Bishop Stratford for the interment of the victims of the giant pestilence in the fourteenth century.

CHAPTER III.

ST. JOHN'S GATE, CLERKENWELL, ETC.

TURNING from St. John's Street into St. John's Lane, we face the ancient gateway of the hospital or priory of the Knights of St. John of Jerusalem. In the reign of James the First, this interesting gateway formed the residence of Sir Roger Wilbraham, to whom it was granted by that monarch. From this period little is known of its history till the commencement of the last century, when it had become the private residence of the well-known Cave, the proprietor of the *Gentleman's Magazine,* the first number of which issued from St. John's Gate.

Boswell, in mentioning the feelings of "reverence" with which Doctor Johnson first gazed upon the old gateway, attributes it to its association with the *Gentleman's Magazine.* "I suppose," he says, "that every young author has had the same kind of feeling for the magazine or periodical publication which has first entertained him. I myself recollect such impressions from the *Scots' Magazine.*" But when Doctor Johnson gazed with "reverence" on St. John's Gateway, the *Gentleman's Magazine* had, in all probability, but little place in his thoughts. "If," writes Mr. Croker, "Johnson, as Boswell supposes, looked at St. John's Gate as the printing-office of Cave, surely a less emphatical term than reverence would have been more just. The *Gentleman's Magazine* had been at this time but six years before the public, and its contents were, until Johnson himself contributed to improve it, entitled to anything rather than reverence; but it is more probable that Johnson's reverence was excited by the recollections connected with the ancient gate itself, the last relic of the once extensive and magnificent priory of the heroic Knights of the Order of St. John of Jerusalem, suppressed at the dissolution, and destroyed by successive dilapidations."

In connection with Doctor Johnson and St. John's Gate, Malone relates a rather curious anecdote. Shortly after the publication of Johnson's "Life of Savage," Walter Harte, the author of the "Life of Gustavus Adolphus," dined with Cave. A few days afterward, when Harte and Cave again met, the latter observed: "You made

a man
that he
but
during
behind
who wa
ting do
versati
encoun

The
of Jeru
John F
The
upper

The
chastit
devoti
periors
renounc
stock;
ministe
joined
it to th

To
the Kr
occupy
subjec
must
themse
territor

a man very happy the other day." "How could that be?" said Harte; "there was no one there but ourselves." Cave then reminded him that during dinner a plate of victuals had been sent behind a screen. They were for Johnson, he said, who was dressed so shabbily that he declined sitting down to table, but who had overheard the conversation, and was highly delighted with Harte's encomiums on his work.

The military Order of the Knights of St. John of Jerusalem was founded about the year 1100, by John Briset, a Norman baron, and Muriel, his wife. The dress of the Order was originally a black upper garment, with a white cross in front.

The knights were required to take an oath of chastity; to be rigid in the performance of their devotions; to yield implicit obedience to their superiors; to defend Christians against pagans; to renounce all property independent of the common stock; and lastly, to relieve the needy and to administer to the sick. They were especially enjoined, as the champions of the cross, to fight for it to the last gasp of their lives.

To enumerate the heroic exploits performed by the Knights of St. John in the Holy Land would occupy far more space than we can devote to the subject. Even when the cause of the Crusade must have appeared almost desperate even to themselves, they continued to defend the sacred territory almost inch by inch against the immense masses of infidels who confronted them. The same heroic gallantry which had distinguished them in the early period of their history, at the sieges of Ascalon and Gaza, shone no less conspicuous at the sieges of Azotus and St. Jean d'Acre. Of the ninety knights who defended Azotus, when that fortress was at length taken by assault, not one was found alive. The dead body of the last served as a stepping-stone to the advancing infidels.

It was in the year 1310, after a long and bloody contest with the desperate piratical inhabitants of the island of Rhodes, that the Knights of St. John invested themselves with the sovereignty of that island. Here they remained — carrying on a continual warfare with the Mohammedans, and enriching themselves by commerce — till the year 1522, when the sultan, Solyman the Fourth, appeared before the island with an overwhelming armament. The details of the protracted and bloody siege which followed — in which the Turks lost one hundred thousand men — are well known. The last bulwark which was blown up was that of the English knights, who on four different occasions drove back the Turks from the breach, and tore down the crescent which they had planted on the walls. The last who consented to capitulate was the grand master, the venerable L'Isle Adam. When at length the Sultan Solyman subsequently entered Rhodes as a conqueror, he paid a visit to the heroic old man, with whose misfortunes he is said to have deeply sympathised. "It is not without pain," he said, "that I force this Christian at his time of life to leave his dwelling." By the terms of the capitulation, the surviving knights were allowed to quit Rhodes unmolested, and to retire whithersoever they chose. Accordingly, in 1530, they took possession of the island of Malta, which had been conceded to them by the Emperor Charles the Fifth, where they continued till the extinction of their Order.

One of the most remarkable features in the history of the Knights of St. John, was the long and bitter rivalry which existed between them and the Knights Templars. So intense, indeed, was their mutual hatred, that, forgetful of the common cause which enjoined them to fight side by side against the infidel, they more than once, on the plains of Palestine, pointed their lances against one another. The last and most sanguinary of these combats took place in 1259, when the Knights of St. John obtained a complete victory over their rivals, leaving scarcely a Templar alive on the field of battle. When, about half a century afterward, the Knights Templars ceased to exist as an Order, the greater portion of their possessions was conferred by the Pope and the other European sovereigns on the Knights of St. John. Among the property thus transferred to them was the temple in Fleet Street, which in the reign of Edward the Third they leased to the students of law. The prior at this period ranked as first baron of England.

The Order of St. John, like that of the Knights Templars, was in the first years of its existence distinguished by the austerities, the chastity, and the self-denial practised by its members. "Receive the yoke of the Lord," were the words of the principal to a proselyte knight; "it is easy and light, and you shall find rest for your soul. We promise you nothing but bread and water, a simple habit and of little worth." By degrees, however, as their riches increased, so also did luxury and licentiousness take root among this once ascetic and self-denying Order. To the lower classes, the notorious vices of many of the knights, and their arrogant display of wealth, rendered them especially obnoxious. When, in the reign of Richard the Second, the celebrated riots broke out under the direction of Wat Tyler, the property of the Knights of St. John was among the first which fell a sacrifice to the fury of the rebels. "They burnt," writes Stow, "all the houses belonging to St. John's; and then burnt the fair priory of the hospital of St. John, causing the same to burn the space of seven days after." King Richard, it appears, witnessed the conflagration from a turret of the Tower. Of those who fell victims to the popular fury one was the prior of St. John's, Sir Robert Hales, who perished by the axe of the rebels. A few days previously, when the assem-

bled rebels at Blackheath had sent to demand a
conference with their sovereign, it was the prior
of St. John's who had been the first to urge his
royal master to hold no converse with such " barelegged ribalds."

These events occurred in 1381, within a quarter
of a century from which time a new priory arose
from the ashes of the old, apparently far surpass-
ing it in magnificence. It was not, however, till
the end of the fifteenth century that the present
gateway was built, nor was the church completed
till 1504.

The Order of St. John of Jerusalem was suppressed by Henry the Eighth, in the thirty-second
year of his reign. On the last prior, Sir William
Weston, — who died, it is said, of a broken heart
on the day his Order was suppressed, — the king
conferred a pension of a thousand a year, and
on the knights smaller annuities. The remainder
of their large possessions Henry seized for the
" augmentation of his crown." "The priory,
church, and house of St. John," writes Stow,
" were preserved from spoil or downpulling so
long as King Henry the Eighth reigned, and were
employed as a storehouse for the king's toils and
tents for hunting, and for the wars. But in the
third of King Edward the Sixth, the church, for
the most part, — to wit the body and side-aisles,
with the great bell-tower, a most curious piece of
workmanship, graven, gilt, and enamelled, to the

great beautifying of the city, and passing all other that I have seen, — was undermined and blown up with gunpowder. The stone thereof was employed in building of the lord protector's house at the Strand."

In the succeeding reign of Queen Mary an attempt was made to revive the Order, and to place it on its ancient footing. The choir of the church, and some of the side chapels which still remained, were repaired, and Sir Thomas Tresham, knight, appointed lord prior. But the glory of the Order of St. John had passed away, and on the accession of Queen Elizabeth it was for ever abolished in England. The priory, which was of great extent, stood on the ground now occupied by St. John's Square, on the south side of Clerkenwell Green.

On the opposite, or north, side of the green stood the Benedictine Nunnery of St. Mary, founded so early as the year 1100, by one Jorden Brisset, as an establishment for Black Nuns of the Order of St. Benedict. The first prioress was Christina. The last was Isabella Sackville, niece of Thomas, first Earl of Dorset. On the site of this convent, which was dissolved in 1570, arose the present parochial church dedicated to St. James. As late as the days of Pennant, a part of the cloisters of the old convent and also of the nuns' refectory, still remained.

The old conventual church contained many

costly and interesting monuments, many of which
were unfortunately destroyed during the progress
of rebuilding the church.   Among these may be
mentioned the monument of Sir William Weston,
the last Lord Prior of the Order of St. John, and
that of the last Prioress of St. Mary's, Isabella
Sackville; of Elizabeth Drury, widow of William
Cecil, Earl of Exeter; of Elizabeth, wife of Sir
Maurice Berkeley, standard-bearer to Henry the
Eighth and to Queen Elizabeth; and of the celebrated antiquary and collector of funeral inscrip-
tions, John Weever, who died in 1634.[1]   The
epitaph on Weever's tomb, composed by himself,
is as quaint as any of those which he delighted to
collect.   The inscription concludes:

> " Lancashire gave me breath,
>   And Cambridge, education;
> Middlesex gave me death,
>   And this church my humation;
> And Christ to me hath given
> A place with Him in Heaven.
>   Ætatis suæ 56."

The present church was erected between the
years 1788 and 1792.

Another eminent person who lies buried in this
church is the historian, Gilbert Burnet, Bishop of
Salisbury, who died in St. John's Square on the

---

[1] The tombs of Prior Weston and of Lady Berkeley are still
preserved in the vaults of the church.

17th of March, 1714–15. John Langhorne, the poet, was for some time curate and lecturer of St. James's, Clerkenwell.

The neighbouring and uninteresting church of St. John Clerkenwell was consecrated on the 27th of December, 1723; the crypt forming a part of the choir of the ancient church of St. John's Priory. It was from the vaults of this church that the famous Cock Lane ghost was presumed to issue in the dead hour of the night.

Clerkenwell derives its name from its vicinity to one of those pure and sparkling springs, or wells, of which there were formerly several in the northern suburbs of the metropolis, and at which the parish clerks of London used anciently to perform their mysteries, or sacred dramas. For instance, in the old records we find the convent church of St. Mary repeatedly styled, *Ecclesia Beatæ Mariæ, de fonte Clericorum.* "There are about London," writes Fitzstephen, "on the north of the suburbs, choice fountains of water, sweet, wholesome, and clear, streaming forth among the glistening pebble stones. In this number, Holywell, Clerkenwell, and St. Clement's Well, are of most note, and frequented above the rest when scholars and the youth of the city take the air abroad in the summer evenings." This and other springs in the neighbourhood pursued their murmuring course till they flowed into the Fleet River, then a pure and limpid stream, and which from this circumstance obtained its name of the " River of Wells."

In the days when Fitzstephen wrote, the Clerk's Well bubbled in the midst of verdant meadows and shady lanes; the richly wooded uplands of Hampstead and Highgate rising behind them. Such was Clerkenwell when, in 1390, the clerks performed here during three successive days in the presence of Richard the Second, his queen, and the nobility; and again when, in 1409, in the reign of Henry the Fourth, the Creation of the World formed the subject of their drama, and when, in the words of Stow, there flocked "to see the same the most part of the nobles and gentles in England." Close to Ray Street, Clerkenwell, are some houses which still retain the rural denomination of Coppice Row. Here also is a dilapidated-looking pump, on which an inscription informs us that the water which it supplies flows from the " Clerk's Well." [1]

As late as 1780, Clerkenwell, to the north of the upper end of St. John's Street, was bounded by fields, through which a solitary road led to

[1] The inscription is as follows : " A. D. 1800, William Bound, Joseph Bird, churchwardens. For the better accommodation of the neighbourhood, this pump was removed to the spot where it now stands. The spring by which it is supplied is situated four feet eastward, and round it, as history informs us, the parish-clerks of London, in remote ages, commonly performed sacred plays. That custom caused it to be denominated Clerks'-well, and from whence this parish derived its name."

Islington.   At this recent period, so infested was
the neighbourhood by highwaymen, that travellers
usually preferred sleeping all night at the Angel
Inn at Islington, to journeying by this dangerous
thoroughfare after dark.   Those whose business
called them into the country at a late hour used
to assemble at the upper end of St. John's Street,
where there was an avenue of trees called Wood's
Close, and where they waited till they were rein-
forced by other travellers, when they were escorted
by an armed patrol to Islington.

In the middle of the last century, when any
extraordinary performance at Sadler's Wells Theatre was likely to tempt thither the nobility and
gentry from the fashionable quarters of London, it
was the custom to announce in the playbills that
a horse-patrol would be stationed for that particular night in the New Road, and also that the
thoroughfare leading to the city would be properly
guarded.

In January, 1559, we find Sir Thomas Pope, the
virtuous and high-minded minister of Henry the
Eighth, breathing his last at his mansion at Clerkenwell.   At a much later period, between the
reigns of James the First and Charles the Second,
Clerkenwell was still a fashionable district.   We
have already seen Sir Roger Wilbraham occupying
the old gateway of St. John's in the reign of
James the First; about which time Sir Thomas
Chaloner the younger, tutor to Henry, Prince of

Wales, and eminent as a poet, a scholar, and a statesman, erected a fine mansion in the priory, over which Fuller informs us that he inscribed the following verses :

> " Casta fides superest, velatæ tecta sorores
>   Ista relegatæ deseruere licèt ;
> Nam venerandus Hymen hic vota jugalia servat,
>   Vestalemque forum mente fovere studet."

Sir Thomas was the son of that fine old soldier, Sir Thomas Chaloner, who was knighted by the Duke of Somerset for his heroic gallantry at Musselburgh. He also attended Charles the Fifth in the wars, and, shortly after the unfortunate expedition to Algiers, was shipwrecked in a very dark night on the coast of Barbary. At the moment when he was exhausted with swimming, and when his arms were rendered entirely powerless, he suddenly came in contact with the cable of a ship. With great presence of mind he caught hold of it with his teeth, and with the loss of several of them was drawn up into the vessel. His gifted son, Sir Thomas the younger, by his knowledge of chemistry and natural history, was enabled, when at Rome, to distinguish the similarity of soil between that on his own estate at Gisborough and the soil used in the alum works of the Pope. Having with great care made himself master of the process of manufacture, and having bribed several of the workmen to accompany him to England, for which

he was afterward solemnly anathematised by the
Pope, he overcame every difficulty, and at a great
expense established an alum manufactory in England.   Just, however, as the result promised to be
eminently successful, his lands, on pretence that
he was interfering with the prerogative of the
royal mines, were seized by the Crown.   As a
recompense, indeed, for his loss, he received the
appointment of governor of the Prince of Wales,
but gratifying as was the compliment, it offered
but a slight compensensation to his family for the
loss of wealth which they had unquestionably sustained.   When, some forty years afterward, two of
his sons, Thomas and James, signed the warrant
for the execution of Charles the First, may it not
have been the recollection of this act of royal
injustice which guided their pens?

Compton Street and Northampton Square point
out the site of what was formerly the London
residence of the Comptons, Earls of Northampton, the square having been built on the site of
the garden and orchards which were situated to
the rear of the old mansion.   Aylesbury Street,
too, leading from Clerkenwell Green into St. John's
Street, covers the site of the mansion and gardens
of Aylesbury House, which so late as the days of
Charles the Second was the town residence of the
Bruces, Earls of Aylesbury.

In Clerkenwell Close, on the site of the mansion
built by Sir Thomas Chaloner, stood Newcastle

House, the residence of William, Duke of New-castle, the brave and devoted follower of Charles the First. The site is still pointed out by the buildings known as Newcastle Place. After the Restoration of Charles the Second, the duke, we are told, "spent nearly the whole remainder of his life in the retirement afforded by his seat at Clerkenwell, where he took much pleasure in literary pursuits and paid some necessary attention to repairing the injuries sustained by his fortune." Newcastle House was, at different periods, the residence of two of the most eccentric women of their day. The first was Margaret, Duchess of Newcastle, the authoress of thirteen folio volumes, consisting of poetry, plays, and philosophy, in which perplexity of ideas and pomposity of expression are the principal characteristics. The other lady was the wealthy heiress of the Newcastle family, Lady Elizabeth Ogle, who married first, Christopher, Duke of Albemarle, and afterward Ralph, first Duke of Montagu. In our account of old Montagu House, now the British Museum, will be found a notice of this fantastic lady. After the death of the duchess, Newcastle House became the property of her sister Margaret, who had married John Holles, subsequently created Duke of Newcastle. As late as the year 1683 it continued to be the London residence of that nobleman.

On the opposite side of Clerkenwell Close stood within the last half-century a large house which, according to tradition, was inhabited by Oliver Cromwell; the site is pointed out by Cromwell Place. In 1631 John Weever, the antiquary, was residing in Clerkenwell Close.

To the left of St. John Street was the Red Bull Theatre, the arena where, during the reign of the Puritans, the persecuted players occasionally ventured to perform, and whence they were not unfrequently dragged to prison. At the Cross Keys Inn in this street the unfortunate Richard Savage occasionally passed his social hours.

A part of the ground adjoining Clerkenwell to the north was formerly in the possession of a Miss Wilkes, the daughter of a gentleman of fortune in the reign of Queen Elizabeth, and subsequently the wife of Sir Thomas Owen, one of the judges of the Common Pleas. She was the munificent foundress of a school and some almshouses at Islington, in reference to which foundation a singular anecdote is related by Stow. The young lady was one day walking in the fields with her maid, when, being seized with a fancy to learn how to milk a cow, she was in the act of stooping down for this purpose, when an arrow, shot at random by a gentleman who was practising archery in an adjoining field, pierced her high-crowned hat and carried it away. But for this act of stooping, the shot might have proved a fatal one, and accordingly so affected was she by the narrowness of her escape, as to express her determination, should Providence ever place it in her power, to raise some pious monument near the spot in token of her gratitude. Such an opportunity was afforded her on her becoming the wife of Sir Thomas Owen, when not only did she purchase the ground which had been the scene of her almost miraculous escape, but by her will, dated in 1613, bequeathed to the Brewers' Company sufficient funds to build on it and endow ten almshouses and a free grammar school. Altogether, Lady Owen by her will devoted no less than £2,300 to acts of charity; a very considerable sum when we take into consideration the relative value of money in the days of James the First and in our own time.

In Clerkenwell the father of John Wilkes carried on business as an opulent distiller, and here, in 1727, the celebrated demagogue was born. Whether he was of the same family as the charitable lady just mentioned we know not.

Coppice Row leads us into Cobham Row, the site of the suburban residence of the ill-fated Sir Thomas Oldcastle, afterward Lord Cobham, the chief of the Lollards, or disciples of Wickliffe, in the reign of Henry the Fifth. For professing their tenets he was executed in St. Giles's-in-the-Fields in February, 1418. Having been suspended alive from a gibbet by a chain fastened around his body, a fire was lighted beneath him, by which he was slowly burnt to death. To the last he is said to have expressed his conviction that he would rise again on the third day.

Close to Coppice Row are Cold Bath Fields, so named from a spring or well of cold water, which has long since been built over. In Dorrington Street, Cold Bath Fields, resided Carey, the musical composer, and the author of that pleasing song, "Sally in Our Alley;" and in Warner Street, in the immediate neighbourhood, he perished by his own hand, on the 4th of October, 1743. In a sponging-house, in Eyre Street Hill, Cold Bath Fields, died, in 1806, the celebrated painter, George Morland.

Within a short distance from Clerkenwell stood, till recently, the well-known place of amusement, Bagnigge Wells, formerly famous for its medicinal spring. It was first opened as a place of public entertainment in 1767. The old house, of which the writer witnessed the demolition, was said to have been the residence of Nell Gwynn. Among the persons buried in the neighbouring church of St. James, Clerkenwell, appears the name of Richard Gwynn, who died February 16, 1691. Probably he was an occupant of the house in question, which may have originated the tradition that it was the residence of his frail namesake. Colman speaks of

> ". . . drinking tea, on summer afternoons,
>   At Bagnigge Wells, with china and gilt spoons."

At Sadler's Wells, within no great distance of Bagnigge Wells, is another medicinal spring, formerly held in high repute not only among the citizens in the neighbourhood, but by the wealthiest and noblest in the land. In the last century, Sadler's Wells might be seen crowded every morning by five or six hundred persons, among whom were the daughters of George the Second, who came from St. James's every day to drink the waters.

The spring from which Sadler's Wells derives its name was discovered in the reign of Charles the Second, in the garden of one Sadler, who made a considerable sum of money by opening a place of entertainment near the spot, afterward superseded by the present theatre. "Here," writes Noorthouck, in 1773, "apprentices, journeymen, and clerks, dressed to ridiculous extremes, entertain their ladies on Sundays, and to the utmost of their power, if not beyond their proper power, affect the dissipated manners of their superiors. Bagnigge Wells and the White Conduit House — two other receptacles of the same kind, with gardens laid out in miniature taste — are to be found within the compass of two or three fields, together with Sadler's Wells, a small theatre for the summer evening exhibition of tumbling, rope-dancing, and other drolls, in vulgar style." On the 15th of October, 1807, Sadler's Wells Theatre was the scene of a fearful catastrophe. A cry of "fire" having been raised, the terrified audience in the gallery made a simultaneous rush to the doors;

the result being that no fewer than eighteen persons were killed, and several others seriously injured.

At Sadler's Wells, in front of the Hugh Myddleton Tavern, is laid the scene of Hogarth's "Evening." For many years the theatre was celebrated for its aquatic exhibitions, which were contrived by the removal of the boards from the stage, and the introduction of a flow of water from the New River. Here for many years, the famous clown, Grimaldi, performed his inimitable antics.

Not far from Clerkenwell Green is Hockley in the Hole, immortalised by Pope, Gay, Fielding, and the *Spectator*. From the days of Charles the Second, almost to our time, it continued to be the resort of bull-baiters, bruisers, and dog-fighters; the headquarters, in fact, of most of those barbarous diversions which tend to degrade man below the nature of brutes.

CHAPTER IV.

HOLBORN, ST. ANDREW'S CHURCH, GRAY'S INN LANE, ETC.

Cock Lane Ghost — Holborn — William Dobson — Death of John Bunyan — Snow Hill — Shoe Lane — Gunpowder Alley — Lovelace and Lilly — Fetter Lane — Residents in Fetter Lane — Hatton Garden — Ely House — Southampton Buildings — St Andrew's Church — Brooke Street — Gray's Inn Lane — Celebrated Residents There — Blue Boar Inn — Anecdote of Charles the First and Cromwell — Birth of Savage — King Street — John Bampfylde.

PASSING from Smithfield through Giltspur Street, on the right hand is Cock Lane, the scene of the vagaries of the celebrated Cock Lane ghost. The person to whom the apparition was said to have presented itself was a girl of twelve years of age, of the name of Parsons, the daughter of the parish clerk of St. Sepulchre, who resided in a wretched hovel, since demolished, about half-way down Cock Lane, on the north side. The ghost was said to be that of a young married lady, who had been poisoned by her husband, and who lay buried in the vaults of St. John's Church, Clerkenwell.

The extraordinary sensation created by this impudent imposition, as well as the credulity of persons of all ranks of society, almost exceed belief. To George Montagu, Horace Walpole writes, on the 2d of February, 1762: " I went to hear the ghost, for it is not an apparition, but an audition. We set out from the opera, changed our clothes at Northumberland House, — the Duke of York, Lady Northumberland, Lady Mary Coke, Lord Hertford and I, all in one hackney-coach, — and drove to the spot. It rained torrents, yet the lane was full of mob, and the house so full we could not get in. At last they discovered that it was the Duke of York, and the company squeezed themselves into one another's pockets, to make room for us. The house — which is borrowed, and to which the ghost has adjourned — is wretchedly small and miserable. When we opened the chamber, in which were fifty people, with no light but one tallow candle at the end, we tumbled over the bed of the child to whom the ghost comes, and whom they are murdering by inches in such insufferable heat and stench. At the top of the room are ropes to dry clothes. I asked if we were to have rope-dancing between the acts. We had nothing. They told us, as they would at a puppet-show, that it would not come that night till seven in the morning, that is, when there are only prentices and old women. We stayed, however, till half an hour after one. The Methodists have promised them contributions ;

spot. It rained torrents, yet, the lane was full of mob, and the house so full we could not get in. At last they discovered that it was the Duke of York, and the company squeezed themselves into one another's pockets, to make room for us. The house — which is bu.. o

. . wt.o .ne} — is w

fifty

. . . . the

inches in such insufferable heat and stench. At the top of the room are ropes to dry clothes. I asked if we were to have any dancing between the acts. We had nothing. They told us, as they would at a' puppet-show, that it would not come out night till seven in the morning, that is, when .... are only prentices and old women. We stayed, however, till half an hour after one. The them contributions ;

provisions are sent in like forage, and all the taverns and ale-houses in the neighbourhood make fortunes."

The affair of the ghost-story ended in the detection and punishment of the persons concerned in it. According to Boswell, Doctor Johnson took great credit to himself for the share which he had in exposing the imposition.

Till recently the steep descent of Snow Hill led us into Holborn, which derives its name from the Saxon words, old bourne, or old river. The great painter, Vandyke, was one day passing down Snow Hill, when his attention was attracted by a picture which was exposed for sale in one of the shop windows. Struck with its merits, he made inquiries respecting the artist, and was informed that he was then employed at his easel in a miserable apartment in the attics. Vandyke ascended the stairs; and thus took place his first introduction to William Dobson, then a young man unknown to fame, but whose celebrity as a portrait-painter was afterward second only in England to that of Vandyke. The great artist not only generously released him from a condition so unworthy his merits, but subsequently introduced him to Charles the First, who, after the death of Vandyke, conferred on him the appointments of his sergeant-painter and groom of the chamber. His prosperity, however, lasted but a short time. The decline of the royal cause, combined with his unfortunate

addiction to a life of pleasure, occasioned his falling into difficulties and being thrown into gaol.
Hence he was released by the generosity of a
Mr. Vaughan of the exchequer, but died shortly
afterward at the early age of thirty-six.

At the sign of the Star on Snow Hill, then the
residence of his friend, Mr. Strudwick, a grocer, died John Bunyan, the illustrious author of
the " Pilgrim's Progress." On his return from the
country, whither he had been summoned for the
pious purpose of effecting a reconciliation between
a father and son, he was overtaken by excessive
rains, which on his arrival at his lodging on Snow
Hill had wetted him to the skin. A fever was the
consequence, which put a period to his existence
on the 31st of August, 1688, in the sixty-first year
of his age.

On Snow Hill anciently stood one of the city
conduits, a structure ornamented with Corinthian
columns and surmounted by the figure of a lamb,
a rebus on the name of one Lamb, from whom
Lamb's Conduit Street derives its name. Anciently on days of great rejoicing the city conduits were made to run with red and white wine.
The last occasion on which the conduit on Snow
Hill thus flowed was on the anniversary of the
coronation of George the First, in 1727.

West of Farringdon Street is Shoe Lane, running from Holborn into Fleet Street. In the
burial-ground of Shoe Lane workhouse was in-

terred the ill-fated poet, Thomas Chatterton. The ground in which he lies buried now forms a part of Farringdon Market, but unfortunately the exact site of his resting-place is unknown.

Running out of Shoe Lane is Gunpowder Alley, a miserable spot associated with the miseries of a poet scarcely less gifted or unfortunate, Richard Lovelace. According to Anthony Wood, he was "accounted the most beautiful and amiable person that ever eye beheld; a person, also, of minute modesty, virtue, and courtly deportment, which made him, especially when he retired to the great city, much admired and adored by the female sex." Having exhausted his fortune in the cause of Charles the First, and twice suffered imprisonment as the penalty of his loyalty, he retired to the Continent, where, having raised a regiment for the French king, he was so severely wounded at Dunkirk that in England it was long believed that he was dead. Anthony Wood draws a painful picture of Lovelace's condition at the close of life. "Having consumed all his estate, he grew very melancholy, which at length brought him into a consumption; became very poor in body and purse; was the object of charity; went in ragged clothes, — whereas, when he was in his glory, he wore cloth of gold and silver; and mostly lodged in obscure and dirty places more befitting the worst of beggars than the poorest of servants." Lovelace died in a very mean lodging

in Gunpowder Alley in 1658, and was buried at
the west end of St. Bride's Church.

Another remarkable person who lived in Gunpowder Alley was William Lilly, the astrologer,
who here served his apprenticeship in the occult
sciences under one Evans, a clergyman of indifferent repute.

Fetter Lane, running from Holborn Hill into
Fleet Street, parallel with Shoe Lane, has been
supposed to derive its name from the fetters of
criminals. Such, however, is not the case. In the
reign of Charles the First it was called Fewtor's
Lane, a name which Stow derives from its having
been the resort of fewtors, as idle and disorderly
persons were then styled, — a corruption from
"defaytors" or defaulters.

Fetter Lane is rendered especially interesting
from its having been for some time the residence of
the immortal Dryden.   No. 16, though apparently
on insufficient evidence, is said to have been the
house which he occupied.   In this street Thomas
Hobbes, of Malmesbury, was residing at the period
when he published his celebrated "Leviathan."   In
Three Leg Alley, too, in the immediate neighbourhood, Thomas Flatman, the poet, breathed his last.
The name has since been dignified into Pemberton
Row.

In Fetter Lane Dr. Robert Levet, the grave
and well-known friend of Doctor Johnson, was
inveigled into that extraordinary marriage with a

woman of the town, which Doctor Johnson used to say presented as marvellous features as anything to be found in the "Arabian Nights." Levet, it appears, when nearly sixty years of age, had made the acquaintance of the female in question; and though her habitation was merely a small coal-shed in Fetter Lane, she had art enough to persuade him that she was nearly related to a man of fortune, who had defrauded her of her birthright. Levet, completely duped, made her his wife. They had scarcely, however, been married four months when a writ was issued against him for debts contracted by his wife, and for some time he was compelled to keep himself in close concealment in order to avoid the horrors of a gaol. Not long afterward his wife ran away from him, and having been taken into custody for picking pockets, was tried at the Old Bailey, where she pleaded her own cause, and was acquitted. A separation now took place between Levet and his wife, when Doctor Johnson took Levet into his own home, where he afforded him an asylum during the remainder of his life; and at his death celebrated the virtues of his friend in those beautiful elegiac lines, which when once read are never forgotten:

> " Well tried through many a varying year,
>   See Levet to the grave descend;
>   Officious, innocent, sincere,
>   Of every friendless name the friend."

Boswell informs us that Doctor Johnson himself lived at one time in Fetter Lane.

The celebrated Praise-God Barebone was another resident in Fetter Lane. His turbulence and fanaticism could scarcely have impaired his fortune, for in some evidence which he gave at a trial, it was shown that he was in the habit of paying forty pounds a year for house rent, — no inconsiderable sum in the reign of Charles the Second. There are said to have been three brothers in the family, each of whom had a sentence for his name: "Praise-God Barebone," "Christ-came-into-the-world-to-save Barebone," and, "If-Christ-had-not-died-thou-hadst-been-damned Barebone." For the sake of brevity, either the friends or the enemies of the latter are said to have merely styled him "Damned Barebone," omitting the former part of the sentence.

Running parallel with Fetter Lane is Castle Street, formerly called Castle Yard. In this street, in 1710, at the house of his father, a master-tailor, Paul Whitehead, the poet, was born.

Nearly opposite to Fetter Lane, on the north side of Holborn Hill, is Hatton Garden, which derives its name from being the site where the house and gardens of the Hatton family formerly stood. Hatton House was originally built by Sir Christopher Hatton, lord keeper in the reign of Queen Elizabeth; a man as much distinguished for his graceful person and fine dancing, as for all the qualities essential to constitute an orator and a statesman. Here the great lord keeper breathed his last, on the 20th of September, 1591, the victim, it is said, of a broken heart, occasioned by a stern demand of Elizabeth for the amount of an old debt due to her, which it was not in his power to pay.

In Hatton Garden resided the beautiful Letitia, Countess of Drogheda, who, about the year 1680, conferred her hand on the witty and handsome dramatist, William Wycherley. He was originally introduced to Lady Drogheda under somewhat peculiar circumstances in a bookseller's shop at Tunbridge Wells. Satisfied that he had made an impression on her heart, he followed her on her return to London, visited her at her house in Hatton Garden, and in a short time obtained her consent to marry him. It is almost needless to remark that their union was productive of happiness to neither party.

In 1669 the celebrated physician, Doctor Bate, who attended Oliver Cromwell in his last moments, breathed his last in his house in Hatton Garden.

Close to Hatton House stood Ely House, the ancient town residence of the Bishops of Ely, of which interesting habitation an account will presently be found.

On the south side of Holborn, between Fetter Lane and Chancery Lane, are Southampton Buildings, so called from their having been built on the

site of Southampton House, the residence of the
Wriothesleys, Earls of Southampton. The old
mansion was almost entirely destroyed in 1652,
but small portions of it are said still to exist, and
to form part of the adjoining houses. It was in
Southampton Buildings that the celebrated republican general, Edmund Ludlow, lay concealed till
he found means to effect his escape to Geneva.

Not far from Hatton Garden, on the south side
of Holborn, is the church of St. Andrew. Originally built in the reign of Henry the Sixth, it
escaped the great fire of London, but falling into
a ruinous state, was rebuilt, with the exception of
the tower, in 1686. The exterior of St. Andrew's
possesses but little merit, while, on the other hand,
the interior, displaying the magnificent taste of
Sir Christopher Wren, has been much admired.
Over the communion-table is a large painted window, by Joshua Price, which, though of modern
date (1718), is distinguished by the glowing rich-
ness of its colouring. In the lower part is represented the Last Supper, and in a compartment
above, the Resurrection of our Saviour from the
grave.

In St. Andrew's Church, of which he was for
some years the parish clerk, lies buried John
Webster, the gifted author of " The White Devil,"
" The Duchess of Malfey," and of other plays
which will not " willingly be let die ! " The celebrated Doctor Sacheverel, and Joseph Strutt, the

author of the "Sports and Pastimes of the People of England," were also interred in this church. The resting-place of Sacheverel is pointed out by an inscribed stone in the chancel.

Among the eminent persons who have held the rectory of St. Andrew's may be mentioned John Hacket, Bishop of Lichfield, who wrote the well-known "Life of Lord Keeper Williams;" Edward Stillingfleet, Bishop of Worcester; and Doctor Sacheverel.

Let us not omit to mention that the parish register of St. Andrew's, under the date of 18th January, 1696–97, records the christening of the unfortunate poet, Richard Savage, the supposititious child of the profligate Anne, Countess of Macclesfield, by Earl Rivers. According to Doctor Johnson, the entry was made in the register by Lord Rivers's own direction. The parish registers contain also the following interesting events; the marriage, in 1598, of the great lawyer, Sir Edward Coke, to Lady Elizabeth Hatton, sister of Lord Burleigh; the marriage, in 1638, of Colonel Hutchinson, to Lucy Apsley, the authoress of the charming "Memoirs;" the burial, in 1643, of Nathaniel Tomkins, who was executed for his share in Waller's plot to surprise the city; and lastly, the interment, on the 28th of August, 1770, of the unfortunate Thomas Chatterton.

Opposite to St. Andrew's Church is Brooke Street, deriving its name — as also does Greville

Street, which adjoins it — from Fulke Greville, Lord Brooke, the accomplished poet and courtier of the reigns of Elizabeth and James the First, as well as the intimate friend of Sir Philip Sydney, as recorded on the tomb of the former at Warwick. It was in Brooke House, which stood on the immediate site of Brooke Street and Greville Street, that on the 1st of September, 1628, its noble owner met with his tragical fate. He had been attended for many years by one Ralph Haywood, a gentleman by birth, who had expected that Lord Brooke would have rewarded his long services by bequeathing him a handsome legacy. For some cause, however, Lord Brooke not only omitted Haywood's name in his will, but unfortunately allowed him to become cognisant of the fact. Irritated at this circumstance, and, moreover, having been sharply rebuked by his master for some real or imaginary offence, Haywood entered Lord Brooke's bedchamber, and terminated a violent scene of asperity and recrimination by stabbing him in the back. The assassin then retreated to his own apartment, in which, having locked himself in, he committed suicide by killing himself with the same weapon with which he had stabbed his master. Lord Brooke survived for a few days.

Brooke Street is rendered especially interesting from the circumstance of Chatterton having met with his untimely end at No. 4, in this street.

His kind-hearted landlady, Mrs. Angel, aware how long he had fasted, and that he was without a shilling in the world, offered him some dinner on the day preceding his death, which his pride, superior to his sufferings, induced him to decline. A few hours afterward he swallowed poison, and the next day, the 25th of August, 1770, was found dead in his bed. He was only in his eighteenth year. The house in which Chatterton expired is no longer in existence, the site being now occupied by a furnishing warehouse.

Philip Yorke, the first celebrated Lord Hardwicke, previously to his being entered at the Middle Temple, was for some time articled to an attorney of the name of Salkeld in Brooke Street.

Running parallel with Brooke Street is Gray's Inn Lane, interesting as having contained the residences of many celebrated persons. The first whose name occurs to us is the celebrated dramatic poet, James Shirley. He was educated at St. John's College, Oxford, where he obtained the friendship and affection of Archbishop Laud, then president of the college. Contrary to the advice of Laud he entered into holy orders; an unfortunate step for him, inasmuch as not long afterward he was induced to exchange the religion of the Church of England for that of Rome, when, throwing up a preferment which he held near St. Albans, he established himself as teacher of a grammar school in that town. This employment proving too irksome for him, he repaired to London, and, taking up his abode in Gray's Inn Lane, commenced the composition of those dramatic writings which have conferred such celebrity on his name. Happily he lived in a reign in which genius was seldom left to linger long in obscurity. Charles the First appreciated his genius, and invited him to his court. Henrietta Maria conferred on him an appointment in her household. If Charles in the days of his prosperity extended his smiles and his bounty to the poets, the latter, when the sky of royalty became overcast, displayed no want of gratitude or affection toward their unhappy sovereign. On the breaking out of the civil troubles Shirley bade adieu to his wife and children, and enlisted himself beneath the banner of the Duke of Newcastle. On the downfall of the royal cause he returned to London a ruined man. Plays had in the interim been alike prohibited by the government and denounced from the pulpit, and accordingly it was only by the kindness of Thomas Stanley, the author of the "History of Philosophy," that he was saved from becoming the inmate either of a workhouse or a gaol. In this revolution in his fortunes, Shirley reverted to his former profession of teacher, and opened a grammar school in White Friars. Then followed the Restoration, and with it the revival of his plays on the stage; bringing back, however, no long career of prosperity to the poet. His house in Fleet having been burnt to the ground in the great fire of 1666, he was compelled to seek refuge in the neighbouring village of St. Giles's-in-the-Fields, whither, however, he retired only to die. As has been already mentioned, the loss of his property, added, probably, to the horrors of the terrible conflagration which he had witnessed, gave such a shock to his constitution that he survived the event scarcely twenty-four hours.

Another unfortunate poet whose name is associated with Gray's Inn Lane is John Ogilby, now principally remembered by his translation of Homer, a task in which he was assisted by his friend Shirley. Ogilby served his apprenticeship to a dancing-master in Gray's Inn Lane, in which undignified profession he acquired so great a proficiency, that in a short time he was able to purchase his discharge from his apprenticeship, as well as to obtain the liberty of his father, who was a prisoner in the King's Bench. His talents as a dancer led to his introduction at court; a circumstance so far unfortunate for him that, in cutting a caper at a masque given by the Duke of Buckingham, he fell to the ground, and so severely strained one of the sinews of his leg as ever afterward to continue lame. He now turned author by profession, and after suffering great vicissitudes, succeeded, toward the close of life, in obtaining the appointments of cosmographer and geographic printer to Charles the Second, the emoluments of which offices probably enabled him to end his days, if not in affluence, at least not in actual want.

There remains to mention but one more poet, the Rev. John Langhorne, in connection with Gray's Inn Lane. He lived before the days of "clubs," when men of the learned professions, and even clergymen, were accustomed to assemble at particular taverns, where they could enjoy the society which best suited them, and the beverage which they most loved. The favourite haunt of Langhorne was the Peacock, in Gray's Inn Lane, famous in the last century for its Burton ale, a beverage to which he was so partial, that an over-indulgence in it is said to have hastened his end. The affliction which he suffered at the loss of his beloved wife — the "Constantia" of Cartwright's verse, and whom he himself so pathetically and poetically lamented — probably laid the foundation of the unhappy infirmity which he had contracted.

About the year 1756, in the days of his penury and distress, Doctor Johnson was a resident in Gray's Inn Lane.

In 1640, at the period when the illustrious Hampden was heading the great struggle in defence of the liberties of his country, he was a resident of Gray's Inn Lane. At the same time, too, from a house almost adjoining that of his friend,

Pym might be seen sallying forth day after day to conduct the impeachment and prosecution of his arch-enemy, Lord Strafford. In 1673, John Aubrey, the antiquary, was lodging in Gray's Inn Lane.

In the immediate neighbourhood of Gray's Inn, in the days of his ignominy and disgrace, lived Lord Bacon. The name of Verulam Buildings, Gray's Inn, still points out the spot where stood the last London residence of the fallen but still immortal philosopher.

> " If parts allure thee, think how Bacon shined,
> The wisest, brightest, meanest of mankind."

The Blue Boar Inn, in High Holborn, now No. 270, was the scene of a curious passage in the life of Charles the First. A secret compact is said to have been entered into between Charles on the one side, and Cromwell and Ireton on the other, by which the king guaranteed to Ireton the lieutenancy of Ireland, and to Cromwell the Garter, £10,000 a year, and the earldom of Essex, on condition of their restoring him to liberty and power. His spirited consort, Henrietta Maria, who was then in France, wrote to reproach him for these unworthy concessions. Her letter is said to have been intercepted by Cromwell and Ireton, who, having informed themselves of its contents, forwarded it to the unsuspecting monarch, whose reply they anxiously awaited, and also in due time intercepted. The proofs which it contained of Charles's insincerity are said to have sealed the king's fate. So far, he said, was it from being his intention to keep faith with "the rogues," that in due time, "instead of a silken garter, they should be fitted with an hempen cord." "The letter," said Cromwell to Lord Orrery, "was sewn up in the skirt of a saddle, and the bearer of it was to come with the saddle upon his head, about ten of the clock that night, to the Blue Boar Inn, in Holborn, for there he was to take horse, and go to Dover with it. This messenger knew nothing of the letter in the saddle, but some persons in Dover did. We [Cromwell and Ireton] were at Windsor, and immediately Ireton and I resolved to take one trusty fellow with us, and with troopers' habits, to go to the inn in Holborn ; which accordingly we did, and set our man at the gate of the inn, where the wicket only was open, to let people in and out. Our man was to give us notice when any person came there with a saddle, whilst we, in the disguise of common troopers, called for cans of beer, and continued drinking till about ten o'clock ; the sentinel at the gate then gave notice that the man with the saddle was come in. Upon this we immediately arose, and as the man was leading out his horse saddled, came up to him with drawn swords, and told him that we were to search all that went in and out there, but as he looked like an honest man, we would only search his saddle, and so dismiss him. Upon that, we ungirt the saddle, and carried it into the stall where we had been drinking, and left the horseman without sentinel; then ripping up one of the skirts of the saddle, we there found the letter of which we had been informed; and having got it into our own hands, we delivered the saddle again to the man, telling him he was an honest man, and bidding him go about his business. The man, not knowing what had been done, went away to Dover." This singular story must doubtless be received with caution. Nevertheless, that such a letter, in the handwriting of Charles the First, was intercepted either by Cromwell or by his emissaries, there exists reasonable grounds for believing. Lord Oxford, in fact, assured Lord Bolingbroke that he had read it, and offered for it no less a sum than £500.

Diverging from the east side of Gray's Inn Lane is Fox Court, in which wretched alley the profligate Countess of Macclesfield was delivered of her illegitimate child, Richard Savage. In "The Earl of Macclesfield's Case," presented to the House of Lords in 1690, will be found some curious particulars respecting the *accouchement* of the countess, and the birth of the future poet. From this source it appears that Anne, Countess of Macclesfield, under the name of Madam Smith, was delivered of a male child in Fox Court, Holborn, by a Mrs. Wright, a midwife, on Saturday, the 16th of January, 1697, at six o'clock in the morning; that the child was baptised on the Monday following, and registered by Mr. Burbridge, assistant-curate of St. Andrew's, Holborn, as the son of John Smith; that it was christened on Monday, the 18th of January, in Fox Court, and that, from the privacy maintained on the occasion, it was supposed by Mr. Burbridge to be a " by-blow." During her delivery Lady Macclesfield wore a mask. By the entry of the birth in the parish register of St. Andrew's, it appears that the child's putative father, Lord Rivers, gave his son his own Christian name. " January 1696-97. Richard, son of John Smith and Mary, in Fox Court, in Gray's Inn Lane, baptised the 18th."

Adjacent to the entrance into Chancery Lane stood the Old Temple, the inn of the Knights Templars from the time of its erection, in 1118, till their removal to the New Temple in Fleet Street, in 1184. According to Stow, about the year 1595 one Agaster Roper, while employed in erecting buildings on the spot, discovered the ruins of the old church, which were of Caen stone, and built in a circular shape.

In 1597 the eminent botanist, John Gerarde, was residing in Holborn, then a suburb of London, where he had a good garden behind his house, in which he cultivated his rare exotics. Another remarkable person who resided in Holborn was the eccentric Sir Kenelm Digby. "The fair houses in Holborn," says Aubrey, "between King Street and Southampton Street, were built anno 1633, by Sir Kenelm, where he lived before the civil wars."

King Street, running out of Holborn, and now forming part of Southampton Row, is connected with the fate of an unfortunate poet, John Bampfylde, whose sonnets Mr. Dyce has thought worthy of being included in his selection of the choicest in the language. "He was the brother of Sir Charles, as you say," writes Southey to Sir Egerton Brydges, on the authority of Jackson, of Exeter, "and you probably know that there is a disposition to insanity in the family. At the time when Jackson became intimate with him he was just in his prime, and had no other wish than to live in solitude and amuse himself with poetry and music. He lodged in a farmhouse near Chudleigh, and would oftentimes come to Exeter in a winter morning, ungloved and open-breasted, before Jackson was up, with a pocket full of music or poems, to know how he liked them. His relations thought this was a sad life for a man of family, and forced him to London. The tears ran down Jackson's cheeks when he told the story. 'Poor fellow,' said he, 'there did not live a purer creature, and if they would have let him alone he might have been alive now.' When he was in London, his feelings having been forced out of their natural

and proper channel, took a wrong direction, and
he began soon to suffer the punishment of debauch-
ery. The Miss Palmer (afterward Lady Inchi-
quin) to whom he dedicated his sonnets was niece
to Sir Joshua Reynolds. Whether Sir Joshua ob-
jected to his addresses on account of his irregu-
larities in London, or of the family disposition to
insanity, I know not, but this was the commencement of his madness. He was refused admittance
into the house; upon this, in a fit of half anger
and half derangement, he broke the windows, and
was (little to Sir Joshua's honour) sent to Newgate. Some weeks after this had happened, Jackson went to London, and one of his first inquiries
was for Bampfylde. Lady B., his mother, said she
knew little or nothing about him, — that she had
got him out of Newgate, and he was now in some
beggary place. 'Where?' 'In King Street,
Holborn,' she believed, 'but she did not know the
number of the house.' Away went Jackson, and
knocked at every door till he found the right. It
was a truly miserable place; the woman of the
house was one of the worst class of women in
London. She knew that Bampfylde had no money,
and that at that time he had been three days without food. When Jackson saw him, there was all
the levity of madness in his manners. His shirt
was ragged, and black as a coalheaver's, and his
beard of a two months' growth. Jackson sent out
for food, said he was come to breakfast with him,

and turned aside to a harpsichord in the room, literally, he said, to let him gorge himself without being noticed. He removed him from hence, and, after giving his mother a severe lecture, obtained for him a decent allowance, and left him, when he himself quitted town, in decent lodgings, earnestly begging him to write. But he never wrote. 'The next news was that he was in a private madhouse, and I never saw him more.' After twenty years' confinement," adds Southey, "he recovered his senses, but not till he was dying of a consumption. The apothecary urged him to leave Sloane Street, where he had always been as kindly treated as he could be, and go into his own country, saying that his friends in Devonshire would be very glad to see him. But he hid his face, and answered, 'No, sir! They who knew me what I was shall never see me what I am.'"

It remains to mention one or two celebrated men who were residents in Holborn, but in what exact locality is not known.

Milton at two different periods of his life was a resident in Holborn, and on both occasions, as was his custom, occupied houses looking upon the green fields. The first time that he resided here was in 1647, in a house which "opened backward into Lincoln's Inn Fields," and here it was that he principally employed himself in writing his virulent tirades against monarchy and Charles the First. The second occasion of his residing in Holborn was after the Restoration of Charles the Second, when his house looked into Red Lion Fields, the site of the present Red Lion Square. After residing here a short time he removed to Jewin Street, Aldersgate Street.

From Boswell we learn that Doctor Johnson, during a part of the time he was employed in compiling his great work, the English Dictionary, was a resident in Holborn. Here, too, was born the once popular actor and poet, George Alexander Stevens; a man whose misfortunes were only equal to his misconduct, — at one time the idol of a Bacchanalian club, and at another the inmate of a gaol; at one moment writing a drinking-song, and at another a religious poem. Stevens is now, perhaps, best remembered from his "Lectures on Heads," a medley of wit and nonsense, to which no other person but himself could have given the proper effect. The lecture was originally designed for Shuter, who entirely failed in the performance. Stevens, however, no sooner attempted the task himself, than it became instantly popular. His songs are now nearly forgotten; yet one or two of them are not without merit, especially the one entitled the "Wine Vault," commencing:

"Contented I am, and contented I'll be,
    For what can this world more afford,
Than a lass that will sociably sit on my knee,
    And a cellar as sociably stored?
                                My brave boys.

" My vault-door is open, descend and improve,
    That cask, — ay, that we will try;
' Tis as rich to the taste as the lips of your love,
    And as bright as her cheek to the eye,
                        My brave boys."

CHAPTER V.

ELY HOUSE, GRAY'S INN, THAVIE'S INN, STAPLE INN, BARNARD'S INN.

Ely House in Its Splendour — Its Inhabitants — Protector Glou-
cester — Bishops of Ely — Feastings in Ely House — Sir
Christopher Hatton and the Bishops of Ely — Gray's Inn
and Gardens — Masques Performed at Gray's Inn — Famous
Masque — Celebrated Men Who Studied at Gray's Inn —
Thavie's Inn — Furnival Inn — Staple Inn — Barnard's Inn
— Gordon Riots.

ON the north side of Holborn Hill are Ely Place
and Hatton Garden; the former deriving its name
from the episcopal palace of the Bishops of Ely,
which stood here for nearly four centuries, and the
latter from the adjoining residence of Sir Christopher Hatton, the graceful courtier and eminent
statesman of the reign of Queen Elizabeth.

Ely House, in the days of its splendour, — for at
one period its palace and gardens covered an area
of nearly twenty acres, — consisted of a spacious
paved court, the approach to which was through a
stately gateway. On the left side of the court was
a small garden; on the right were the offices, supported by a colonnade; and, at the extremity, the
noble old hall, associated in our minds with many

past scenes of revelry and splendour. To the northwest of the hall was a quadrangular cloister, and, adjoining it, a small meadow, in which stood the chapel, dedicated to St. Etheldreda, the patron saint of the Cathedral Church of Ely. The gardens of Ely House, long famous for their strawberries and roses, corresponded in size and beauty with the adjoining palace.

Ely House was originally founded by John de Kirkeby, who, dying Bishop of Ely in 1290, bequeathed some landed property of considerable value for the purpose of erecting a suitable residence for his successors in the see. Considerable additions and improvements were made by successive prelates, and more especially by John de Hotham, Bishop of Ely in the reign of Edward the Third, till at length Ely House became one of the most magnificent mansions in the metropolis. Of the ancient building, all that now remains is the interesting chapel of St. Etheldreda, which, though it has suffered much from the lapse of ages, and has been sadly disfigured by modern improvements, still retains many traces of its pristine beauty. Its crypt also, of the same length as the chapel, and its east window, looking into Ely Place, have been deservedly admired. Evelyn, in his " Diary," more than once notices Ely Chapel. On the 14th of November, 1668, he writes : " I was invited to the consecration of that excellent person, the Dean of Ripon, Doctor Wilkins, now made Bishop of Chester. It was at Ely House, the Archbishop of Canterbury, Doctor Cosin, Bishop of Durham, the Bishops of Ely, Salisbury, Rochester, and others officiating. Doctor Tillotson preached. Then we went to a sumptuous dinner in the hall, where were the Duke of Buckingham, judges, secretaries of state, lord keeper, council, noblemen, and innumerable other company, who were honourers of this incomparable man, universally beloved by all who know him." Again, Evelyn inserts in his " Diary," 27th of April, 1673 : " My daughter Susanna was married to William Draper, Esq., in the chapel of Ely House, by Doctor Tenison, Bishop of Lincoln, since Archbishop. I gave her in portion £4,000. Her jointure is £500 per annum. I pray Almighty God to give his blessing to this marriage."

In Ely House resided, at the close of his eventful life, John, Duke of Lancaster,

" Old John o' Gaunt, time-honoured Lancaster."

Here he breathed his last in 1399; and here Shakespeare represents him admonishing with his dying breath his dissipated nephew, Richard the Second :

" A thousand flatterers sit within thy crown,
　Whose compass is no bigger than thy head ;
　And yet, incaged in so small a verge,
　The waste is no whit lesser than thy land.
　O, had thy grandsire with a prophet's eye

Seen how his son's son should destroy his sons,
From forth thy reach he would have laid thy shame;
Deposing thee before thou wert possessed,
Which are possessed now to depose thyself.
Why, cousin, wert thou regent of the world,
It were a shame to let this land by lease:
But for thy world enjoying but this land,
Is it not more than shame to shame it so?
Landlord of England art thou, and not king."
                    — *King Richard II.*, Act ii. Sc. 1.

Under what circumstances Ely House became the residence of John o' Gaunt is not known. It seems probable, however, that it was either lent or leased to him by Bishop Fordham after the duke's own palace in the Savoy had been burnt by the insurgents in Wat Tyler's riots. It was leased, indeed, on more than one occasion to men of high rank. Here Henry Ratcliffe, third Earl of Sussex, was residing in 1547. In the following reign it was in the occupation of John Dudley, Earl of Warwick, afterward Duke of Northumberland, and here it was that he carried on those famous intrigues which brought the Protector Somerset to the block.

Were it from no other circumstance than the connection of Ely Place with the pages of Shakespeare, we should look upon it as hallowed ground. We allude, not only to the death-bed admonitions of John o' Gaunt, but to the famous scene in the council-chamber at the Tower, in which the Protector, Richard, Duke of Gloucester, after jesting with the Bishop of Ely on the excellence and early growth of his strawberries at Ely House, concludes the tragical farce by exposing his shrivelled arm, and sending Lord Hastings, "without time for confession or repentance," to the block.

> " My Lord of Ely, when I was last in Holborn,
>   I saw good strawberries in your garden there;
>   I do beseech you send for some."

"Gladly, my lord," was the bishop's reply; "would to God I had some better thing as ready to your pleasure as that!" And therewithal, we are told, "in all haste he sent his servant for a mess of strawberries." Such was the first scene of that memorable drama, which was followed by the arrest of Lord Stanley and of Jane Shore, the execution of Lord Hastings, and the dethronement and death of the ill-fated Edward the Fifth!

Not unfrequently we find the Bishops of Ely, in the true spirit of hospitality, lending their fine old hall for the purposes of feasting and revelry, to the sergeants at law, the halls of the Inns of Court being apparently too small to accommodate the required number of guests. It was on one of these occasions, in 1495, that Henry the Seventh was feasted with his consort, Elizabeth of York, with great ceremony and magnificence. "The king," writes Bacon, "to honour the feast, was present with his queen at the dinner; being a prince that was ever ready to grace and countenance the professors of the law." But a feast, on a far greater scale of splendour, took place here in November, 1531, at which King Henry the Eighth and his queen, Catherine of Aragon, sat as guests; while at the tables below the dais sat the lord mayor, aldermen, and principal merchants of London; the foreign ambassadors, the judges, masters in Chancery, the sergeants at law and their wives, besides the principal nobility, and numerous knights and esquires. The entertainment lasted five days; the king and queen dining in the hall only on the principal day, the 13th of November. The bill of fare, which has been preserved, is alike curious, as evincing the vast scale of the entertainment, and the relative value of money in our own time and in the days of Henry the Eighth. Among other items are:

Twenty-four beeves, each . . .	26s.	8d.	
One carcase of an ox from the shambles	24	0	
One hundred fat muttons, each . .	2	10	
Fifty-one great veals, each . . .	4	8	
Twenty-four porkes, each . . .	3	3	
Ninety-one pigs, each	0	6	
Ten dozen capons of Greece . .	1	8	per doz.
Nine dozen and six capons of Kent .	1	0	"
Seven dozen and nine cocks of grose .	0	8	"
Nineteen dozens of capons course .	0	6	"
Seven dozen and nine fat cocks . .	0	8	"
Thirty-seven dozen of pigeons . .	0	2	"
Thirteen dozens of swans . . .	———		
Three hundred and forty dozen of larks	0	5	"

Prynne informs us that the last "Mystery" represented in England — that of "Christ's Passion" — was performed at Ely House before Gondomar, the Spanish ambassador, in the reign of James the First.

It was a great misfortune to Ely House when, in the reign of Queen Elizabeth, her favourite, Sir Christopher Hatton, prevailed upon his royal mistress to demand from Bishop Cox a considerable portion of the buildings and garden to enable him to enlarge his own adjoining mansion, Hatton House. Earnestly and respectfully the bishop implored the queen to spare a property which for three centuries had been the pride and delight of his predecessors. "In his conscience," he said, "he could not do it, being a piece of sacrilege. When he became Bishop of Ely, he had received certain farms, houses, and other things, which former pious princes had judged necessary for that place and calling; that these he had received by the queen's favour from his predecessors, and that of these he was to be a steward, not a scatterer. That he could not bring his mind to be so ill a trustee for his successors, nor to violate the pious wills of kings and princes, and, in effect, rescind their last testaments." All his entreaties and arguments, however, proved of no avail. Elizabeth continued fixed in her resolve, and, consequently, after demurring for a considerable time, we find the bishop compelled to make the required conveyance to the Crown for the sum of £100 ; reserving, however, to himself and to his successors the use of the gateway, the melancholy pleasure of taking exercise in the garden, and the right to gather twenty bushels of roses annually.

On the death of Doctor Cox, his successor, Dr. Martin Heton, showed himself quite as averse to complete the bargain as his predecessor had been, and accordingly it was on this occasion that Elizabeth addressed to the latter prelate the following memorable epistle :

" PROUD PRELATE : — I understand you are backward in complying with your agreement, but I would have you know that I, who made you what you are, can unmake you ; and if you do not forthwith fulfil your engagement, by G—d I will immediately unfrock you.

"ELIZABETH."

In Hatton House Sir Christopher Hatton breathed his last on the 20th of November, 1591 ; dying, it is said, of a broken heart occasioned by the stern demand of his royal mistress for repayment of the sum of £40,000 which she had formerly lent him, and which he was unable to repay. Elizabeth, it is further said, not only repented of her cruelty when it was too late, but paid a visit to Sir Christopher in his extremity at Hatton House, and even administered his " cordial-

broths" to him with her own hand. His names
are still preserved in Christopher Street, as well as
in Hatton Garden.

Ely Place continued to be the London residence
of the Bishops of Ely till 1772, when an act of the
legislature empowered them to dispose of the
ground to the Crown. Since that date their
episcopal residence in London has been in Dover
Street, Piccadilly.

In Cross Street, Hatton Garden, lived the eminent divine, William Whiston; and in Charles
Street died, on the 16th of October, 1802, Joseph
Strutt, the author of the popular work, the " Sports
and Pastimes of the People of England."

The Inns of Court in Holborn, or in its immediate vicinity, consist of Gray's Inn, Furnival's Inn,
Thavie's Inn, Staple Inn, and Barnard's Inn. Of
these the most important is Gray's Inn, situated
close to Gray's Inn Lane. Like more than one of
the Inns of Court, it derives its name from having
been originally the residence of a noble family;
the word "inne" having been anciently the usual
denomination of the town houses in which persons
of rank resided when summoned to attend either
Parliament or their sovereign.

Gray's Inn stands upon the site of a property
anciently know as the Manor of Portpoole, or Pur-
poole, and derives its name from having been the
residence of the Lords Gray of Wilton from 1315
to 1505. The name of the ancient manor is still

preserved in Portpoole Lane, running from Gray's Inn Lane into Leather Lane.   In 1505 it was sold by Edmund, the ninth baron, to Hugh Denny, Esq., who about eight years afterward disposed of it to the prior and convent of East Sheen in Surrey. The convent leased the mansion to the students at law, whose tenure was subsequently rendered somewhat insecure by the dissolution of the religious houses.   Henry the Eighth, however, took the property into his own hands, allowing the students at law to become tenants of the Crown on payment of an annual rent.

This important Inn of Court consists of a spacious court, and a large garden, laid out about the year 1600, and shaded by lofty trees.   The domain of the society extends over a large tract of ground between Holborn and King's Road. It has its hall, built in 1560, its chapel, and library ; but, if we except the hall, they are distinguished by no extraordinary architectural merit. We must not omit to mention, however, that the bench tables in the hall are said to have been the gift of Queen Elizabeth, who not only took great pleasure in the dramatic performances of the gentlemen of Gray's Inn, but, according to tradition, on one occasion partook of a banquet in their hall.   We may add that in our own time the only toast which is ever publicly drunk by the society, is "to the glorious, pious, and immortal memory of Queen Elizabeth," and this only on state occasions, and then with great formality. Three benchers rise and drink the toast. They then sit down, and two others rise, and in this manner the toast passes down the bar table, and thence to the table of the students.

To the gateway of Gray's Inn a certain interest is attached from its having contained the shop of the celebrated bookseller, Jacob Tonson, who appears to have resided here between the years 1697 and 1712, in which latter year he removed to a shop opposite Catherine Street, in the Strand.

Tonson was succeeded in his shop by another eminent bookseller, Thomas Osborne, whose name more than once occurs in the " Dunciad," especially where he is introduced as contending for the prize among the booksellers, and carrying it off :

" Osborne, through perfect modesty o'ercome,
Crowned with the jordan, walks contented home."

Osborne is perhaps best remembered from his well-known feud with Doctor Johnson. "It has been confidently related with many embellishments," writes Boswell, "that Johnson one day knocked Osborne down in his shop with a folio, and put his foot upon his neck. The simple truth I had from Johnson himself. ' Sir, he was impertinent to me, and I beat him. But it was not in his shop ; it was in my own chamber.' " Johnson says of Osborne, in his " Life of Pope," that he was

entirely destitute of shame, without sense of any
disgrace but that of poverty.   He is said to have
combined the most lamentable ignorance with
extraordinary expertness in all the petty tricks
of his trade.

The most interesting spot connected with Gray's
Inn are the gardens, which, as late as 1633, commanded a very pleasing view of the high grounds
of Hampstead and Highgate; the entire country
to the north consisting of pasture-land.   This spot
was a favourite resort of the immortal Bacon during the period he resided in Gray's Inn.   It appears,
by the books of the society, that he planted the
greater number of the elm-trees which still afford
their refreshing shade; and also that he erected
a summer-house on a small mound on the terrace,
where it is not improbable that he often meditated
and passed his time in literary composition.   From
the circumstance of Lord Bacon dating his essays
from his "Chamber in Graies Inn," it is not improbable that the charming essay in which he dwells
so enthusiastically on the pleasures of a garden,
was composed in, and inspired by, the floral beau-
ties of this his favourite haunt.   "God Almighty,"
he says, "first planted a garden; and indeed it
is the purest of human pleasures.   It is the greatest refreshment to the spirits of man, without
which buildings, and palaces are but gross handy-
works."   And he adds, "Because the breath of
flowers is far sweeter in the air, where it comes and

goes like the warbling of music, than in the hand, therefore nothing is more fit for that delight than to know what be the flowers and plants that do best perfume the air." As late as the year 1754 there was standing in the gardens of Gray's Inn an octagonal seat covered with a roof, which had been erected by Lord Bacon to the memory of his friend, Jeremiah Bettenham. To the seat was attached the following inscription :

"Franciscus Bacon, Regis Solicitor Generalis, executor testamenti Jeremiæ Bettenham, nuper Lectoris hujus hospitii, viri innocentis, abstinentis, et contemplativi, hanc sedem in memoriam ejusdem Jeremiæ extruxit, anno Dom. 1609."

Howell, writing in 1621, speaks of the walks in Gray's Inn Gardens as "the pleasantest place about London." Hither, in May, 1662, — when Mrs. Pepys was about to purchase some new articles of dress, — her gossiping husband mentions his bringing her, in order to observe "the fashions of the ladies ; " and here Addison, in the *Spectator*, mentions Sir Roger de Coverley walking on the terrace, "hemming twice or thrice to himself with great vigour ; for he loves to clear his pipes in good air, to make use of his own phrase, and is not a little pleased with any one who takes notice of the strength which he still exerts in his morning hems."

We have already alluded in our notices of Lincoln's Inn to the famous masques, revels, and

Christmasings of which the halls of the Inns of
Court were anciently the scene; to the days of
the yule-wood, of boars' heads and barons of beef,
when the Lord of Misrule and the King of the
Cockneys performed their fantastic fooleries, and
when, in the words of Justice Shallow:

> "'Twas merry in hall,
>   When beards wag all."

During the reigns of Henry the Eighth and
Queen Elizabeth, masques and other goodly "dis-
guisings" appear to have been frequently performed
at Gray's Inn.   The first of which we have any
record was a masque composed by one John Roo,
sergeant at law, which was performed at Gray's Inn
in 1525.   It was principally remarkable from the
great offence which it gave to Cardinal Wolsey,
whose ambition and misgovernment it was supposed that the author intended to satirise.   According to the old chronicler, Hall, " This play
was so set forth with rich and costly apparel, and
with strange devices of masks and morrishes, that
it was highly praised by all men, except by the
cardinal, who imagined that the play had been
devised of him.   In a great fury he sent for Master Roo, and took from him his coif, and sent him
to the Fleet, and afterward he sent for the young
gentlemen that played in the play, and highly rebuked and threatened them, and sent one of them,
called Thomas Moyle, of Kent, to the Fleet; but

by means of friends, Master Roo and he were delivered at last. This play sore displeased the cardinal, and yet it was never meant for him, wherefore many wise men grudged to see him take it so to heart; and even the cardinal said that the king was highly displeased with it, and spake nothing of himself."

It may, or may not have been the case that Roo, when he composed his masque, intended to "devise" the cardinal. From the following passage, however, in Fox's "Acts and Monuments," it is evident that the performers were fully aware that Wolsey would in all probability conceive himself to be the object of its satirical pleasantries. Fox, writing of Simon Fish, of Gray's Inn, author of the "Supplication of the Beggars," observes : "It happened the first year that this gentleman came to London to dwell, which was about the year of our Lord 1525, that there was a certain play or interlude made by one M. Roo, of the same inn, gentleman, in which play partly was matter against the Cardinal Wolsey; and when none durst take upon them to play that part which touched the said cardinal, this aforesaid M. Fish took upon him to do it. Whereupon great displeasure ensued against him on the cardinal's part, in so much as he, being pursued by the said cardinal, the same night that this tragedy was played, was compelled of force to void his own house, and so fled over the sea to Tindal."

During the period that Fish was residing in Germany, a copy of his " Supplication of the Beggars "— a satire on the monastic orders in England — was shown by Anne Boleyn to Henry the Eighth, who was so much pleased with it that he not only permitted the author to return to England but took him under his protection.   Fish, however, survived his recall only a short time, dying of the plague in 1531.

As a specimen of those costly entertainments with which the courts of law were anciently in the habit of regaling their sovereigns, the following account may not be unacceptable to the reader. The masque to which we allude was performed in the palace of Whitehall, before Charles the First and Henrietta Maria, at Allhallowtide, in 1633, on the occasion of the birth of the Duke of York, afterward James the Second.   It was given by the members of the four principal Inns of Court, — Lincoln's Inn, Gray's Inn, and the Middle and Inner Temple, — the hall of Ely House being the place where the masquers assembled and whence the motley procession set out in long array for Whitehall.   "On Candlemas day, in the afternoon, the masquers, horsemen, musicians, dancers, and all that were actors in this business, met at Ely House in Holborn; and when the evening was come, all things being in full readiness, they began to set forth in this order down Chancery Lane to Whitehall.   The

first that marched were twenty footmen in scarlet
liveries with silver lace, each one having his sword
by his side, a baton in one hand, and a torch
lighted in the other. There were the marshal's
men, who cleared the streets, made way, etc.
After them came the marshal, Mr. Daniel, afterward knighted by the king. He was of Lincoln's
Inn, an extraordinary handsome, proper gentleman.
He was mounted on one of the king's best horses
and richest saddles, and his own habit was exceed-
ingly rich and glorious. His horsemanship was
very gallant; and, besides his marshal's men, he
had two lackeys, who carried torches by him, and a
page in livery that went by him carrying his cloak.

"After the marshal followed a train of a hundred young gentlemen, selected on account of
their showy and handsome appearance, from the
different Inns of Court, all of them mounted on
gallant horses sumptuously caparisoned, which had
been furnished for the occasion from the king's
stables and those of the principal nobility. Then
followed the chariots of the inferior masquers,
after which came the first chariot of the grand
masquers, which was not so large as those that
went before, but most curiously framed, carved,
and painted with exquisite art, and purposely for
this service and occasion. The form of it was
after that of the Roman triumphant chariots.
The colours of the first chariot were silver and
crimson, given by lot to Gray's Inn; the chariot

was drawn with four horses all abreast, and they were covered to their heels all over with cloth of tissue of the colours of crimson and silver, huge plumes of red and white feathers on their heads; the coachman's cap and feather, his long coat, and his very whip and cushion of the same stuff and colour. In this chariot sat the four grand masquers of Gray's Inn, their habits, doublets, trunkhose, and caps of most rich cloth of tissue, and wrought as thick with silver spangles as they could be placed; large white stockings up to their trunkhose, and rich sprigs in their caps, themselves proper and beautiful young gentlemen. On each side of the chariot were four footmen, in liveries of the colour of the chariot, carrying huge flambeaux in their hands, which, with the torches, gave such a lustre to the paintings, spangles, and habits, that hardly anything could be invented to appear more glorious.

" After this chariot came six more musicians on foot, and clothed in habits like the former. These were followed by the second chariot, as the lot fell, for the Middle Temple. This differed not in anything from the former but in colours only, which were of this chariot silver and blue. The chariot and horses were covered and decked with cloth of tissue of blue and silver. In this second chariot were the four grand masquers of the Middle Temple, in the same habits as the other masquers, and with the like attendance of torches and flam-

beaux with the former. After these followed the
third and fourth chariots, and six musicians between each chariot, habited, on foot; clothes
and horses as before. The chariots were all of
the same make and alike carved and painted,
differing only in the colours. In the third chariot rode the grand masquers of the Inner Temple;
and in the fourth chariot went those of Lincoln's
Inn, according to the lot drawn by each of them.
The habits of the sixteen grand masquers were all
the same, their persons most handsome and lovely,
the equipage so full of state and height of gallantry that it never was outdone by one repre-
scntation mentioned in our former stories.

"The march was slow in regard of their great
number, but more interrupted by the multitude of
spectators in the streets, besides [those at] the
windows, and they all seemed loath to part with
so glorious a spectacle. In the meantime, the
Banqueting House at Whitehall was so crowded
with fair ladies glittering with their rich clothes
and richer jewels, and with lords and gentlemen of
great quality, that there was scarce any room for
the king and queen to enter in.

"The gallery behind the state was reserved for
the gentlemen of the four Inns of Court who came
to see the masque. The king and queen stood at
a window to see the procession, and being so delighted with the noble bravery of it, desired that it
might turn about the tilt-yard, that their Majesties

might have a double view of it. The king and queen and all their noble train being come in, the masque began, and was incomparably performed in the dancing, speeches, music, and scenes. The dancing, figures, properties, the voices, instruments, songs, airs, composures, the words, and the actions, were all of them exact, and none failed in their parts of them, and the scenes were most curious and costly.

"The queen did the honour to some of the masquers to dance with them herself, and to judge them as good dancers as she ever saw, and the great ladies were very free and civil in dancing with all the masquers as they were taken by them. Thus they continued in their sports until it was almost morning, and then the king and queen retiring to their chamber, the masquers and Inns-of-Court gentlemen were brought to a stately banquet, and after that was dispersed every one departed to their own quarters."

This famous masque, the expense of which is said to have been about £21,000, is described by Garrard, in one of his letters to Lord Strafford, as "far exceeding, in bravery, any masque that had formerly been presented by these societies." "In their company," he writes, "there was one Mr. Read, of Gray's Inn, whom all the women, and some men, cried up for as handsome a man as the Duke of Buckingham. They were all well used at court by the king and queen, and no dis-

gust given them. Only this one accident fell.
Mr. May, of Gray's Inn, a fine poet, he who
translated Lucan, came athwart my lord chamberlain in the Banqueting House, and he broke
his staff over his shoulder, not knowing who he
was. The king was present, who knew him, for
he calls him his poet, and told the chamberlain of
it, who sent for him next morning, and fairly excused himself to him, and gave him fifty pounds
in pieces." The lord chamberlain here referred
to was the choleric Philip Herbert, Earl of Pembroke and Montgomery, — the "memorable simple-
ton" of Horace Walpole, — of whom Anthony
Wood quaintly observes, that he broke many
wiser heads than his own. May was a spirited
and an accomplished gentleman, as well as a poet;
indeed, according to Wood, had it not been for
the earl's high office and the place they were in,
"it might have been a question whether the earl
would ever have struck again." Lord Clarendon
says of this boisterous peer: "There were few
great persons in authority who were not frequently offended by him by sharp and scandal-
ous discourses and invectives against them behind
their backs; for which they found it best to receive satisfaction by submissions and professions
and protestations, which was a coin he was plenti-
fully supplied with." Early in life the earl had
been publicly horsewhipped on the race-course at
Croydon by Ramsey, a Scotch gentleman, after-

ward created Earl of Holderness; and nearly forty years afterward we find him using such insolent language to Lord Mowbray in the House of Lords as to provoke the latter to throw an inkstand at his head. Both lords were sent to the Tower, the earl apparently having been the greater sufferer of the two, in consequence of the king depriving him of his post of lord chamberlain.

Of the lawyers of the olden time who were members of Gray's Inn, the name which is perhaps the most familiar to us is that of Sir William Gascoigne, as eminent for his private virtues as for his integrity as a judge, and immortalised in the pages of Shakespeare in connection with the frolics of Falstaff and Prince Henry. Every one remembers the fine scene in which the future victor of Agincourt, after his accession to the throne, first meets with the independent judge who had been bold enough to commit him to prison.

"*King.* You are right, Justice, and you weigh this well;
Therefore still bear the balance and the sword;
And I do wish your honours may increase,
Till you do live to see a son of mine
Offend you and obey you, as I did.
. . . You did commit me:
For which, I do commit into your hand
The unstained sword that you have used to bear;
With this remembrance, — That you use the same
With the like bold, just and impartial spirit
As you have done 'gainst me."
— *King Henry IV.*, Part II., Act v. Sc. 2.

The account given by one of our old chroniclers of the prince's committal to prison by Sir William Gascoigne differs but little from that of Shakespeare. "It happened," we are told, "that a servant of Prince Henry, afterward the fifth English king of that Christian name, was arraigned before this judge for felony, whom the prince, then present, endeavoured to take away, coming up in such fury that the beholders believed he would have stricken the judge. But he, sitting without moving, according to the majesty he represented, committed the prince prisoner to the King's Bench, there to remain until the pleasure of the prince's father were further known. Who, when he heard thereof by some pick-thank courtier, who probably expected a contrary return, gave God thanks for his infinite goodness, who, at the same instant, had given him a judge who could minister and a son who could obey justice.

> "Happy am I, that have a man so bold,
>   That dares do justice on my proper son;
>   And not less happy, having such a son,
>   That would deliver up his greatness so,
>   Into the hands of justice."

Sir William Gascoigne was reader of Gray's Inn till 1398, when he was called to the degree of king's sergeant at law, and on the 15th of November, 1401, was constituted Chief Justice of the King's Bench. He died on the 17th of December, 1413.

Among other eminent members of Gray's Inn may be mentioned Sir Anthony Fitzherbert, Lord Chief Justice of the Court of Common Pleas in the reign of Henry the Eighth, Sir Nicholas Bacon, lord keeper of the Great Seal during the first twenty-five years of the reign of Elizabeth, and father of the great Lord Bacon, John Bradshaw, who sentenced Charles the First to the block in Westminster Hall, John Cooke, who, as Solicitor-General of the Commons of England, conducted the prosecution against the king at his mock trial, and, nearer our own time, Sir Samuel Romilly, Sir John Bayley, and Sir William Garrow. The latter lived for many years in No. 11 Gray's Inn Place, leading to the gardens.   Lord Bacon, whom we have already mentioned as a member of Gray's Inn, lived at No. 1 Coney Court, which was unfortunately burnt down in 1678.   The site is occupied by the present row of buildings at the west end of Gray's Inn Square, adjoining the gardens in which the great philosopher took such delight.

Besides the eminent lawyers we have mentioned, some of our most celebrated statesmen, prelates, and poets have been members of Gray's Inn. Here resided the great statesman, Thomas Cromwell, afterward Earl of Essex, who succeeded Wolsey in the favour of Henry the Eighth, and to whom the disgraced cardinal addressed his famous apostrophe :

"O Cromwell, Cromwell!
Had I but served my God with half the zeal
I served my king, he would not in mine age
Have left me naked to mine enemies."
— *King Henry VIII.*, Act iii. Sc. 2.

Cromwell was admitted a member of Gray's Inn in 1524. In 1535 he commenced his career of greatness, and only five years afterward, on the 24th of July, 1540, he fell by the stroke of the executioner on Tower Hill. Two other celebrated statesmen who were members of this inn were the great Lord Burghley, who was admitted a student in 1540, and his son, Robert Cecil, Earl of Salisbury, secretary of state to Queen Elizabeth, and first minister to James the First.

Among the distinguished prelates who have been members of Gray's Inn we find the merciless Stephen Gardiner, Bishop of Winchester, whose name is associated with so many fearful scenes of human suffering; Whitgift and Bancroft, successively Archbishops of Canterbury; Lord Keeper Williams, Bishop of Lincoln and afterward Archbishop of York; his implacable enemy, Laud, Archbishop of Canterbury; Joseph Hall, Bishop of Norwich, author of the well-known "Satires" and "Contemplations;" James Usher, Archbishop of Armagh, whose political hostility was forgiven by Oliver Cromwell in admiration of his private virtues; and, lastly, William Juxon, Bishop of London and afterward Archbishop of

Canterbury, who attended Charles the First upon the scaffold.

Of the literary men, and especially the poets, who were members of Gray's Inn, we have a still longer list. Among these let us mention the graceful and chivalrous Sir Philip Sydney, Edward Hall, the chronicler, George Gascoigne, a popular poet in the reign of Elizabeth, George Chapman, the translator of Homer, James Shirley, the dramatic poet, Thomas Rymer, author of the "Fœdera," and also no contemptible poet, Thomas May, the translator of Lucan's "Pharsalia," Samuel Butler, the author of "Hudibras," and Arthur Murphy, the dramatist and translator of Tacitus. Lastly, among the eminent men who belonged to the society of Gray's Inn, let us not omit to mention John Lambert, the distinguished parliamentary general in the civil wars, and the still more celebrated George Monk, Duke of Albemarle.

Of the other Inns of Court in the neighbourhood of Holborn but little remains to be said, and that little possesses no extraordinary interest.

Thavie's Inn, which stood on the south side of Holborn, was the hostel or inne, in the reign of Edward the Third, of one Job Thavie, who leased it to the students at law, and who, by his last will, directed it to be sold in order to maintain a chaplain, who was to pray for his soul and that of his wife, Alice. In the reign of Edward the Sixth it

came into the possession of Gregory Nicholas, who
made a grant of it to the society of Lincoln's Inn,
by whom it was erected into an Inn of Chancery,
on condition of paying the annual sum of £3 6s.
4d., as an acknowledgment of its dependency on
the mother house. In 1771 it was disposed of by
the benchers of Lincoln's Inn to a private individual, and having been subsequently destroyed by
fire, a range of private buildings was erected on
its site.

Furnival's Inn, near Brook Street, another
former appendage of Lincoln's Inn, stands on the
site of the princely inne of the Lords of Furnival,
that valiant family whose names so often occur in
the annals of chivalry, from Gerard de Furnival,
who fought by the side of Richard Cœur de Lion
on the plains of Palestine, to Thomas de Furnival,
the companion of the Black Prince on the field of
Cressy. In 1383, the race having become extinct
in the male line, Furnival's Inn fell by marriage
into the possession of the Earls of Shrewsbury.
In their hands it remained till the reign of Edward
the Sixth, when, on the 1st of December, 1548,
Francis, Earl of Shrewsbury, disposed of the mansion to the society of Lincoln's Inn, who converted
it into a separate Inn of Court on the condition of
the payment of an annual sum of £3 6s. 8d. The
inn was rebuilt in the reign of James the First,
but having fallen into a ruinous state in the present century, and a portion of it having been des-

troyed by fire, the old inn was taken down in
1817, and the present handsome pile of building
erected on its site. It no longer however, exists
as an Inn of Chancery. It adds to the interest of
the spot that Sir Thomas More filled for three
years the office of reader in Furnival's Inn.

Staple Inn, dependent on Gray's Inn, situated
on the south side of Holborn, is known to have
been an Inn of Chancery, at least as early as the
reign of Henry the Fifth. It has been supposed
to derive its name from having been anciently a
staple, or emporium, where the merchants of England exposed for sale their wool, cloth, and other
commodities; the society, in fact, having still for
their arms a woolpack argent. Stow, however,
confesses that the derivation of its name had escaped his researches. Staple Inn is divided into
two courts, with a pleasant garden behind. On
the 27th of November, 1756, a fire broke out at
No. 1, which destroyed four sets of chambers,
two females and two children perishing in the
flames. The hall, which fortunately escaped destruction, is a small but handsome building, in
which are portraits of Charles the Second, Queen
Anne, the Earl of Macclesfield, Lord Chancellor
Cowper, and Lord Camden. To Miss Porter, Doctor Johnson writes, on the 23d of March, 1759:
"I have this day moved my things, and you are
now to direct me at Staple Inn, London." The
removal in question was from Gough Square, Fleet

Street, where Johnson had resided for ten years. In Staple Inn (No. 11) resided Isaac Reed, the commentator on Shakespeare; and here he formed his rare and valuable collection of books.

Barnard's Inn, also on the south side of Holborn, was originally called Mackworth's Inn, from John Mackworth, Dean of Lincoln, whose executors made it over to the Dean and Chapter of Lincoln, on condition of their finding a priest to perform divine service in the chapel of St. George in that cathedral where the dean lies interred. In the lifetime of Dean Mackworth it was leased to one Lionel Barnard, who seems to have been the last person who resided in it before it was converted into an Inn of Chancery, and from whom it derives its present name. In the hall is a fine full-length portrait of the upright and learned Lord Chief Justice Holt, for some time principal of Barnard's Inn; and also of Lord Burleigh, Lord Bacon, Lord Keeper Coventry, and other eminent men.

During the famous Gordon Riots Barnard's Inn very nearly fell a sacrifice to one of those nightly and fearful acts of incendiarism, by which, on the eventful night of the 7th of June, 1780, so many public and private edifices were devoted to the flames. It adjoined the extensive premises of Mr. Langdale, an opulent distiller, who on two accounts was exposed to the fury of the mob; both as professing the Roman Catholic religion, and from the temptation of the intoxicating liquors on his premises.

The attack on Langdale's distillery, and its subsequent destruction by fire, — rendered the more awfully vivid from the quantity of ardent spirits which fed the flames, — was not among the least striking of those frightful scenes which occurred in various parts of the metropolis. Many of the rioters are said to have literally drunk themselves dead; women and children were seen on their knees drinking from the kennels, which flowed with gin and other intoxicating liquors; and many of the rabble, who had drunk themselves into a state of insensibility, perished in the flames. Doctor Warner, who passed the night in his chambers in Barnard's Inn, writes on the following morning to George Selwyn : "The staircase in which my chambers are is not yet burnt down, but it could not be much worse for me if it were. However, I fear there are many scores of poor creatures in this town who have suffered this night much more than I have, and with less ability to bear it. Will you give me leave to lodge the shattered remains of my little goods in Cleveland Court for a time? There can be no living here, even if the fire stops immediately, for the whole place is a wreck; but there will be time enough to think of this. But there is a circumstance which distresses me more than anything; I have lost my maid, who was a very worthy creature, and I am sure would never have deserted me in such a situation by her own will; and what can have become of her is horrible to think! I fervently hope that you and yours are free from every distress.

"Five o'clock. The fire, they say, is stopped, but what a rueful scene has it left behind! *Sunt lachrymæ rerum*, indeed; the sentence that struck me upon picking up a page of Lord Mansfield's Virgil yesterday in Bloomsbury Square. *Sortes Virgilianæ!*[1]

"Six o'clock. The fire, I believe, is nearly stopped, though only at the next door to me. But no maid appears. When I shall overcome the horror of the night, and its consequence, I cannot guess. But I know if you can send me word that things go well with you, that they will be less bad with me."

Such was the result of one of those disgraceful scenes which, under the pretext of zeal for the interests of the Protestant religion, disgraced, only ninety years since, the character of the English people. "Our danger is at an end," writes Gibbon, "but our disgrace will be lasting; and the month of June, 1780, will ever be marked by a dark and diabolical fanaticism, which I had supposed to be extinct, but which actually subsists in Great Britain, perhaps beyond any country in Europe." Fortunately we live in a more enlightened age. Scarcely sixty years had elapsed after Gib-

---

[1] Lord Mansfield's house in Bloomsbury Square, together with his lordship's fine library, had been burnt the day before by the mob.

bon penned his indignant tirade, when a body of London masons were to be seen quietly engaged in erecting the high altar of a magnificent Roman Catholic Cathedral on the very spot in St. George's Fields where the insane eloquence of Lord George Gordon excited that popular frenzy which very nearly had the effect of reducing London to a heap of ashes.

CHAPTER VI.

RED LION SQUARE, GREAT ORMOND STREET, BLOOMSBURY SQUARE, ETC.

Cromwell's Supposed Grave in Red Lion Square — Lamb's-Conduit Fields — Great Ormond Street — Queen Square — Southampton Row — Bloombsbury Square — Burning of Lord Mansfield's House — Celebrated Persons Who Lived in Bloomsbury Square — Highway Robberies — Great Russell Street — Montague House, now the British Museum — Duchess of Montague.

FORMERLY there existed a favourite tradition among the inhabitants of Red Lion Square and its vicinity, that the body of Oliver Cromwell was buried in the centre of their square, beneath an obelisk which stood there till within a few years.[1] The likelihood of such a fact strikes us,

[1] Pennant speaks of the "clumsy obelisk" in Red Lion Square, and mentions that it was inscribed with the following lines:

"Obtusum
Obtusioris Ingenù
Monumentum.
Quid me respicis, viator?"
Vade.

Could this quaint inscription have any hidden reference to the bones of Cromwell lying beneath it? We think not; but they are meant to mystify, and what, therefore, do they mean?

at first thought, as improbable enough, and yet, on consideration, we are inclined to think that beneath this spot not improbably moulder, not only the bones of the great Protector, but also those of Ireton and Bradshaw, whose remains were disinterred at the same time from Westminster Abbey, and exposed on the same gallows.

As regards the last resting-place of these remarkable men, the contemporary accounts simply inform us that on the anniversary of the death of Charles the First their bodies were borne on sledges to Tyburn, and after hanging till sunset, they were cut down and beheaded; that their bodies were then flung into a hole at the foot of the gallows, and their heads fixed upon poles on the roof of Westminster Hall. From the word Tyburn being here so distinctly laid down, it has usually been taken for granted that it was intended to designate the well-known place for executing criminals, nearly at the north end of Park Lane, or, as it was anciently styled, Tyburn Lane. As has been already mentioned, however, when we read of a criminal in old times having been executed at Tyburn, we are not necessarily to presume that it was at this particular spot; the gallows having unquestionably been shifted at times from place to place, and the word Tyburn having been given indiscriminately, for the time being, to each distinct spot. For instance, sixty years before the death of Cromwell, the gallows were frequently erected at the extremity of St. Giles's parish, near the end of the present Tottenham Court Road; while, for nearly two centuries, the Holborn end of Fetter Lane, within a short distance of Red Lion Square, was no less frequently the place of execution. Indeed, in 1643, only a few years before the exhumation and gibbeting of Cromwell, we find Nathaniel Tomkins executed at this spot for his share in Waller's plot to surprise the city.

In addition, however, to these surmises, is the curious fact of the bodies of Cromwell and Ireton having been brought in carts, on the night previous to their exposure on the gibbet, to the Red Lion Inn, Holborn, from which Red Lion Square derives its name, where they rested during the night. In taking this step it is surely not unreasonable to presume that the government had in view the selection of a house in the immediate vicinity of the scaffold, in order that the bodies might be in readiness for the disgusting exhibition of the following morning. Supposing this to have been the case, the place of their exposure and interment could scarcely have been the end of Tyburn Lane, inasmuch as the distance thither from Westminster is actually shorter than the distance from Westminster to Red Lion Square. The object of the government could hardly have been to create a sensation by parading the bodies along a populous thoroughfare, inasmuch as the ground between St. Giles's Pound and Tyburn, a distance of a mile and a half, was at this period almost entirely open country. The author has dwelt longer, perhaps, on the subject than such vague surmises may seem to deserve. The question, however, is not altogether an uninteresting one, and there may be others, probably, who may have the means of, and who may take a pleasure in, further elucidating it.

In Bedford Row, running parallel with Red Lion Street, Bishop Warburton was residing in 1750; and here, at No. 14, lived the eminent surgeon, John Abernethy.

Lamb's-Conduit Street derives its name from one William Lamb, an eminent cloth-worker, who erected a water conduit on its site in 1577.[1] It was taken down in 1746. As late as the reign of Queen Anne, Lamb's-Conduit Fields formed a favourite promenade for the citizens of London, on a portion of the site of which was erected, in 1739, the present Foundling Hospital for the reception of "exposed and deserted children." The founder was Capt. Thomas Coram, a merchant-seaman, from whom Great Coram Street derives its name. This excellent person, having passed

---

[1] This munificent individual purchased and bequeathed to the Cloth-workers the hermitage of St. James-in-the-Wall, situated at the north corner of Monkwell Street, Cripplegate. He died in 1577. Stow styles him "one of the gentlemen of the king's chapel, citizen and cloth-worker of London."

a long life in the performance of acts of charity and benevolence, found himself in his old age reduced to comparative penury. Under these circumstances the object of his friends was to raise a subscription for him, but fearful of offending him, they inquired of him in the first instance whether he was averse to such a measure. The reply was worthy of the man. "I have not wasted," he said, "the little wealth of which I was formerly possessed in self-indulgence or vain expenses, and am not ashamed to confess that in my old age I am poor." This excellent man, whose death took place on the 29th March, 1751, at his lodgings near Leicester Square, by his own wish was buried in the vaults under the chapel of the Foundling Hospital. The Foundling Hospital contains some very interesting pictures by Hogarth, Sir Joshua Reynolds, Gainsborough, and others, and is altogether well worthy of a visit.

In Doughty Street, Foundling Hospital, the Rev. Sydney Smith, the wit, was residing in 1805.

Lamb's-Conduit Street leads us into Great Ormond Street, the site of which was formerly occupied by Powys House, the residence in the reign of William the Third of the Herberts, Marquises of Powys. Their name is still preserved in Powys Place. In the reign of Queen Anne, Powys House was occupied by the French ambassador, the Duc d'Aumont, and having been

burnt down during his occupancy, was rebuilt
with considerable splendour at the expense of
Louis the Fourteenth. The second mansion,
which was of brick, ornamented with fluted pi-
lasters, was remarkable for its having a large
reservoir on the roof, which served the double
purpose of *piscatorium* and of supplying water
in case of fire. Powys House, which for twenty
years was the residence of Lord Chancellor Hardwicke, was pulled down in 1777, a portion of the
present street having been previously erected in
the reign of Queen Anne. Even as late as
some eighty years since, the north side of Great
Ormond Street commanded views of Islington,
Hampstead, and Highgate. In this street, at
No. 49, resided the celebrated physician, Doctor
Mead, and here he kept his fine collection of
books, drawings, medals, and antiquities. He
died here in 1754. In this street also resided
Dr. George Hickes, the scholar and divine, who
died in 1715; Robert Nelson, the author of the
" Fasts and Festivals," who died at Kensington,
the same year; Doctor Stukeley, previously to
his removal to Queen Square; Dr. John Hawkesworth; Zachary Macaulay, at No. 50; Lord
Chancellor Thurlow, at No. 45; and lastly, here,
in 1832, died Charles Butler, the author of the
agreeable " Reminiscences " which bear his name.

From Great Ormond Street we pass into Queen
Square, which, from its having been principally

built in the reign of Queen Anne, was named in
honour of that sovereign.   Here lived and died the
indefatigable, but somewhat fanciful, antiquary,
William Stukeley, who held the neighbouring living of St. George the Martyr.   The death of the
amiable old man was characteristic of his blameless
life.   On the 27th of February, 1765, on his return from his favourite country-house at Kentish
Town, to which he was in the habit of paying frequent visits, he lay down, according to his usual
custom, on his couch in Queen Square, waiting
for his housekeeper to come and read to him.
Subsequently, some occasion calling her from the
apartment, on her return he observed with a cheerful look : " Sally, an accident has happened since
you have been absent."   " Pray what is that, sir ? "
" No less than a stroke of the palsy."   " I hope
not, sir," she replied, and began to weep.   " Nay,
do not trouble yourself," he said, " but get some
help to carry me up-stairs, for I never shall come
down again but on men's shoulders."   " Soon
after," adds his biographer, Collinson, " his facul-
ties failed him ; but he continued quiet and composed, as in a sleep, until Sunday following, the
3d of March, 1765, and then departed, in his
seventy-eighth year, which he attained by his remarkable temperance and regularity."   By his own
wish he was buried in a particular spot in the
churchyard of West Ham, Essex.   It was his
further desire that the turf might be laid smoothly

over him, but that no monument should be raised over his grave.

Another eminent person who resided in Queen Square, was the learned physician, Dr. Anthony Askew, who formed here his rare and valuable collection of books, which at his death, in 1784, sold for £5,000.   In this square, also, Alderman Barber, the printer, died in 1741 ; here Jonathan Richardson, the painter, breathed his last in 1745, at the age of eighty; and here his son, "the younger Richardson," died in 1770.   Doctor Johnson mentions his frequent visits to John Campbell, the author of "The Lives of the Admirals," at the residence of the latter in Queen's Square.   "I used to go pretty often to Campbell's, on a Sunday evening, till I began to consider the shoals of Scotchmen who flocked about him might probably say, when anything of mine was well done, 'Ay, ay, he has learned this of Cammell.'"   Campbell's residence was at the northwest corner of Queen Square, and here he died in December, 1775. In Queen Street, Bloomsbury, George Vertue, the engraver, was residing in 1712.   Campbell, Jonathan Richardson and his wife, and Robert Nelson, lie buried in the churchyard of St. George the Martyr.   Here also were interred the celebrated Nancy Dawson, who died at Hampstead in May, 1767 ; Edward Dilly, the bookseller, and friend of Doctor Johnson ; and the late Zachary Macaulay.   This church, which is otherwise as uninteresting as it is unsightly, was built in 1706, and was constituted a parish church in September, 1723.

From Queen Square let us pass into Southampton Row, where we find Gray, the poet, lodging at one period, at a Mr. Jauncey's, in the same house which had previously been occupied by Doctor Warton. The space between Southampton Row and Montague Street was formerly occupied by the fair gardens of Southampton House. This splendid mansion, which extended along the whole of the north side of Bloomsbury Square, with a spacious courtyard in front, toward Holborn, was, in the days of Charles the First and Second, the princely residence of the Wriothesleys, Earls of Southampton, after their removal from their old mansion above Holborn Bars. The spot recalls many interesting associations. Here, "at his house near Holburne, in the suburbs of London," breathed his last, in 1667, the wise and virtuous Thomas Wriothesley, the last earl of that ancient race, who, as the faithful friend and upright minister of Charles the First, played so prominent a part at the closing period of that unhappy reign. Here, too, passed the childhood of that tender wife and heroic woman, Lady Rachael Russell, —

"... that sweet saint who sat by Russell's side, — "

and here, after her marriage to Lord Russell, she spent the happiest years of her life. Her devotion to her ill-fated lord, the personal assistance which she rendered him at his trial, their agonising interviews in the Tower, her heroic calmness at their last parting, and her passionate bursts of grief when all was over and when she had no longer to dread that her presence might unnerve her beloved one, are among the most touching passages in history. Lady Russell passed many years of her widowhood in Southampton House, and hence many of her interesting letters are dated. Southampton House after her death became the property of the Dukes of Bedford, on which occasion it changed its name to Bedford House. On the 9th of February, 1665, Evelyn inserts in his "Diary:" "Dined at my lord treasurer's, the Earl of Southampton, in Bloomsbury, where he was building a noble square, or piazza, a little town. His own house stands too low. Some noble rooms, a pretty cedar chapel, a naked garden to the north, but good air." It was in the fields behind Southampton House that, in the reign of William the Third, the London gallants were in the habit of settling their disputes with the sword. The old mansion was taken down at the commencement of the present century, when the north side of Bloomsbury Square was erected on its site. In Southampton Street, running from Bloomsbury Square into Holborn, Colley Cibber informs us that, on the 6th of November, 1671, he first saw the light.

Bloomsbury Square, originally called Southampton Square, derives its name from the manor and
village of Lomesbury, or Bloomsbury, now occupied by the square and its surrounding streets.
At Lomesbury, at the time when it was a retired
village, our early monarchs had a large establishment for their horses and hawks ; indeed, as late
as the middle of the last century it would seem
to have been still kept up as a branch of the
royal stables.   Doctor Radcliffe, the celebrated
physician ; Richard Baxter, the non-conformist
divine ; Doctor Akenside ; Sir Hans Sloane ; and
Lord Chief Justice Ellenborough, resided at different periods in this square.   Here also, at the
northeast angle, was the residence of the great
Lord Mansfield.   He was living here at the time
of the Protestant riots in 1780, when the mob
attacked and set fire to the house.   Not only did
his valuable pictures and library perish in the
flames, but the earl himself and Lady Mansfield
had a narrow escape from falling into the hands
of the infuriated populace.   "I was personally
present," writes Sir Nathaniel Wraxall, in his
"Memoirs of his own Time," "at many of the
most tremendous effects of popular fury on the
memorable 7th of June, the night on which it
attained its highest point.   About nine o'clock
on that evening, accompanied by three other
gentlemen, we set out from Portland Place, in
order to view the scene.   Having got into a

hackney-coach, we drove first to Bloomsbury Square, attracted to that spot by a rumour generally spread that Lord Mansfield's residence, situate at the northeast corner, was either already burnt or destined for destruction. Hart Street and Great Russell Street presented each to the view, as we passed, large fires composed of furniture taken from the houses of magistrates or other obnoxious individuals. Quitting the coach, we crossed the square, and had scarcely got under the wall of Bedford House, when we heard the door of Lord Mansfield's house burst open with violence. In a few minutes all the contents of the apartments being precipitated from the windows, were piled up and wrapped in flames. A file of foot-soldiers arriving, drew up near the blazing pile; but without either attempting to quench the fire or to impede the mob, who were indeed far too numerous to admit of being dispersed, or even intimidated by a small detachment of infantry. The populace remained masters."

After having witnessed the sacking and burning of Mansfield House, Sir Nathaniel and his companions proceeded into Holborn, where the first object which presented itself was the flames bursting from the dwelling-house and warehouses of an obnoxious Roman Catholic gentleman of the name of Langdale. "They were altogether," writes Wraxall, "enveloped in smoke and flame. In front had assembled an immense multitude of both sexes, many of whom were females, and not a few held infants in their arms. All appeared to be, like ourselves, attracted as spectators solely by curiosity, without taking any part in the acts of violence. Spirituous liquors in great quantity ran down the kennel of the street, and numbers of the populace were already intoxicated with this beverage. So little disposition, however, did they manifest to riot or pillage, that it would have been difficult to conceive who were the authors and perpetrators of such enormous mischief, if we had not distinctly seen at the windows of the house men, who, while the floors and rooms were on fire, calmly tore down the furniture and threw it into the streets, or tossed it into the flames. They experienced no kind of opposition during a considerable time that we remained at this place, but a party of the horse-guards arriving, the terrified crowd instantly began to disperse, and we, anxious to gratify our further curiosity, continued our progress on foot along Holborn to Fleet Market. I would in vain attempt adequately to describe the spectacle which presented itself when we reached the declivity of the hill close to St. Andrew's Church. The other house and magazines of Mr. Langdale, who as a Catholic had been selected for the blind vengeance of the mob, situated in the hollow space near the north end of Fleet Market, threw up into the air a pinnacle of flame resembling a volcano. Such was the beautiful and brilliant effect of the illumination, that St. Andrew's Church appeared to be almost scorched by the heat of so prodigious a body of fire; and the figures designated on the clock were as distinctly perceptible as at noonday. It resembled, indeed, a tower rather than a private building in a state of conflagration, and would have inspired the beholder with a sentiment of admiration allied to pleasure, if it had been possible to separate the object from its causes and its consequences. The wind, however, did not augment its rage on this occasion, for the night was serene and the sky unclouded, except when it became obscured by the volumes of smoke, which, from time to time, produced a temporary darkness. The mob, which completely blocked up the whole street in every part and in all directions, prevented our approaching within fifty or sixty yards of the building; but the populace, though still principally composed of persons allured by curiosity, evidently began here to assume a more disorderly and ferocious character. Troops, either horse or foot, we still saw none; nor, in the midst of this combination of tumult, terror, and violence, had the ordinary police ceased to continue its functions. While we stood by the wall of St. Andrew's Churchyard, a watchman, with his lantern in his hand, passed us, calling the hour as if in a time of profound tranquillity."

The residence of another eminent lawyer, Lord Ellenborough, before he removed to St. James's Square, was at the corner house of Bloomsbury Square and Orange Street. Number 6 Bloomsbury Square was the residence of the late Isaac Disraeli, the author of the "Curiosities of Literature and the "Quarrels of Authors."

In Bedford Place died, in May, 1811, the celebrated dramatic writer, Richard Cumberland; and in Charlotte Street, now Bloomsbury Street, on the east side, Theodore Hook first saw the light.

The church of St. George, Bloomsbury, consecrated in 1731, is the work of Nicholas Hawksmoor, a pupil of Sir Christopher Wren. It possesses no interest and but little merit. The portico, supported by pillars of the Corinthian order, has indeed been much admired; but the tower, surmounted by a pyramid with George the First at the top, and with lions and unicorns, with their tails and heels in the air, at the base, affords a specimen of architecture which Walpole justly styles a masterpiece of absurdity. This church must not be confounded with the neighbouring one of St. George the Martyr, Bloomsbury.

In the reign of Queen Anne, this part of London constituted one of its most fashionable localities, disputing the palm in this respect with Lincoln's Inn Fields, Soho Square, and Queen Square, Westminster. In 1708, for instance, we find the Duke of Bedford, the Earl of Northampton, the Earl of Chesterfield, and Lords Paget and Castleton, occupying houses in Bloomsbury Square; while in Great Russell Street stood Montague House and Thanet House. Let us not forget that in this latter street lived at one period the great artist, Sir Godfrey Kneller. Strype speaks of Great Russell Street as having "on the north side gardens behind the houses, and the prospect of the pleasant fields up to Highgate and Hampstead, insomuch that this place, by physicians, is named the most healthful of any in London."

So late as the middle of the last century the neighbourhood of Russell Square appears to have been still the resort of highwaymen. To Sir Horace Mann, Horace Walpole writes on the 31st of January, 1750: "You will hear little news from England, but of robberies. The numbers of disbanded soldiers and sailors have all taken to the road, or rather to the street. People are almost afraid of stirring after it is dark. My Lady Albemarle was robbed the other night in Great Russell Street by nine men. The king [George II.] gave her a gold watch and chain the next day. She says, 'the manner was all;' and indeed so it was, for I never saw a more frippery present, especially considering how great a favourite she is, and my Lady Yarmouth's friend." So infested at this period were even the more populous thoroughfares of London with highwaymen, that, on the very day preceding the date of Walpole's letter, we find a proclamation in the *London Gazette* offering a reward of £100 for the apprehension of any such offender against the laws. The fact is that, favoured by the ill-lighted and ill-protected state of the streets, highway robberies were committed in the heart of London, up to a much later period than is usually supposed. Only some sixty years ago a near relative of the author, accompanied by a friend, was on his way to Ranelagh, when, in Piccadilly, opposite to St. James's Church, the hackney-coach in which they were was suddenly stopped; at the same time, two men with pistols presented themselves, one at each door, while a third jumped on the box to overawe the coachman. Without the means of defence, they were compelled to satisfy the ruffians by delivering up their watches and money, their next step being to drive to the nearest police-station in order to give information of the robbery. Here but little hopes of redress were held out to them. Not only was their tale listened to as if it had been one of common occurrence, but, as regarded the evidence of the coachman, they were told that very little doubt existed, but that he was in league with the robbers.

' To return to Great Russell Street. In this street John Le Neve, the antiquary, was born, on the 27th of December, 1679; and here, in February, 1768, died Speaker Onslow. Here, too, was the residence of the great actor, John Philip

Kemble, principally conspicuous from its double windows in the library, which drew from the late James Smith the following lively lines :

> " Rheumatic pains make Kemble halt;
> He, fretting in amazement,
> To counteract the dire assault,
> Erects a double casement.

> " Ah ! who from fell disease can run ?
> With added ills he's troubled ;
> For when the glazier's task is done,
> He finds his panes are doubled."

Kemble's house, No. 89, — afterward the residence of Sir Henry Ellis, the principal librarian of the British Museum, — was taken down in 1847, to make room for the new buildings required by the museum. At No. 72 Great Russell Street Sir Sidney Smith was residing in 1828.

The chief object of interest in Great Russell Street is unquestionably Montague House, now converted into the British Museum. This magnificent mansion was originally built in 1678, by Ralph, first Duke of Montague, ambassador to France in the reign of William the Third. A few years afterward we find it leased by the duke, then Lord Montague, to William, fourth Earl of Devonshire, during whose occupancy it was destroyed by fire, on the morning of the 19th of January, 1686. The countess and her children, after a very narrow escape with their lives, were carried in blankets to

Southampton House, where they were hospitably received by their neighbour, Lady Russell, who in one of her letters to Doctor Fitzwilliam has left us an account of the catastrophe. The mansion was shortly afterward rebuilt by Lord Montague with increased splendour. The architect was a M. Poughet, who laid out the buildings and gardens entirely on the French model. Even the staircase and ceilings at Montague House were painted by French artists.

In Montague House resided for many years the eccentric Lady Elizabeth Cavendish, daughter and coheir of Henry, Duke of Newcastle, afterward successively Duchess of Albemarle and Montague. She had been contracted in early youth to Christopher, only son of the celebrated George Monk, Duke of Albemarle. This marriage had been a favourite project of the old duke, and accordingly, feeling himself dying without its having taken place, he resolved on having it solemnised in his sick-chamber, which was accordingly done on the 30th of December, 1669, only four days before he breathed his last; the bridegroom being at the time only sixteen, and the bride probably considerably younger. Their union was not a happy one, the duke's life being embittered by the fretfulness and ill temper of his imperious wife. After his death his duchess, whose wealth must have been immense, publicly expressed her determination to marry no one but a sovereign prince. Among her

suitors were the reprobate Lord Rosse, and Lord
Montague.   In order to flatter her insane fancies,
the latter is said to have courted her as Emperor
of China, which produced from his angry competi-
tor the following lines :

> " Insulting rival ! never boast
>   Thy conquest lately won ;
> No wonder if her heart was lost,
>   Her senses first were gone.

> " From one that's under Bedlam's laws,
>   What glory can be had ?
> For love of thee was not the cause,
>   It proves that she was mad."

Of her insanity there can be no doubt ; indeed,
her second husband placed her in confinement
with an allowance of £3,000 a year.   To the
last she was indulged in her fantasies, especially
being served on the knee as a sovereign princess.   The apartments which she occupied in
Montague House were on the ground floor.   Her
death took place in 1734, at a very advanced
age, at Newcastle House, Clerkenwell, her pater-
nal property.

It was in the meadows behind Montague House
that Aubrey mentions the following incident as
having occurred in 1694.   " The last summer,"
he writes, " on the day of St. John the Baptist,
I accidentally was walking in the pasture behind
Montague House.   It was twelve o'clock.   I saw

there about two or three and twenty young women, most of them well habited, on their knees, very busy, as if they had been weeding. I could not presently learn what the matter was; at last a young man told me that they were looking for a coal under the root of a plantain, to put under their heads that night, and they should dream who would be their husbands. It was to be found that day and hour."

In the middle of the last century the ground behind the northwest of Russell Street was occupied by a farm belonging to two old maiden sisters of the name of Capper. According to Mr. Smith, in his "Book for a Rainy Day," "They wore riding-habits and men's hats. One rode an old gray mare, and it was her spiteful delight to ride with a pair of shears after boys who were flying their kites, purposely to cut their strings; the other sister's business was to seize the clothes of the lads who trespassed on their premises to bathe."

In Bolton House, formerly the corner house of Russell Square, turning into Great Guildford Street, resided Lord Chancellor Loughborough. The residence of Sir Thomas Lawrence was on the east side of Russell Square, No. 65, four doors from that of Lord Loughborough. In this square Sir Samuel Romilly destroyed himself, in 1818. At No. 2 Bernard Street, Russell Square, resided Joseph Munden, the comedian.

No. 6 Bedford Square was for some time the residence of Lord Eldon. At that period, when the punishment of death was much more common than in the present day, it happened that a foot-pad had been sentenced to be hanged on account of a street robbery which he had committed close to Lord Eldon's house in this square. When the recorder subsequently presented his report to the king, all the ministers, with the exception of one, gave it as their opinion that the man should be left for execution. The king, however, observing that Lord Eldon had been silent, called upon him for his opinion, which the chancellor gave in favour of mercy. "Very well," said the king; "since his lordship, who lives in Bedford Square, thinks there is no great harm in committing robberies there, the poor fellow shall not be hanged." In Store Street, Bedford Square, the celebrated actor, Thomas King, breathed his last in December, 1805.

Before quitting this neighbourhood, let us not omit to mention that in Charlotte Street, Fitzroy Square, lived John George Morland and Richard Wilson, the painters, and that in Buckingham Street, Fitzroy Square, John Flaxman, the sculptor, breathed his last. Let us not forget also the residence of the delightful actor, Jack Bannister, who lived and died in Gower Street. A strange superstition had impressed itself on his mind that he should die at the age of sixty-five, the number corresponding with that of his house in Gower Street. He survived, however, till his seventy-seventh year.

In Gower Street, Lord Eldon lived for thirteen years, and here also resided John Adolphus, the historian, and Harley, the comedian.

CHAPTER VII.

CHEAPSIDE.

Cheapside at an Early Period Called the "Crown Field"—
Tournaments Held There—Persons Executed at the Stand-
ard in Cheapside—"Evil May-day"—Elizabeth's Coro-
nation Procession—The Cross—The Conduit—Celebrated
Residents in Cheapside—Streets in the Vicinity—Mermaid
Tavern—Guildhall—Trial-scenes, and Entertainments
There—St. Mary-le-Bow—"Crown Seld"—Watling Street
—Goldsmiths' and Coachmakers' Hall.

LET us retrace our steps into Cheapside. This
celebrated street, which derives its name from
" chepe," a market, was in the middle of the thir-
teenth century an open space, called the "Crown
Field," from the Crown Inn, which stood at the east
end of it. In the reign of Edward the Fourth the
sign of the Crown in Cheapside was kept by
one Walter Walker, who happened to observe in
joke that he intended to make his son "heir to the
crown." The words reached the jealous ears of
royalty. The foolish equivoque was construed into
the crime of high treason, and the man was hanged
opposite to his own door.

In the days of our Norman sovereigns, when
Cheapside was still the "Crown Field," it shared

with Smithfield the honour of witnessing those
gorgeous tournaments of which the old chroniclers
have bequeathed us such vivid descriptions. There
is, in fact, no street in London more intimately
associated with the romantic history of the past.
Here, in 1329, between Wood Street and Queen
Street, Edward the Third held a solemn tournament in honour of the French ambassadors; the
street being covered with sand to prevent the
horses from slipping, while across it ran a scaffold,
richly decorated, in which sat Queen Philippa and
her ladies, in all the blaze of beauty and precious
stones. The king, surrounded by the rank and
chivalry of the land, was also present; while apart
sat the lord mayor, aldermen, and common council
in their scarlet robes and chains of massive gold.
Unfortunately, in the midst of the tilting the gallery on which the queen and her ladies sat suddenly gave way, "whereby," writes Stow, "they
were, with some shame, forced to fall down."
Some injuries occurred to the knights and others
who were standing close to the gallery, but happily the ladies escaped unhurt. The king,
nevertheless, was so exasperated against the
master-carpenter who had erected the scaffolding,
that he ordered him to be forthwith led to the
gallows. The queen, however, threw herself on
her knees, and so pathetically pleaded to the king
to save the life of the offender, that with some
difficulty he consented. Philippa's reward for her

generous interference was a unanimous shout of applause from the surrounding multitude.

In the same reign (1339) we find Cheapside the scene of a sanguinary encounter between the rival companies of the Skinners and Fishmongers. In the heat of the fray, the lord mayor arrived on the spot with a band of armed citizens, but it was in vain that he attempted to restore quiet. The rival factions, making common cause, drove him and his men-at-arms from the field; nor was it till the sheriffs made their appearance with a large re-inforcement that the riot was quelled and the ringleaders were seized. On the following day seven of them were hanged in Cheapside without even the pretence of a trial.

Edward the Third died in 1377, shortly after which event his grandson, Richard the Second, proceeded in great state through Cheapside in his way from the Tower to his coronation at West-minster. In the centre of a brilliant assemblage of peers, knights, and esquires, the young king, clad in white robes, rode solemnly, we are told, through the "public ways" till he came "to the noble street called the Chepe," the houses of which were hung with tapestry and cloth of arras, and thence to "Flete-strete," and so direct to the royal palace of Westminster. Similarly animated was the scene at Cheapside when, four years afterward, Richard conducted his young betrothed, Anne of Bohemia, through London, on her way to her

bridal and coronation at Westminster.   At the
upper end of Cheapside, we are told, was erected
a castle, from which flowed fountains of wine, and
from which beautiful maidens blew gold leaf in the
faces of the king and queen, and threw florins of
counterfeited gold over their horses' heads.

During Wat Tyler's insurrection we find several
persons beheaded by the infuriated mob at the
Standard in Cheapside.   Here also, in 1450, when
Jack Cade made himself master of the metropolis,
Lord Say, High Treasurer of England, was put to
death by the insurgents.   It was to little purpose
that he claimed the privilege of being tried by his
peers.   Having been wrested from the officers of
justice, he was hurried to the Standard at Cheapside, where he was decapitated, after which his
head was carried in triumph through the streets
of London.

"*Say.*   Tell me wherein have I offended most?
Have I affected wealth or honour? speak.
Are my chests filled with extorted gold?
Is my apparel sumptuous to behold?
Whom have I injured, that ye seek my death?
These hands are free from guiltless blood-shedding;
This breast from harbouring foul deceitful thoughts.
O, let me live!
    Cade. [*Aside*] I feel remorse in myself with his words:
but I'll bridle it; he shall die, an it be but for pleading so
well for his life.   Away with him! he has a familiar under
his tongue; he speaks not o' God's name.   Go, take him
away, I say, and strike off his head presently: and then

break into his son-in-law's house, Sir James Cromer, and strike off his head, and bring them both upon two poles hither.

All.   It shall be done!

Say.   Ah, countrymen! if when you make your prayers,
God should be so obdurate as yourselves,
How would it fare with your departed souls?
And therefore yet relent, and save my life!

Cade.   Away with him, and do as I command ye."
— *King Henry VI.*, Part II., Act iv. Sc. 7.

Another notorious political offender whose fate is associated with Cheapside was the handsome and accomplished Perkin Warbeck. After his arrest in the priory of Sheen, in Surrey, he was brought to London, and compelled to sit for a whole day in the stocks before the entrance of Westminster Hall. On the following day he was brought to Cheapside, where he was again placed in the stocks, and forced to read a confession which he is said to have written with his own hand. At night he was lodged in the dungeons of the Tower, where he remained till the 23d of November, 1499, when he was led forth to be hanged at Tyburn.

The Standard in Cheapside — anciently the spot where criminals were executed — is said to have stood in the middle of the street, near Bow Church. The date of its foundation remains unascertained; but inasmuch as so early as the reign of Henry the Fourth it was in such a ruinous state that it was necessary to rebuild it, the presumption is that it was of considerable antiquity. It was at

the Standard in Cheapside that William Fitz-
Osbert, commonly called William Longbeard, —
· after having been dragged with his concubine from
the neighbouring church of St. Mary-le-Bow, where
he had defended himself by force of arms, — was
executed in 1199.   Here, also, Walter Stapleton,
Bishop of Exeter, was beheaded by the mob in the
reign of Edward the Second.   Here, in 1293, we
find three men decapitated for rescuing an offender
from the officers of justice; and here, in 1461,
John Davy had his hand cut off for striking a
man before the judges at Westminster.   It was at
the Standard that Henry the Fourth, in 1399,
caused the blank charter of Richard the Second to
be publicly burnt; and, lastly, from this spot it
was that Eleanor Cobham, wife of Humphrey,
Duke of Gloucester, when convicted of sorcery
and witchcraft, was compelled to walk with a
sheet over her, and a taper in her hand, to St.
Paul's Cross.

Cheapside is intimately associated with the celebrated riots which took place on the 1st of May,
1517, and which obtained for that day the name
of "Evil May-day."   "A great heart-burning
and malicious grudge," writes Stow, "had grown
among the Englishmen of the city of London
against strangers; the artificers finding themselves
much aggrieved because such a number of strangers were permitted to resort hither with their
wares, and to exercise handicrafts, to the great

hindrance and impoverishing of the king's liege
people." The "heart-burnings" thus excited had
not only for some time threatened a popular out-
break, but, according to Stow, a general impression
got abroad that "on May-day next following, the
city would slay all the aliens, insomuch that diverse
strangers fled out of the city." At length, the
fears of the corporation being thoroughly aroused,
they issued orders, strictly enjoining every house-
holder to close his habitation on the evening of
the 1st of May, and after nine o'clock at night to
keep his sons, apprentices, and servants within
doors. A trifling incident, however, threw the
city into convulsions. One of the aldermen, in
passing through Cheapside a few minutes after
nine o'clock, happened to observe two apprentices
playing at "bucklers" in the middle of the street,
when, instead of quietly expostulating with them
on the impropriety of their conduct, he threatened,
in a peremptory tone of voice, to send them to the
Compter unless they instantly desisted from their
sport. An insolent reply on the part of one of
the apprentices led to the alderman attempting to
seize one of the offenders, when the bystanders
raised the formidable and then familiar war-shout
of the youths of London, " Prentices, prentices!
clubs, clubs!" Almost in an instant every door
in the neighbourhood was thrown open, and numbers of persons, consisting principally of apprentices, servants, and watermen, rushed to join the

fray. A temporary triumph awaited them. Having succeeded in beating every reinforcement which the lord mayor was able to bring against them, they dispersed in different directions, for the purpose of plundering and destroying the houses and warehouses of the unoffending foreigners, a work of havoc which lasted till break of day. At length, exhausted by fatigue, the majority of the rioters returned to their several homes, when the lord mayor seized his opportunity and captured about three hundred of the remainder. A commission was immediately issued to the Duke of Norfolk and other noblemen to try the offenders, of whom their reputed leader, John Lincoln, and twelve others, were subsequently hanged in different parts of London. The remainder, many of whom were women and boys, were also sentenced to death, but were reprieved at the king's pleasure and subsequently pardoned.

On the occasion of Queen Elizabeth proceeding from the Tower to her coronation in Westminster Abbey, we find her received in great state and ceremony at the Standard in Cheapside. Lining the street, which was hung with costly drapery, were arranged the different city companies, "well apparelled with many rich furs, and their livery hoods upon their shoulders." The queen herself — "most honourably accompanied," writes Holinshed, "as well with gentlemen, barons, and other nobility of her realm, as also a notable train of

goodly and beautiful ladies, richly appointed "—
sat in an open chariot sumptuously ornamented.
On reaching the Standard, the Recorder of London,
in the name of the city, presented her with a purse
of crimson velvet containing a thousand marks in
gold, as a token of its affectionate loyalty.   At the
same time, a child, intended to personify Truth,
having been made to descend by machinery as if
from heaven, presented her with an English translation of the Bible, which she accepted with the
greatest reverence.   It was a gift, she said, which
gave her more real gratification than all the other
endearing proofs which she had that day experienced of her people's love.

Besides the Standard, there were anciently two
other remarkable buildings in Cheapside, the Cross
and the Conduit.   The Cross, which stood nearly
opposite to Wood Street, was one of those beautiful architectural memorials raised by Edward the
First, in 1296, to mark the several spots where
the remains of his beloved consort, Eleanor of
Castile, rested in their progress to Westminster
Abbey.   Falling into decay, it was rebuilt in 1441
at the expense of John Hatherley, Lord Mayor of
London, John Fisher, mercer, and other persons.
Subsequently, in consequence of its being decorated with popish images, it was much injured by
the populace in 1581, but was again repaired in
1591.   Its final demolition took place in May,
1643, when it shared the fate of many other relig-

ious crosses in England, the destruction of which was voted by the Parliament. On that day, a troop of horse and two companies of foot having surrounded the Cross, the work of destruction commenced. At the moment that the cross at the top fell beneath the blows of the workmen, the drums beat and the trumpets sounded, the multitude at the same time throwing their caps into the air, and raising a general shout of joyful acclamation. On the night of the 6th, the leaden pipes were melted on the spot amidst the ringing of bells and the renewed shouts of the populace. The destruction of this "stately cross" was witnessed by Evelyn, who mentions it in his "Diary" with expressions of great regret.

The Conduit in Cheapside stood in the middle of the street, rather to the east of the Cross, and close to the Poultry. It was built about the year 1281, was of stone, and richly decorated. Having fallen into decay, it was rebuilt in 1479 by Thomas Ilam, Sheriff of London, from which time it continued in use till about the year 1613, when it was superseded by the great work of Sir Hugh Myddelton, who had accomplished his project of supplying London with water from the New River. There was also a "lesser conduit" in Cheapside, known as the Little Conduit, which stood in the middle of the street, near the east end of Paternoster Row.

The following incident in connection with Cheapside is related by Anthony Wood as having taken place during the agitation caused by the famous "Popish Plot" in 1679. "In the evening," he writes, "when the Duke of York returned from his entertainment in the city, Oates and Bedloe were got into the balcony of one Cockerill, a blink-eyed bookseller in Cheapside, and a great rabble about them. As the duke passed by, they cried out, 'A Pope, a Pope,' upon which, one of the duke's guard cocked his pistol, and rode back, saying, 'What factious rogues are these?' Upon which, they cried out, 'No Pope, no Pope;' 'God bless his Highness.' So the king's worthy evidence, Oates and Bedloe, sneaked away."

In Cheapside was born, in 1591, one of the sweetest of lyric poets, Robert Herrick. In his "Tears to Thamasis," he writes:

"Never again shall I with finnie oar
   Put from, or draw unto, the faithful shore;
   And landing here, or safely landing there,
   Make way to my beloved Westminster;
   Or to the golden Cheapside, where the earth
   Of Julia Herrick gave to me my birth."

The expression of the "golden" Cheapside has apparently reference to the father of the poet, Nicholas Herrick, having carried on the business of a goldsmith in this street. He survived the birth of his gifted son little more than a year, dying on the 9th of November, 1592, of injuries which he received by a fall from an upper window of his house in Cheapside. From the circumstance of his will having been made only two days before this event, it has been conjectured that the fall was not altogether accidental.

Another poet whose name is associated with Cheapside is Sir Richard Blackmore, who first commenced practice as a physician in this street. "His residence," writes Doctor Johnson, "was in Cheapside, and his friends were chiefly in the city. In the early part of Blackmore's time a citizen was a term of reproach, and his place of abode was another topic to which his adversaries had recourse in the penury of scandal."

In Cheapside the pure-minded philosopher and angler, Isaak Walton, carried on for some years the trade of a sempster. According to Anthony Wood, he resided here till 1643, at which time, "finding it dangerous for honest men to be there, he left the city, and lived sometimes at Stafford, and elsewhere, but mostly in the families of the eminent clergymen of England, by whom he was much beloved."

Another celebrated person who lived in Cheapside was Sir Christopher Wren, whose residence is said to have been at No. 73. In this street also died, in March, 1769, in his eighty-eighth year, Mr. David Barclay, the last surviving son of Robert Barclay, the author of the "Apology for the Quakers." He carried on the business of a mercer, and had the singular honour of receiving at his house, No. 108 Cheapside, three successive monarchs on the occasion of their severally visiting the city on lord mayor's day.

At No. 3 Cheapside, at the corner of Paternoster Row, lived John Beyer, a linen-draper, the original of Cowper's admirable ballad of John Gilpin, who hence is said to have set out on his memorable ride.

> " So three doors off the chaise was stayed,
>   Where they did all get in;
> Six precious souls, and all agog,
>   To dash through thick and thin.
>
> " Smack went the whip, round went the wheels,
>   Were never folk so glad;
> The stones did rattle underneath,
>   As if Cheapside were mad.
>
> " John Gilpin at his horse's side,
>   Seized fast the flowing mane,
> And up he got in haste to ride,
>   But soon came down again."

During more than three centuries — from the day when the old Benedictine monk, John Lydgate, penned his " London Lykpenny," to those in which Cowper charmed the world with his " John Gilpin " — we find Cheapside the great resort of the linen-drapers and haberdashers of London.

" Then to the Chepe I began me drawne,
    Where mutch people I saw for to stande;
One ofred me velvet, sylke, and lawne,
    An other he taketh me by the hand,
' Here is Parys thread, the fynest in the land.'
I never was used to such thyngs indede,
And wantyng mony I myght not spede."

The streets in the immediate vicinity of Cheapside are no less associated with eminent names than Cheapside itself. In Milk Street — the site of the London residence of the Staffords, Dukes of Buckingham — Sir Thomas More first saw the light; and in Bread Street, on the opposite side of Cheapside, lived the father of Milton, under whose roof in this street the great poet was born. Almost every house in London had anciently its distinguishing sign. That of Milton's father, who was a scrivener, was a spread eagle, — the armorial bearing of his family, — which was suspended over his door. From Anthony Wood, who was only junior to Milton by a few years, we learn that in his time foreigners used to pay a pilgrimage to the house in Bread Street in which the poet first saw the light. Aubrey also informs us: "The only inducement of several foreigners that came over to England, was to see the Protector Oliver, and Mr. John Milton, and would see the house and chamber where he was born." Milton's father was himself a poet and a musician. "He was an ingenious man," writes Aubrey, "delighted in

music, and composed many songs now in print,
especially that of ' Oriana.' "   Milton himself
addresses him :

> " . . . thyself
> Art skilful to associate verse with airs
> Harmonious, and to give the human voice
> A thousand modulations, heir by right
> Indisputable of Arion's fame.
> Now, say, what wonder is it, if a son
> Of thine delight in verse ; if, so conjoin'd
> In close affinity, we sympathise
> In social arts and kindred studies sweet ? "

The house in which Milton was born was burnt
down in the great fire of 1666.

Bread Street derives its name from the circumstance of a bread market having been anciently
held on its site.   In Stow's time, however, it was
entirely inhabited by "rich merchants," whose
"diverse fair inns be there."   In Basing Lane,
Bread Street, stood formerly Gerard's Hall, corrupted from Gisors Hall.   In 1245 it was the
residence of John Gisors, Lord Mayor of London,
in the possession of whose descendants it long
remained.   "On the south side of Basing Lane,"
writes Stow, "is one great house of old time built
upon arched vaults, and with arched gates of
stone, brought from Caen, in Normandy.   The
same is now a common hostelry for receipt of
travellers, commonly and corruptly called Ger-
rardes-hall, of a giant said to have dwelt there.
In the high-roofed hall of this house sometime

stood a large fir pole, which reached to the roof thereof, and was said to be one of the staves that Gerrarde, the giant, used in the wars to run withal. There stood, also, a ladder of the same length, which, as they say, served to ascend to the top of a staff."   Gerard's Hall, with its curious Norman crypt, stood till 1852 under the name of the Gerard's Hall Hotel, when it was removed to make room for Cannon Street.

In Bread Street stood the famous Mermaid Tavern, endeared to us by its association with some of the most illustrious names in the literature of our country.

> "At Bread Street's Mermaid having dined, and merry,
> Proposed to go to Holborn in a wherry."
>   — *Ben Jonson.*

Here was held the celebrated Mermaid Club, at which Sir Walter Raleigh so often presided; where wit so often flashed from the lips of Shakespeare, Beaumont, and Ben Jonson; and where the author of "The Faerie Queene," as the intimate friend of Raleigh, was doubtless often a guest. Gifford, speaking of the year 1603, observes: "About this time, Jonson probably began to acquire that turn for conviviality for which he was afterward noted. Sir Walter Raleigh, previously to his unfortunate engagement with the wretched Cobham and others, had instituted a meeting of *beaux esprits* at the Mermaid, a celebrated tavern in Friday Street.[1]   Of this club, which combined more talent and genius than ever met together before or since, our author was a member; and here, for many years, he regularly repaired with Shakespeare, Beaumont, Fletcher, Selden, Cotton, Carew, Martin, Donne, and many others whose names, even at this distant period, call up a mingled feeling of reverence and respect."   Beaumont, in a charming poetical epistle addressed to Ben Jonson, describes the "wit-combats" in which they had both of them so often borne a part in the Mermaid Tavern:

> "What things have we seen
> Done at the 'Mermaid.'   Heard words that have been
> So nimble, and so full of subtle flame,
> As if that every one from whence they came
> Had meant to put his whole wit in a jest,
> And had resolved to live a fool the rest
> Of his dull life; then when there hath been thrown
> Wit able enough to justify the town
> For three days past, — wit that might warrant be
> For the whole city to talk foolishly
> Till that were cancelled; and when that was gone
> We left an air behind us, which alone
> Was able to make the two next companies
> Right witty; though but downright fools, more wise."

[1] This appears to be an error. At the time when Jonson penned his couplet there was also a Mermaid Tavern in Cheapside, and possibly another in Friday Street. The Mermaid in Cornhill was also probably in existence at this period. Ben Jonson's expression, however, of "Bread Street's Mermaid," evidently proves that the Mermaid frequented by Jonson and his illustrious associates was in Bread Street.

Ben Jonson has again celebrated the Mermaid Tavern and its delicious Canary in his delightful poem, "Inviting a Friend to Supper:"

> "But that which most doth take my muse and me,
>   Is a pure cup of rich Canary wine,
>   Which is the Mermaid's now, but shall be mine."

And again :

> "Of this we will sup free, but moderately,
>   Nor shall our cups make any guilty men ;
>   But at our parting we will be as when
>   We innocently met.   No simple word
>   That shall be uttered at our mirthful boards
>   Shall make us sad next morning, or affright
>   The liberty that we'll enjoy to-night."

Fuller, speaking of the "wit-combats" between Shakespeare and Jonson, observes: "Many were the wit-combats between him and Ben Jonson, which two I behold like a Spanish great galleon and an English man-of-war. Master Jonson, like the former, was built far higher in learning, solid, but slow in his performances. Shakespeare, with the English man-of-war, lesser in bulk but lighter in sailing, could turn with all tides, tack about, and take advantage of all winds by the quickness of his wit and invention."

Friday Street, running parallel with Bread Street, is said to have been anciently inhabited almost entirely by fishmongers ; its name having been derived from the great quantity of business which was carried on there on a Friday, the fast-day of the Roman Catholics. In this street is the church of St. Matthew, Friday Street, a plain stone structure, rebuilt by Sir Christopher Wren after the destruction of the old edifice by the fire of London.

Nearly opposite to Friday Street is Wood Street, at the corner of which may be seen a solitary tree, presenting a striking and refreshing appearance in this smoky and crowded district. The tree is interesting, moreover, as pointing out the site of the old church of St. Peter's at the Cross, destroyed by the great fire of 1666.

Lad Lane, now forming part of Gresham Street, is said to be a corruption from Our Lady Lane, an image of the Virgin having anciently stood there. Stow, however, tells us that it should properly be called Ladle Street, Ladle Hall having anciently stood on its site.

At the end of King Street, running northward out of Cheapside, is the Guildhall of the city of London. Previously to the year 1411, it was held in the street called Aldermanbury. "I myself," writes Stow, "have seen the ruins of the old court hall, in Aldermanbury Street, which of late hath been employed as a carpenter's yard." The present edifice was commenced in 1410, during the mayoralty of Sir Thomas Knolles, but was not completed till the sixteenth century. It suffered severely in the great fire, but so solid was its masonry that it was able to defy the fury of the raging element, though its fine old oak roof was unfortunately destroyed. "Among other things that night," writes an eye-witness, the Rev. T. Vincent, "the sight of Guildhall was a fearful spectacle, which stood the whole body of it together for several hours, after the fire had taken it, without flames, — I suppose because the timber was of such solid oak, — in a bright shining coal, as if it had been a palace of gold, or a great building of burnished brass." The building was subsequently thoroughly repaired at an expense of £2,500.

The exterior front of Guildhall, though its appearance is sufficiently striking and picturesque when seen from Cheapside, consists of a strange mixture of the Gothic, Grecian, and Oriental styles of architecture. Its principal feature is the great hall, which, notwithstanding the barbarous alterations to which it has from time to time been subjected, presents a very imposing appearance. It measures one hundred and fifty-three feet in length, forty-eight feet in breadth, and fifty-five in height.

The old crypt, too, beneath it, which extends the whole length of the hall, is well worthy of a visit. In the hall are five monuments, — each of considerable pretensions, but of indifferent merit,— to the memory of the great Earl of Chatham; his illustrious son, William Pitt; Lord Nelson; the Duke of Wellington; and Alderman Beckford.

Here also are conspicuous the fantastic-looking figures, known as Gog and Gogmagog, but whose real names and identity have long been a difficulty with antiquaries. Comparatively speaking, they are of modern date, having been carved by Richard Saunders, and set up no later than 1708. As early, however, as the reign of Henry the Fifth, we find it the custom of the citizens of London to display a couple of gigantic figures in their pageants, to which custom the Gog and Gogmagog in Guildhall evidently owe their origin. For many years, Guildhall continued to be decorated with the banners and other trophies captured at the battle of Ramillies, which were brought hither with great state and ceremony, but which have long since disappeared.

Another interesting building connected with old Guildhall was its ancient chapel, dedicated to St. Mary Magdalen and All Saints, which stood on the site of the present law courts. It had anciently an establishment consisting of a warden, seven priests, three clerks, and four choristers. It was built as early as the year 1299, and was pulled down in the year 1822.

The trial-scenes of many celebrated persons have taken place in Guildhall. Among these may be mentioned that of the fair martyr, Anne Askew, who perished in the flames on the 16th of July, 1546. Here, also, severally stood at the bar of justice the beautiful and accomplished Lady Jane

Grey; the gallant and gifted Earl of Surrey; Sir Nicholas Throgmorton, the eminent soldier and statesman, implicated in the Duke of Suffolk's conspiracy to raise Lady Jane Grey to the throne; Garnet, the Jesuit, who was executed for his share in the Gunpowder Plot; and lastly, Edmund Waller, the poet.

When Queen Mary, on the hostile approach of Sir Thomas Wyatt to London in 1533, paid a visit of encouragement to the city, we find her received at Guildhall by the lord mayor, Sir Thomas White, and the aldermen, each clad in complete armour, though wearing over it the civic robe.

The city feasts in Guildhall have been famous for centuries. In this hall, in 1613, the Elector Palatine and his young wife, Elizabeth, daughter of James the First, were entertained with great splendour by the citizens of London. Here, too, in 1641, Charles the First honoured the city with his company at a sumptuous feast. On the 29th October, 1663, "To Guildhall," writes Pepys. . . . "I sat at the merchant strangers' table, where ten good dishes to a mess, with plenty of wine of all sorts: but it was very unpleasing that we had no napkins nor change of trenchers, and drank out of earthen pitchers and wooden dishes."

On the 29th of October, 1689, King William and Queen Mary were entertained at a banquet at Guildhall.

In Guildhall, in 1761, the citizens of London gave an entertainment to George the Third, the cost of which amounted to £6,898. Here, also, on the occasion of the peace in 1814, the city gave a still more magnificent feast to the prince regent, the Emperor of Russia, and the King of Prussia, the total expenditure of which was estimated at the enormous sum of £25,000. The plate alone is stated to have been worth £200,000. On the occasion of Charles the First dining in the city, the number of dishes is said to have been five hundred. At the entertainment given to George the Third, they are stated to have amounted to 414, exclusive of the dessert.

King Street, Cheapside, the small street in which Guildhall is situated, is associated with a curious incident in the early life of the author of " Christabel," then a friendless and ill-fed boy in the Bluecoat School. " From eight to fourteen," he himself writes, " I was a playless day-dreamer, a *helluo librorum*, my appetite for which was indulged by a singular accident. A stranger, who was struck by my conversation, made me free of a circulating library in King Street, Cheapside." The particulars of this " singular accident " are thus explained by Coleridge's biographer, Mr. Gilman : " Going down the Strand," he says, " in one of his day-dreams, — fancying himself swimming across the Hellespont, he thrust his hands before him as in the act of swimming, when his hand came in contact with a gentleman's pocket. The gentleman seized his hand, turned around, and looked at him with some anger: 'What, so young, and so wicked!' at the same time accusing him of an attempt to pick his pocket. The frightened boy sobbed out his denial of the intention, and explained to him how he thought himself Leander swimming across the Hellespont. The gentleman was so struck and delighted with the novelty of the thing, and with the simplicity and intelligence of the boy, that he subscribed, as before stated, to the library, in consequence of which Coleridge was further enabled to indulge his love of reading." The Crown in King Street was the resort of the improvident poet, Richard Savage.

On the south side of Cheapside stands the celebrated church of St. Mary-le-Bow. Who is there who has ever passed along the crowded thoroughfare of Cheapside without turning his eyes toward the belfry of Bow Church, and recalling the nursery days when he listened with childish delight to the legend of Richard Whittington? — how he, a friendless boy, came to London believing that its streets were paved with gold; how disappointed he was when he found himself alone amidst a cold, strange, and unsympathising multitude; how he sat down, disconsolate, upon the milestone at Highgate, and how his face brightened, and his heart beat, when the bells of Bow Church rang their merry and prophetic peal, —

> " Turn again, Whittington,
>   Lord Mayor of London."

"Bow Bells," if we may be allowed to continue the nursery expression, have been famous from time immemorial.   They are, in fact, a vestige of the ancient times when the Norman "curfew tolled the knell of parting day;" of those days when the will of the Conqueror decreed that, at the peril of the citizens of London, every light should be extinguished and every fire raked out by a prescribed hour.   Even as late as the year 1469 we find the common council ordering that Bow Bell shall be rung every night at nine o'clock; a signal, probably, to the London 'prentices that they were at liberty to close their masters' shops and to betake themselves to their amusements. At all events, we have evidence that the sound of the evening bells of Bow Church was formerly anxiously waited for in the neighbourhood of Cheapside.

> " Clerk of the Bow bell, with yellow locks,
>   For thy late ringing thy head shall have knocks."

To which the clerk replies :

> " Children of Cheape, hold you all still,
>   For you shall have the Bow bell rung at your will."

Allusions to the "Bow-bells" may be found in many of our old writers.   Pope, for instance, has the well-known line :

> " Far as loud Bow's stupendous bells resound."

To be born "within the sound of Bow-bells" is
not only an expression of old date, but is still in
use to define a cockney.   Beaumont and Fletcher
speak of "Bow-bell suckers," which has been explained as persons nursed and reared within the
sound of the bells.

Another ancient and interesting custom connected with old Bow Church was one which we
have previously referred to, that of displaying
illuminated lanterns on the summit of its lofty
tower, to serve as beacons to those who journeyed
to London from the north, when the present richly
cultivated uplands of Hampstead and Highgate
consisted of trackless forest-ground, and when the
only means of entering the city were through
some occasional and obscure postern-gate in its
fortified walls.

The church of St. Mary-le-Bow — said to stand
on the site of a Roman temple — was certainly
a place of Christian worship as early as the days
of William the Conqueror.   In the reign of his
successor (1091) occurred that terrific hurricane
which laid low upward of six hundred houses,
destroyed several churches, and which swept
away London Bridge from its foundations.   During its progress, not only was the roof of the
church of St. Mary-le-Bow carried away to a considerable distance, but when it fell it was with
such violence that four of its rafters, each of
twenty-six feet in length, forced their way

through the ground to the depth of upward of twenty feet.

According to Stow, Bow Church derives its name from the circumstance of its having been built on arches of stone, and consequently having been dedicated to St. Mary de Arcubus. Elsewhere, however, he infers that it may have owed its name to the stone arches which anciently supported the lantern on the top of the tower. The Court of Arches derives its name from its having been formerly held in this church.

In the reign of Richard Cœur de Lion, Bow Church was one of the principal scenes of those formidable riots in 1196, which at length were brought to a close by the seizure and execution of the popular idol, William Longbeard. For some time he had succeeded in defending himself against the authorities in Bow Church, till at length the king's justiciary having given orders to fire the steeple, he made a desperate effort to escape at the head of his devoted followers, but he was taken prisoner in the attempt. After a hurried trial he was hanged, as we have already related, in Cheapside.

In 1284, in the reign of Edward the First, Bow Church was the scene of another outrage, also characteristic of the lawlessness of the times. One Lawrence Ducket, a goldsmith, having wounded one Ralph Crepin in Cheapside, the former sought the protection of sanctuary in Bow Church, where

he shut himself up with a youth who had kindly
volunteered to share his solitude.   Unfortunately
for Ducket, the friends of the wounded man discovered the place of his retreat, and accordingly,
having obtained entrance into the church at night,
they dragged him from the steeple, where he had
sought to conceal himself, and put him to death.
They then so disposed of the body, by suspending
it from one of the windows, as to induce the conviction that he had committed suicide; the result
being that the corpse was dragged by the feet to
a ditch without the city walls, and there interred
with every mark of indignity.   The boy, however,
in fear and trembling, had witnessed from his
hiding-place the whole of the transaction; the consequence of which was that several persons were
apprehended, of whom sixteen were hanged, and
one, a woman, the principal instigator of the crime,
burned alive.   This tragedy created so painful a
sensation that not only for a time was divine service discontinued in Bow Church, but the windows
were filled up with brambles.

The old church of St. Mary-le-Bow having been
burnt down in the great fire of 1666, the present
stately edifice was commenced by Sir Christopher
Wren in 1671.   Its great merit is its exterior, and
especially its beautiful steeple.   The latter, surmounted by its conspicuous gilt ball and dragon,
is 225 feet in height.   The old Norman crypt still
exists, and has been much admired.

Bow Church, both as regards its sepulchral monuments and the persons interred within its walls, is singularly deficient in interest. It contains, indeed, a stately monument to Bishop Newton, who was rector of the church for twenty-five years, but his remains lie buried in St. Paul's Cathedral.

Over the doorway of Bow Church, as seen from the side of Cheapside, may be observed a small balcony, to which considerable interest is attached. In consequence of the accident which we have mentioned as having happened to Queen Philippa and her ladies at the great tournament in 1329, King Edward the Third had caused to be "strongly made of stone," on the north side of old Bow Church, a shed called the Crown-sild, "for himself, the queen, and other estates to stand on, and there to behold the joustings and other shows at their pleasure." To this shed, then, it is supposed that the balcony in the modern church owes its origin; Sir Christopher Wren having apparently been desirous to preserve in the new edifice the distinguishing feature of the old. It was in the old Crown-sild that, for centuries, the Kings of England were accustomed to sit as spectators, not only at tournaments, but on occasions of great or rich processions passing through the streets of the city. It was in the Crown-sild, for instance, in 1509, that Henry the Eighth, disguised in the garb of a yeoman of the guard, sat to witness the

procession of the city watch at night, on the eve
of St. John. "The city music," we are told, "preceded the lord mayor's officers in party-coloured
liveries; then followed the sword-bearer, on horseback, in beautiful armour, before the lord mayor,
mounted also on a stately horse, richly caparisoned,
and attended by a giant and two pages on horseback, three pageants, morrice-dancers, and footmen. The sheriffs marched next, preceded also
by their officers in proper liveries, and attended
by their giants, pages, morrice-dancers, and pageants; then followed a large body of demi-lancers,
in bright armour, on stately horses; and after them
a body of carabineers in white fustian coats, with
the city arms upon their backs and breasts; a
division of archers, with their bows bent, and
shafts of arrows by their side; a party of pikemen
in crosslets and helmets; a body of halberdiers,
also in crosslets and helmets; and a great party of
billmen, with helmets and aprons of mail, brought
up the rear. The whole consisted of about two
thousand, in several divisions, with musicians,
drums, standards, and ensigns, ranked and answer-
ing each other in proper places, who marched
from the Conduit, at the west end of Cheapside,
through Cheapside, Poultry, Cornhill, and Leaden-
hall Street, to Aldgate; and back again through
Fenchurch Street, Gracechurch Street, Cornhill,
and so back to the Conduit from whence it first
set out; illuminated with 940 cressets, or large

lanthorns, fixed at the ends of poles, and carried on men's shoulders; of which two hundred were provided at the expense of the city; five hundred at the expense of the incorporated companies, and 240 at the expense of the city constables. And besides these, the streets were well lighted with a great number of lamps hung against the houses on each side, decorated with garlands of flowers and greens." So delighted was King Henry with the spectacle, that on the occasion of the next procession, which took place on the eve of St. Peter and St. Paul, he carried the queen and her ladies to witness the sight from the "Crown-slld" in Cheapside.

Charles the Second, King William and his consort, and Queen Anne, are severally mentioned as witnessing the pageantry of lord mayor's day from "a balcony" in Cheapside, as also did George the First, George the Second, and George the Third; but then it was not, of course, from the "Crown-sild," but from a private residence opposite Bow Church.

The dragon which surmounts the steeple of Bow Church has long been famous. Otway, for instance, in his comedy of "The Soldier's Fortune" (1681), makes Sir D. Dunce exclaim: "Oh, Lord! here are doings; here are vagaries! I'll run mad; I'll climb Bow steeple presently, bestride the dragon, and preach cuckoldom to the whole city." Again, in the "State Poems," we find:

" When Jacob Hall,[1] on his high rope, shews tricks,
   The dragon flutters; the lord mayor's horse kicks;
   The Cheapside crowds and pageants scarcely know
   Which most t' admire — Hall, hobby-horse, or Bow."

There are one or two other churches in the immediate vicinity of Cheapside which require a passing notice.   On the east side of Bread Street, at the corner of Watling Street, stands, on the site of an edifice of far more ancient date, the church of Allhallows, or All Saints, Bread Street, erected by Wren in 1680.   In this church, in 1531, a discreditable quarrel took place between two priests, in which the blood of one was shed by the other, when, in order to purify it from the sacrilege, it was ordered to be closed for the space of a month.   In the meantime, the two offenders, who had been committed to prison, were led forth, bareheaded, barefooted, and barelegged, and, with beads and books in their hands, compelled to do penance by walking from St. Paul's Cathedral along Cheapside and Cornhill, to the eastern limit of the city.   In the old church Milton was baptised.

In Bread Street, Cheapside, a little below Basing Lane, stands the parish church of St. Mildred, so called from having been dedicated to Mildred, a Saxon saint, daughter of a prince of West Anglia, and abbess of a monastery in the isle of Thanet.

---

[1] A famous rope-dancer in the reign of Charles the Second, on whom the Duchess of Cleveland is said to have conferred her favours.

The present edifice, the interior of which has been much admired, is another of Sir Christopher Wren's churches, built shortly after the destruction of the old place of worship in 1666. Its principal feature, however, is its fine altar-piece, and its beautifully carved pulpit and sounding-board, which, if they are not the work of Grinling Gibbons, would at least have reflected no discredit upon that eminent artist.

Running parallel with, and to the south of Cheapside, is Watling Street, a name, according to Leland, corrupted from Atheling, or Noble Street, so called from its contiguity to the Old Change, where a mint was established in the reign of the Saxon kings. According to other authorities, it derives its name from Adeling, a Saxon nobleman; whence Watheling and Watling. This street forms the site of part of the Roman road which anciently traversed England from Dover to South Wales. At the northwest end of it is the church of St. Augustine, Watling Street, dedicated to St. Augustine, a Roman monk of the order of St. Benedict, who, in 596, was sent to England by the Pope, for the purpose of converting the Anglo-Saxons to Christianity. It was anciently styled *Ecclesia Sancti Augustini ad Portam*, from its vicinity to the southeast gate of St. Paul's Cathedral. The old church having been burnt down in 1666, the present uninteresting edifice was erected in 1682, after designs by Sir Christopher Wren.

St. Anthony's, vulgarly called St. Antholin's, Watling Street, is a religious foundation of great antiquity. In 1399 it was rebuilt, principally at the expense of Sir Thomas Knowles, grocer and lord mayor, to whose memory there was formerly a monument in the church, with the following quaint inscription:

" Here lyeth graven under this stone,
   Thomas Knowles, both flesh and bone;
   Grocer and Alderman, years forty;
   Sheriff and twice Mayor truly.
   And (for he should not lye alone),
   Here lyeth with him his good wife Joan.
   They were together sixty year,
   And nineteen children they had in fear."

The tower and spire of this church, though not in the purest style of architecture, have been much admired.

Opposite to Old Change, on the north side of Cheapside, is Foster Lane, in which stands the church of St. Vedast, an ancient foundation dedicated to Vedast, Bishop of Arras, in the province of Artois, about the close of the fifth or the commencement of the sixth century. The old church having been burnt down in 1666, the present edifice was erected by Wren between the years 1694 and 1698. St. Vedast's Church, with its graceful spire and its panelled roof richly decorated with imitations of fruits and flowers, and its magnificent altar-piece, is well worthy of a visit.

In Foster Lane stands that noble modern edifice, the Goldsmiths' Hall; while in Noble Street, Foster Lane, is the Coachmans' Hall, interesting as having been the spot in which the Protestant Association held its meetings previously to the breaking out of the disgraceful riots of 1780. In the Goldsmiths' Hall are three busts, by Chantrey, of George the Third, George the Fourth, and William the Fourth; as also some well-executed portraits of our modern sovereigns, and an original portrait, by Jansen, of Sir Hugh Myddelton.

At the west end of Cheapside, at the end of Paternoster Row, stood, till 1666, the ancient parish church of St. Michael le Querne, or St. Michael at the Corn Market. Having been burnt down in the great fire, the site of it was appropriated to enlarge the great thoroughfare of Cheapside; the parish at the same time being incorporated by act of Parliament with that of St. Vedast, Foster Lane. In the parish of St. Michael le Querne the celebrated antiquary, John Leland, long carried on his laborious literary pursuits, and here, on the 18th of April, 1552, he breathed his last. He was interred in St. Michael's Church, as was also Francis Quarles, the author of the "Emblems." Sir Thomas Browne, author of the famous "Religio Medici," and of the "Treatise on Vulgar Errors," was baptised in this church.

CHAPTER VIII.

NEIGHBOURHOOD OF ST. PAUL'S.

Old Church of St. Martin's-le-Grand — Abuse of Privilege
of Sanctuary There — Northumberland House — St. Paul's
Churchyard a Residence of Publishers — Burning of Books
There during the Great Fire — Execution of Sir Everard
Digby — Queen Anne — Paternoster Row — Lovell's Court
— Warwick Lane — Archbishop Leighton — St. Paul's School
— Heralds' College — Doctors' Commons — Ludgate Hill —
The Belle Sauvage — Nell Gwynn — St. Martin, Ludgate.

AT the western extremity of Cheapside, close to
St. Paul's Cathedral, runs northward the street
called St. Martin's-le-Grand, so styled from the
famous church and sanctuary which anciently occupied the site of the present general post-office.
A collegiate church, dedicated to St. Martin, is
said to have been founded on this spot by Wythred,
King of Kent, as far back as 700; the epithet of
"le Grand" having been derived from the extraordinary privileges of sanctuary conferred upon it
by successive monarchs. The old monastery and
church were rebuilt about the year 1056 by two
brothers of a noble Saxon family, named Ingelric
and Edward, at which period the religious establishment consisted of a dean and several secular
canons.

In 1068 William the Conqueror not only confirmed to the college all its ancient privileges, but, moreover, rendered it independent of all other ecclesiastical jurisdiction whatsoever, whether regal or papal. Thus an isolated spot, in the centre of a large city, grew to acquire a peculiar government of its own, subject in the first instance to the collegiate dean, and, at a later period, to the Abbots of Westminster, to whom Henry the Seventh thought proper to transfer the jurisdiction. In consequence of the extraordinary immunities which it enjoyed as a sanctuary, St. Martin's-le-Grand became not only a place of refuge for every description of criminal and miscreant, but in periods of political convulsion we find the rioters, when defeated by the city train-bands, safely establishing themselves within the liberty of St. Martin's, and setting all law and authority at defiance. At length, during the tumults and convulsions which prevailed in 1456, the repeated outrages committed by the inhabitants of this privileged district had so entirely exhausted the patience of the respectable portion of the community, that the magistrates took upon themselves the responsibility of forcing an entrance into the monastic territory with an armed force, and succeeded in capturing the principal rioters. The Abbot of Westminster vehemently inveighed against this violation of the rights of the church, but apparently to little purpose.

On the romantic occasion of Richard, Duke of
Gloucester, discovering his future queen, Anne
Neville, in an obscure street in London disguised
as a serving-maid, it was to the sanctuary of St.
Martin's-le-Grand that he conducted her, where
she remained in security till taken under the protection of her uncle, George Neville, Archbishop
of York.   Here, too, according to Sir Thomas
More, "rotted away piecemeal," Miles Forest, one
of the reputed murderers of the two young princes
in the Tower.

The magnificent church of St. Martin's-le-Grand
was pulled down at the surrender of the monastery
to Edward the Sixth, in 1548, shortly after which
period a large tavern was erected on its site.   This
church — as well as those of St. Mary-le-Bow, St.
Giles's Cripplegate, and Allhallows Barking — had,
for some reason or other, the privilege extended to
them of tolling the curfew-bell long after this
ancient feudal custom had become dormant in
every other parish of London.

Not only did St. Martin's afford an asylum for
every description of offender, but for the space of
at least two centuries the immunities which it
enjoyed rendered it a safe and convenient place
for the fraudulent manufacture of all kinds of
counterfeit plate, coins, and jewels.   As early as
the reign of Edward the Fourth, — on the occasion
of an edict being issued against the manufacturers
of debased and counterfeit precious metals, — St.

Martin's was significantly exempted from the operation of the enactment. Long, indeed, after the dissolution of the religious houses we find, from the following passage in "Hudibras," that St. Martin's-le-Grand continued to harbour the peculiar class of people who earned a livelihood carrying on this illicit manufacture:

> "'Tis not those paltry counterfeits,
>   French stones, which in our eyes you set,
>   But our right diamonds that inspire,
>   And set your amorous hearts on fire.
>   Nor can those false St. Martin's beads, —
>   Which on our lips you place for reds,
>   And make us wear like Indian dames, —
>   Add fuel to your scorching flames;
>   But those true rubies of the rock,
>   Which in our cabinets we lock."

It was in the house of one of Milton's relations in St. Martin's - le - Grand, that the reconciliation took place between the poet and his first wife, Mary Powell, when unexpectedly she threw herself at the poet's feet and implored his forgiveness.

Between the church of St. Martin and Aldersgate Street stood Northumberland House, the residence of Harry Hotspur, Lord Percy, immortalised by the genius of Shakespeare and by his own valour. From Stow we learn that Henry the Fourth, in the seventh year of his reign, conferred the mansion, "with the tenements thereunto appertaining," on his consort, Queen Jane, from which

period it was called the Queen's Wardrobe. When
Stow wrote, it was a printing-house.

In the reign of Queen Elizabeth, St. Paul's
Churchyard appears to have been no less the resort
of booksellers than at the present day. Of Henry
Howard, Earl of Northampton, it is related that,
when reduced to penury by the attainder and
execution of his brother, the Duke of Norfolk,
those hours which were passed by others in enjoying the luxuries of the table were occupied by him
in poring over the contents of the booksellers'
stalls in St. Paul's Churchyard.

Many of Shakespeare's immortal plays and
poems were first published at the signs of the
Green Dragon, the Fox, the Angel, and at other
publishers' in St. Paul's Churchyard. On the 21st
of November, 1660, nearly half a century after the
death of Shakespeare, we find Pepys inserting in
his "Diary:" "In Paul's Church Yard I bought
the play of 'Henry the Fourth,' and so went to
the new theatre and saw it acted; but, my expec-
tation being too great, it did not please me, as
otherwise I believe it would; and my having a
book I believe did spoil it a little." Again he
writes, on the 10th of February, 1662: "To
Paul's Church Yard, and there I met with Doctor
Fuller's 'England's Worthies,' the first time that
I ever saw it; and so I sat down reading in it;
being much troubled that (though he had some
discourse with me about my family and arms) he

says nothing at all, nor mentions us either in Cambridgeshire or Norfolk; but I believe, indeed, our family was never considerable."

The great fire of 1666 occasioned fearful havoc among the great emporium of books in St. Paul's Churchyard. Evelyn, for instance, bitterly laments the loss of the vast magazine of books belonging to the stationers, which had been deposited for safety in the vaults of St. Faith's Church, under St. Paul's Cathedral. Pepys also writes on the 26th of September, immediately after the fire: "By Mr. Dugdale I hear of the great loss of books in St. Paul's Church Yard, and at their hall also, which they value at about £150,000; some booksellers being wholly undone, and, among others, they say, my poor Kirton." Again he writes, on the 5th of the following month: "Mr. Kirton's kinsman, my bookseller, came in my way; and so I am told by him that Mr. Kirton is utterly undone, and made £2,000 or £3,000 worse than nothing from being worth £7,000 or £8,000. That the goods laid in the churchyard fired through the windows those in St. Faith's Church; and those coming to the warehouses' doors, fired them, and burned all the books and the pillars of the church, which is alike pillared (which I knew not before); but being not burned, they stood still. He do believe there is above £150,000 of books burned; all the great booksellers almost undone; not only these, but their warehouses at their hall and under Christ Church and elsewhere being all burned. A great want thereof there will be of books, specially Latin books and foreign books; and, among others, the Polyglot and new Bible, which he believes will be presently worth forty pounds apiece."

From Anthony Wood we learn that Gerard Langbaine, the biographer of the dramatic poets, was at one period apprenticed to a bookseller of the name of Nevill Simmons in St. Paul's Church-yard. Here also, or in the immediate neighbour-hood, was born the great architect, Inigo Jones.

One of the most remarkable scenes which this spot has witnessed was the execution, on the 30th of January, 1606, of the once gay and gallant Sir Everard Digby, reputed to be the handsomest man of his day. Three of his fellow conspirators in the famous Gunpowder Plot suffered at the same time with him, namely, the notorious Robert Winter, John Grant, and Thomas Bates. The place of their execution was at the west end of St. Paul's Cathe-dral, apparently nearly on the spot where the statue of Queen Anne now stands. Sir Everard, Winter, and Bates died admitting the justice of their sen-tence, but Grant was stubborn to the last. Sir Everard in particular, we are told, "died penitent and sorrowful for his vile treason, and confident to be saved in the merits of his sweet Saviour Jesus. He prayed, kneeling, about half a quarter of an hour, often bowing his head to the ground. In the same manner they all prayed, but no voice heard, save now and then, 'O Jesu, Jesu, save me, and keep me!' which words they repeated many times upon the ladder." Anthony Wood, on the authority of "a most famous author," whose name, however, he omits to mention, relates the startling fact, that when Sir Everard's heart was plucked from his body by the executioner, — who, according to custom, held it up to the people, exclaiming, "Here is the heart of a traitor!" — Sir Everard made answer, "Thou liest!" The "famous author" here alluded to was apparently no other than Lord Bacon, who, moreover, proceeds to relate other facts quite as incredible. "We ourselves," he writes, "remember to have seen the heart of a man who was embowelled, according to the custom amongst us in the execution of traitors, which, being thrown into the fire, as is usual, sprung up at first six foot high, and continued leaping gradually lower and lower between seven and eight minutes, as far as our memory reaches. There is also an old and credible tradition of an ox that lowed after it was embowelled. But it is more certain that a man, who suffered in the manner we have before mentioned, — his entrails being taken out, and his heart almost torn away, and in the hands of the hangman, — was heard to utter three or four words of a prayer."

Having incidentally alluded to the statue of Queen Anne at the west end of St. Paul's Cathedral, we may mention that among the Cole MSS. in the British Museum are preserved the following lines written upon this statue, having reference to a well-known scandal prevalent in the queen's life-time, that she was too much addicted to intoxicating liquors :

" Here mighty Anna's statue placed we find,
Betwixt the darling passions of her mind ;
A brandy shop before, a church behind.
But why the back turned to that sacred place, —
As thy unhappy father's was, — to grace?
Why here, like Tantalus, in torments placed,
To view those waters which thou canst not taste ?
Though, by thy proffered globe, we may perceive,
That for a dram thou the whole world wouldst give."

And we find in the same collection :

" When brandy Nan became our queen,
    'Twas all a drunken story ;
From noon to night I drank and smoked,
    And so was thought a Tory ;
Brimful of wine, all sober folk
    We damned, and moderation ;
And for right Nantes we pawned to France
    Our goods and reputation."

With regard to the charge thus brought against Queen Anne, it is but fair to remark that Sarah, Duchess of Marlborough, notwithstanding her well-known hostility to the memory of her former royal mistress, hastens to defend her from the imputation.   " I know," writes the duchess, " that in some libels she has been reproached as one who indulged herself in drinking strong liquors, but I believe this was utterly groundless, and that she never went beyond such a quantity of strong wine as her physicians judged to be necessary for her." If there was ever an excuse for an unfortunate woman seeking relief from care and thought in the adventitious excitement produced by strong drinks, it was in the case of Queen Anne, who had not only lost a beloved husband in the prime of his existence, but had seen her numerous offspring — amounting to no fewer than nineteen in number — descend one by one to an untimely grave. It may be mentioned that Doctor Garth, the author of "The Dispensary,' has commemorated the queen's statue in verses which commence more complimentarily than they end:

> "Near the vast bulk of that stupendous frame,
> Known by the Gentiles' great Apostle's name,
> With grace divine great Anna's seen to rise,
> An awful form that glads a nation's eyes," etc.

The statue of Queen Anne in St. Paul's Churchyard is the work of one Francis Bird, whose fame as an artist rests principally on his conspicuous recumbent effigy of Doctor Busby in Westminster Abbey. Neither one nor the other deserves any particular commendation. The former, however, has met with its admirers; Defoe, in his "Journey through England," speaking of it as being "very masterly done," and Garth having commemorated it in some indifferent adulatory verses.

The trees which in the days of Queen Elizabeth were the pride of St. Paul's Churchyard, have long since passed away. Sir John Moore, in a letter addressed to Sir Ralph Winwood, in June, 1611, mentions "an exceeding high wind," which had blown down "the greatest elm in Paul's Church-yard." The last of the ancient grove disappeared a few years since. Mr. Leigh Hunt mentions hav-ing met with a child whose existence was so en-tirely artificial, that it had formed no notion of a tree but from " that single one in St. Paul's Church-yard." This tree is said to have marked the site of the famous Paul's Cross.

On the north side of, and running parallel with, St. Paul's Cathedral is Paternoster Row. "This street," writes Strype, in 1720, " before the fire of London, was taken up by eminent mercers, silkmen, and lacemen ; and their shops were so resorted unto by the nobility and gentry in their coaches, that ofttimes the street was so stopped up that there was no passage for foot-passengers. But since the said fire, those eminent tradesmen have settled themselves in several other parts, especially in Covent Garden, in Bedford Street, Henrietta Street, and King Street. And the inhabitants of this street are now a mixture of tradespeople, and chiefly tirewomen, for the sale of commodes, topknots, and the like dressings for the females.   There are also many shops for mercers and silkmen; and at the upper end some stationers, and large warehouses for booksellers, well situated for learned and studious men's access thither, being more retired and private."

Paternoster Row is said to derive its name from its having anciently been the resort of the venders of paternosters, beads, rosaries, etc., who hawked them to people on their way to mass in St. Paul's Cathedral.   Here, in the reign of Queen Elizabeth, the famous clown, Richard Tarleton, kept his ordinary, known as the "Castle."   He subsequently kept an ordinary known as the "Tabor," in Gracechurch Street.

It was in Paternoster Row that the beautiful but abandoned Frances Howard, Countess of Essex, was in the habit of clandestinely meeting her lover, the Earl of Somerset, to whom she was subsequently married.   Their assignations took place at the house of a Mrs. Turner, who was afterward executed for her share in the murder of Sir Thomas Overbury.   It seems not improbable that Mrs. Turner kept one of those fashionable shops in Paternoster Row for the sale of female attire to which Strype makes allusion, inasmuch as we find her famous in the world of fashion in the reign of James the First as the person who first introduced yellow starch into ruffs.

Between Paternoster Row and Newgate Street is Lovell's Court, standing on the site of a man-

sion of the gallant family of the Lovels, Barons
and Viscount Lovel of Tichmarsh, in Northamp-
tonshire. The last of the race who appears to
have resided here was Francis, first and last viscount, who held the appointments of chamberlain
of the household and chief butler of England in
the reign of Richard the Third. Having had the
good fortune to escape from the battle of Bos-
worth, where he had fought side by side with
Richard, he made his way to the Continent, where
he was received with great kindness and distinc-
tion by Margaret, Duchess of Burgundy, sister to
the late king, Edward the Fourth. We subsequently find him joining the rebellious standard
of the Earl of Lincoln, and acting a conspicuous
part in the sanguinary battle of Stoke, where the
forces of Henry the Seventh proved victorious.
Here again he escaped with his life, and when
last seen was urging his horse across the river,
in hopes of gaining the opposite side. According
to Lord Bacon, he was drowned in making the
attempt; while, if another account is to be cred-
ited, he made his way to a place of concealment
with which he was familiar, in which, either by
the negligence or the treachery of the person to
whom he had confided his secret, he was kept
immured and starved to death. The probability
of there being some truth in these rumours is
borne out by a story related by John, second
Duke of Rutland, in 1728. Six years previously,

said the duke, there having been occasion to raise
a new chimney at Minster Lovel, there was discovered a large subterranean apartment, in which
was the entire skeleton of a man in the attitude
of sitting at a table, with a book, paper, and pen
before him; all the articles being in a state of
great decay.   These were supposed to be the last
remains of the gallant and ill-fated Lord Lovel.
His vast inheritance, which was lost to his family
by his attainder, is now, we believe, chiefly in
the possession of the Marquises of Salisbury and
Northampton.

In the last century, Alderman Brigden, the
intimate friend of Richardson, the author of
"Pamela" and "Sir Charles Grandison," had a
large house in Lovell's Court, in an alcove in
the garden of which the celebrated novelist is
said to have written more than one of his works.

Between Amen Corner and Ludgate Street
stood Abergavenny House, the residence, in the
reign of Edward the Second, of John de Dreux,
Earl of Richmond and Duke of Brittany, and
grandson of Henry the Third.   Subsequently it
became the town mansion of the chivalrous John
Hastings, Earl of Pembroke, who married the
Lady Margaret Plantagenet, fourth daughter of
King Edward the Third; the mansion being then
styled "Pembroke's inne," near Ludgate.   From
the Hastings family it passed to the Nevilles,
Earls of Abergavenny, and from the Nevilles to

the Stationers' Company. The old mansion was destroyed by the great fire of 1666, shortly after which the present unpretending edifice was erected on its site. It contains some interesting portraits of Prior and Steel; of Richardson, the novelist, and his wife; of Bishop Hoadley; and of Alderman Boydell.

In Warwick Lane, between Paternoster Row and Newgate Street, stood the princely mansion or "inne," of the king-maker, Richard, Earl of Warwick, where he exercised that splendid hospitality for which he was so famous. A bas-relief of Guy, Earl of Warwick, may still be seen at the entrance into Warwick Lane.

At the Bell Inn, Warwick Lane, in 1684, died the pious and gentle Robert Leighton, Archbishop of Glasgow. In his old age, at the united and earnest request of Lord Perth and Bishop Burnet, he paid a visit to London. Burnet met him on his arrival. "I was amazed," he writes, "to see him at above seventy look so fresh and well that age seemed as it were to stand still with him. His hair was still black, and all his motions were lively. He had the same quickness of thought and strength of memory, but, above all, the same heat and life of devotion that I had ever seen in him." Burnet congratulating him on his good looks, the venerable prelate shook his head, observing that "he was very near his end, for all that, and that his work and journey were now almost done." He died the following day. He had more than once been heard to express a wish to die at an inn, and the desire was gratified. "He used often to say," writes Burnet, "that if he were to choose a place to die in, it should be an inn. It looked like a pilgrim going home, to whom this world was all as an inn, and who was weary of the noise and confusion in it. He added that the officious tenderness and care of friends was an entanglement to a dying man, and that the unconcerned attendance of those that could be procured in such a place would give him less disturbance. And he obtained what he desired, for he died at the Bell Inn, in Warwick Lane." Burnet was with him to the last. "Both speech and sense," he writes, "went away of a sudden, and he continued panting about twelve hours, and then died without pangs or convulsions. I was by him all the while."

Under the shadow of St. Paul's Cathedral is the celebrated school which bears its name. Its founder was Dr. John Colet, Dean of St. Paul's, who, in 1512, endowed it out of his private fortune for the education of one hundred and fifty-three boys, in allusion to the number of fishes caught by St. Peter. The celebrated grammarian, William Lily, was selected to be the first head master. Although Doctor Colet survived the accomplishment of his noble work scarcely ten years, he had the satisfaction of seeing his school flourish, and his labours rewarded. Among others, Sir Thomas

More wrote to congratulate him on the success which he so well merited, comparing the new school "to the wooden horse of Troy, out of which the Grecians issued to overcome the city." "And so," he added, "out of this your school many have come that have subverted and overthrown all ignorance and rudeness." Erasmus also was amongst the first to do justice to the pious work of the founder. In a letter to Justus Jonas, speaking of Doctor Colet, he writes: "Upon the death of his father, when by right of inheritance he was possessed of a good sum of money, lest the keeping of it should corrupt his mind and turn it too much toward the world, he laid out a great part of it in building a new school in the churchyard of St. Paul's, dedicated to the child Jesus, — a magnificent fabric, — to which he added two dwelling-houses for the two several masters, and to them he allotted ample salaries, that they might teach a certain number of boys free and for the sake of charity. He divided the school into four apartments. The first — the porch and entrance — is for catechumens, or the children to be instructed in the principles of religion, where no child is to be admitted but what can read and write. The second apartment is for the lower boys, to be taught by the second master or usher; the third for the upper forms, under the head master; which two parts of the school are divided by a curtain, to be drawn at pleasure.   Over the master's chair is an image of the child Jesus, of admirable work, in the gesture of teaching, whom all the boys, going and coming, salute with a short hymn; and there is a representation of God the Father, saying, 'Hear ye him,'—these words being written at my suggestion.   The fourth, or last apartment, is a little chapel for divine service.   The school has no corners or hiding-places; nothing like a cell or closet. The boys have their distinct forms or benches, one above another.   Every form holds sixteen, and he that is head or captain of each form has a little kind of desk by way of preëminence.   They are not to admit all boys, of course, but to choose them according to their parts and capacities."

Many great and eminent persons have received their education at St. Paul's School.   Among these may be mentioned John Leland, the antiquary, and Sir Anthony Denny, the well-known statesman in the reign of Henry the Eighth, both of whom were among its first scholars.   Here also were educated the great antiquary, William Camden; John Milton; the gossiping secretary of the admiralty, Samuel Pepys; the learned Richard Cumberland, Bishop of Peterborough; John Strype, the antiquary; the great Duke of Marlborough; the pious Robert Nelson, author of " Fasts and Festivals;" Edmund Halley, the astronomer and mathematician; and the munificent Alured Clarke, Dean of Exeter.   St. Paul's School having been burnt down in the great fire of London, it was shortly afterward rebuilt by the Mercers' Company, in whom, by the decree of the founder, is perpetually vested the care of the funds, as well as the government of the school. Doctor Colet was once asked his reasons for having selected a company of merchants and shopkeepers to be the custodians of his noble charity. "There is no absolute certainty," he replied, "in human affairs; but for my part I have found less corruption in such a body of citizens than in any other order or body of mankind." The present building was erected in 1823.

On the south side of St. Paul's Cathedral is a narrow street, called Paul's Chain, deriving its name from a chain which was formerly drawn across the road to prevent carriages from passing and repassing during the performance of divine service in the cathedral.

Paul's Chain leads us into Knightrider Street, so called, it is said, from the knights usually riding this way from the Tower Royal to the tournaments at Smithfield. On the site of No. 5 in this street lived Thomas Linacre, the celebrated philologist, and physician to Henry the Seventh, who died in 1524, and was buried in St. Paul's Cathedral. In Little Knightrider Street lived Ralph Thoresby, the antiquary.

Close by, on the east side of St. Benet's Hill, is the Heralds' College, a venerable foundation, first formed into a corporate body by Richard the Third, who conferred upon it the stately mansion in Cold Harbour, of which we have already given a notice. Having been arbitrarily driven from this mansion by Henry the Seventh, the heralds remained for some time without a fixed abode, till Queen Mary established them on the site of their present college; "to the end," says the grant, "that the said kings-at-arms, heralds, and pursuivants-at-arms, and their successors, might at their liking dwell together, and at meet times congregate, speak, confer, and agree among themselves, for the good government of their faculty, and that their records may be more safely kept."

The mansion bestowed upon them by Queen Mary had long been the London residence of the Stanleys, Earls of Derby. Here its founder — Thomas, the first earl, who married the mother of King Henry the Seventh — lived and died; and here, according to the charming old ballad, "The Song of Lady Bessy," the Princess Elizabeth of York was for some time the earl's guest, during the usurpation of her uncle, Richard, Duke of Gloucester :—

> "She sojourned in the citie of London
>   That time with the Earl of Derbye."

Here Edward, the third earl, kept up that famous magnificence which has been chronicled by Stow and Holinshed, and which led Camden to remark that "with Edward, Earl of Derby's, death the glory of hospitality seemed to fall asleep." In 1552 Derby House was exchanged by this noble-man with Edward the Sixth for certain lands adjoining his park at Knowsley, in Lancashire; Queen Mary, on the 18th July, 1555, conferring it on the heralds. The old mansion having been burnt down in 1666, the present sombre and venerable-looking edifice was shortly afterward erected, principally at the expense of the officers of the college. The armorial bearings of the Stanleys were, till very recently, to be seen on the south side of the quadrangle.

Close to Heralds' College is Doctors' Commons, so called from its having been originally a college where the law was propounded or taught; the word Commons having been added from its mem-bers living in community together as in other collegiate establishments.

Close to Doctors' Commons stands the church of St. Bennet, or rather St. Benedict, another of the numerous churches rebuilt by Sir Christopher Wren after the great fire in 1666. The only in-terest which attaches itself to this church is the circumstance of the great architect, Inigo Jones, having been interred in the chancel of the old church, in which, upon the north wall, there was a monument to his memory, which was destroyed by the fire. Here also lies interred William Oldys, the author of "The British Librarian."

Retracing our steps to St. Paul's Churchyard, we find ourselves on Ludgate Hill, the site of Lud Gate, one of the ancient entrances into the city of London. Twice it was rebuilt, once by the victorious barons, in the reign of King John, and again in 1586. "It was, in my memory," writes Pennant, "a wretched prison for debtors. It commenced what was called a free prison, in 1373, but soon lost that privilege. It was enlarged, and had the addition of a chapel, by Sir Stephen Forster, on a very romantic occasion. He himself had been confined there, and while begging at the grate was accosted by a rich widow, who asked him what sum would purchase his liberty. She paid it down, took him into her service, and afterward married him. In the chapel was an inscription, in honour of him and Agnes, his wife, dated 1454, the year in which he enjoyed the honour of being lord mayor of the city. Anciently there was to be seen, affixed to the wall of Lud Gate Prison, a copper plate, on which were engraved the following doggerel lines:

" Devout souls, that pass this way,
For Stephen Forster, late Mayor, heartily pray,
And Dame Agnes, his spouse, to God consecrate,
That of pity this house made for Londoners in Ludgate;
So that, for lodging and water, prisoners here nought pay,
As their keepers shall answer at dreadful doom's-day."

It was at Lud Gate that Sir Thomas Wyatt encountered the opposition which gave the final check to his ill-advised insurrection. Finding the gates closed against him, he fell back with the few followers who still remained true to him, and was shortly afterward arrested near the Temple Gate.

Not many years have elapsed since the sign of the Belle Sauvage — representing a large bell with a wild man standing beside it — was a conspicuous object on Ludgate Hill. The old hostelry,— apparently one of the oldest in London,— having been burnt down in the great fire, was rebuilt, and, till its final demolition, retained its ancient name. It was on a bench opposite to this tavern that Sir Thomas Wyatt, on finding the city gates shut against him, is said to have sat and meditated in great despondency on his altered fortunes. By Stow it is conjectured that the name of the Belle Sauvage was derived from one Isabella Savage, a former possessor of the house; whereas the definition suggested by Addison, in the *Spectator*, would seem to be the more correct one. "As for the Bell Savage," he writes, "I was formerly much puzzled upon the conceit of it, till I accidentally fell into the reading of an old romance translated out of the French, which gives an account of a very beautiful woman who was found in a wilderness, and is called in the French 'La belle Sauvage,' and is everywhere translated by our countrymen the Bell Savage."

In the days of his obscurity, the celebrated

artist, Grinling Gibbons, resided in Belle Savage Court, Ludgate Hill. Among other works which he executed at this period is said to have been a vase of flowers of such delicate workmanship that they shook with the motion of the vehicles which passed through the street.

Before the establishment of regular theatres in England, the courtyards of the larger inns — surrounded, as they generally were, on three sides by galleries — formed not incommodious arenas in which the strolling companies erected their temporary stage. "The form of these temporary playhouses," writes Malone, "seems to be preserved in our modern theatre. The galleries in both are ranged over each other on three sides of the building. The small rooms under the lowest of these galleries answer to our present boxes, and it is observable that these — even in theatres which were built in a subsequent period expressly for dramatic exhibitions — still retained their old name, and were frequently called rooms by our ancient writers. The yard bears a sufficient resemblance to the pit, as at present in use." It was in the yard of the Belle Sauvage, in the reign of Queen Elizabeth, that Richard Tarleton, the Grimaldi of that famous age, delighted our forefathers by his unrivalled antics and extempore wit.

Ludgate reminds us of a creditable anecdote related of Nell Gwynn, of whose kindness of heart we have nearly as many proofs as we have of her frailty. She was one day ascending Ludgate Hill in her coach, when her attention was attracted to some bailiffs, who were in the act of hurrying off an unfortunate clergyman to prison. Having ordered her coachman to stop, and made some inquiries into the case, she sent for the persons whom the poor debtor named as attestators to his character, and finding him a proper object of charity, not only discharged his debt, but afterward successfully exerted herself in obtaining preferment for the worthy clergyman.

According to some writers, Lud Gate owed its name to King Lud, who is said to have originally erected the gate, while others, apparently with much more reason, consider its ancient appellation to have been Fludgate, or rather Flodgate, a name derived from the river Fleet, or Flod, which flowed in its immediate vicinity. It may be mentioned that the old gate was sold by order of the commissioners of city lands on the 30th of July, 1760, and in the following November it was razed to the ground.

On the north side of Ludgate Street, opposite to the entrance into Blackfriars, stands the church of St. Martin Ludgate, possessing little interest beyond its antiquity. According to Robert of Gloucester, it was originally built at so remote a period as the seventh century, by the British prince, Cadwallo; speaking of whom, in connection with Ludgate, he writes:

" A chirch of Sent Martyn liuyng he let rere,
    In whych yat men shold goddys seruyse do,
    And sing for his soule and al Christene also."

All, however, that we know for a certainty, is
the fact that a church was standing here in 1322,
when Robert de Sancto Albano was rector.   At
this period the presentation to St. Martin's was
vested in the Abbot and Convent of Westminster,
who continued to enjoy it till the dissolution of
the monasteries, when, Westminster having been
erected into a bishopric, Henry the Eighth conferred the presentation upon the new prelate.
That see having been dissolved in the following
reign, Queen Mary, in 1553, conferred it on the
Bishop of London and his successors, with whom
the patronage still continues.   The old church
having been burnt down in the great fire of London, the present uninteresting edifice was built
after designs of Sir Christopher Wren.   From
the circumstance of several sepulchral stones having been discovered in the immediate neighbourhood, as well as from its vicinity to Watling
Street, the great highway of the Romans, the
church is believed to stand nearly on the site of
a Roman cemetery.   One of the rectors of this
church in the seventeenth century was Samuel
Purchas, the author of the " Pilgrimages."

CHAPTER IX.

ST. PAUL'S CATHEDRAL.

Wren's Discoveries when Digging the Foundation of St. Paul's — Supposed to Have Been Built on the Site of a Roman Temple — History of the Old Structures — Church of St. Faith — Bishop of London's Palace — Lollards' Tower — Wickliffe in St. Paul's — " Paul's Walkers " or " Paul's Men " — Tombs in Old St. Paul's — Paul's Cross — Remarkable Events There — Present St. Paul's — Sir Christopher Wren.

How interesting is the account bequeathed to us by Sir Christopher Wren, of the laying the foundations of his great work, St. Paul's Cathedral! At the greatest depth to which he excavated, he found a substratum of hard clay, the natural soil of the locality, above which, nearly at the level of low-water mark, he discovered water and sand, mixed with sea-shells; thus not only rendering it evident that the sea had once flowed over the high ground on which St. Paul's now stands, but also giving probability to the supposition of the great architect, that the whole country, between Camberwell Hill and the hills of Essex, was once a branch of the sea, forming at low water a sandy bay. Above the sand, on the north

side, Wren found a variety of Roman urns, lamps, and lachrymatories, showing that this had once been a cemetery of that great people. Above these again, affording unquestionable evidence of its having also been a burial-place of the ancient British, he discovered numerous pins of wood and ivory, which had formerly fastened the garments of the dead; and lastly, still nearer to the surface of the earth, he found. stone coffins and graves lined with chalk-stones, the peculiar characteristics of a Saxon cemetery.

Whether there be any truth in the surmise that a temple of Diana anciently stood on the site of the present St. Paul's Cathedral will in all human probability never be satisfactorily settled. As far as the opinion of Sir Christopher Wren is concerned, he decidedly explodes the notion of a pagan temple having ever stood on the spot. He could discover, he says, neither the slightest remains of Roman ornamental architecture, nor the horns of any animal which it was the custom to sacrifice to the Goddess of Chastity. That, after a lapse of upward of twelve centuries, and after the ground had been so repeatedly disturbed by the erection and destruction of successive edifices, no trace was to be found of the graceful cornices and capitals of the Romans is, perhaps, not much to be wondered at. But when we find Sir Christopher himself speaking of the discovery of some ancient foundations, — consisting of " Kentish rubble-stone, artfully worked and consolidated with exceeding hard mortar, in the Roman manner,"— moreover, when we find a Roman burial-place existing in the immediate neighbourhood; when we remember how common it was for the early Christians to convert pagan temples into places of Christian worship; and lastly, when we find it an established fact that the horns of animals used in the sacrifices to Diana have been actually discovered near the spot, though none happened to be found by Wren,— we feel ourselves almost justified in clinging to an ancient tradition which serves to throw so much additional interest over St. Paul's. "Some," writes Bishop Gibson, in his edition of Camden's "Britannia," "have fancied that the temple of Diana formerly stood here, and there are circumstances that strengthen the conjecture; as the old adjacent buildings being called in their records *Dianæ Camera*, the chamber of Diana; the digging up in the churchyard, in Edward the First's reign, as we find by our annals, an incredible number of ox-heads, which the common people at that time, not without great admiration, looked upon to have been Gentile sacrifices, and the learned know that the *Tauropolia* were celebrated in honour of Diana. But much rather I should found this opinion of a temple of Diana upon the witty conceit of Mr. Selden, who, upon occasion of some ox-heads, sacred also to Diana, that were discovered in digging the foundations of a new chapel on the south side of St. Paul's (1316), would insinuate that the name of London imported no more than *Llan Dien*, i. e., *Templum Dianæ*. And against the foregoing conjecture it is urged, that as for the tenements called *Camera Dianæ*, they stood not so near the church as some would have us think, but on St. Paul's Wharf Hill, near Doctors' Commons; and they seem to have taken their denomination from a spacious building, full of intricate turnings, wherein King Henry the Second, as he did at Woodstock, kept his heart's delight, whom he there called Fair Rosamond, and here Diana." Some remains of these "intricate turnings" existed as late as the reign of Elizabeth, as also of an underground passage leading from Baynard's Castle, by which communication it has been presumed that the king was accustomed to find his way to his *Camera Dianæ*, or secret apartment of his beloved mistress.

It has been conjectured that a place of Christian worship existed on the site of the present cathedral as early as the end of the second century, about which time (185) Faganus and Damianus were sent by Pope Eleutherius to convert the natives of Britain to Christianity. This early church, it has been supposed, was destroyed during the famous persecution of the Christians in the reign of Diocletian; it having been the great object of that emperor to efface, throughout the Roman dominions, the name and worship of Christ, and to restore the religion of the heathen gods. It was then, according to some authorities, that a temple dedicated to Diana was erected on this spot. In the words of an old monkish chronicler, Fleta, "the old abomination was restored wherever the Britons were expelled their place. London worshipped Diana, and the suburbs of Thorney offered incense to Apollo." [1]

After the death of the Emperor Diocletian there again arose a place of Christian worship on the site of St. Paul's, which in its turn was destroyed by the pagan Saxons. When, however, early in the seventh century, that people embraced Christianity, it was rebuilt by Ethelbert, King of Kent (610), on its ancient foundations; Melitus, at the instance of St. Augustine, being consecrated first Bishop of London. In 675 we find Erkenwald, son of King Offa, fourth Bishop of London from Melitus, expending large sums of money in repairing and beautifying the ancient edifice, as well as obtaining for it considerable privileges both from the Pope and the Saxon princes of England. For these good deeds, Erkenwald was canonised at his death, and his body placed in a shrine above the high altar,

---

[1] It is needless to remind the reader that by Thorney is meant Westminster Abbey, on the site of which is said to have stood a temple of Apollo; Thorney Island being so called from its having been insulated by a branch of the Thames, and covered with thorns and briars.

where it continued to be an object of adoration till the destruction of the edifice by fire in 1086. William the Conqueror not only secured to St. Paul's its ancient privileges, but appears also to have regarded it with peculiar reverence.

After the destruction of the old church by fire, in 1086, Mauritius, or Maurice, then Bishop of London, commenced rebuilding it on a most extensive and magnificent scale. Interested in his pious work, William Rufus granted him the stones of the old Palatine Tower on the banks of the Thames; while in the following reign we find Henry the First exempting from toll or custom all vessels entering the river Fleet with stones and other materials for the new cathedral. Such, however, was the vastness of the undertaking, that although Bishop Maurice lived twenty years after the commencement of his pious labours, and although his successor, Bishop Beauvages, enjoyed the see twenty succeeding years, and appropriated nearly the whole of his ecclesiastical revenue in advancing this great work, its completion was left to succeeding generations. It was not till 1221 that the steeple was in a finished state, nor the choir till 1240. When completed, this magnificent structure, with the buildings attached to it, covered upward of three acres and a half of ground. Its length was 690 feet; its breadth 130, and its extreme height, to the summit of the spire, 534 feet. The interior of old St.

Paul's corresponded in splendour with the grandeur of its external appearance. The immense length of the vista, the double line of graceful Gothic arches, the gorgeous decorations of the high altar, the sublime effect of the vaulted roof, exquisitely groined and gilt, as well as the beautiful colouring of the painted windows, are said to have presented a spectacle which, in beauty and magnificence, far excelled that of every other religious edifice in England. The high altar, which stood between two columns, under a canopy of wood elaborately carved and painted, was adorned with precious stones and surrounded with images exquisitely wrought. Above the altar was the shrine of St. Erkenwald, which, being inlaid and adorned with gold, silver, and precious stones, made such a splendid and dazzling appearance, that princes and nobles, we are told, came from all parts to visit it, and to offer up their adorations to the Saxon saint. In a wooden tabernacle, on the right side of the high altar, was a picture of St. Paul, said to have been of great excellence; while against a pillar in the body of the church was a beautiful image of the Virgin, before which a lamp was kept constantly burning. In the centre of the cathedral stood a large cross; and if to these we add the splendour of the numerous shrines and altars, and the magnificence of the sepulchral monuments, we shall be able to form some slight notion of old St.

Paul's as it existed in the fourteenth and fifteenth centuries.

Another striking feature in the old cathedral was the beautiful subterranean parish church of St. Faith in the Crypts, commenced in 1356, which, besides several chantries and monuments, had two chapels, severally dedicated to Our Lady and St. Dunstan. Its cemetery was on the south side of the cathedral. Here, on the 29th of December, 1648, "against the door that leadeth into St. Faith's Church," was shot for his loyalty Maj. William Pitcher, a gallant adherent of Charles the First. It was also in St. Faith's cemetery that the remains of Col. Edward Marcus Despard, who was hanged for high treason in February, 1803, were allowed burial. After the fire of London, the parish of St. Faith was united with that of St. Augustine.

The chapter house of the old cathedral, as well as the cloisters, are also said to have been of elaborate workmanship and of great beauty. The latter, with the fine monuments which they contained, were destroyed by the Protector Somerset, in order to furnish materials for constructing his new palace in the Strand.

At the northwest corner of St. Paul's stood the stately inn, or palace, of the Bishops of London, the hospitalities of which appear to have been frequently enjoyed by our earlier sovereigns. Here, for instance, we find Edward the Third and his queen entertained and lodged on the occasion of a magnificent tournament at Smithfield. "There was goodly dancing," writes Froissart, "in the queen's lodging, in presence of the king and his uncles, and other barons of England, and ladies demoiselles, till it was day, which was time for every person to draw to their lodgings, except the king and queen, who lay there in the bishop's palace, for there they lay during all the feasts and jousts." The Bishop of London's palace at St. Paul's was for a short time the residence of the unfortunate Edward the Fifth, previous to his being immured in the Tower. Under its roof, too, it was that the ill-fated Catherine of Aragon, after her marriage to Prince Arthur in the neighbouring cathedral, was conducted to a magnificent banquet, and afterward to her nuptial couch. Here, on the 24th of November, 1588, after having returned tnanks in St. Paul's Cathedral for the dispersion of the Spanish Armada, Queen Elizabeth was entertained at dinner, and hence she returned at night, in state and by torchlight, to Whitehall. Among other eminent persons who have been lodged at different times in this mansion may be mentioned Anne, Duke de Montmorenci, ambassador from Francis the First in 1526; Claude Annibau, ambassador from the same monarch in 1546; and Mary of Guise, Queen Dowager of Scotland, when she visited London, in the reign of Edward the Sixth. It was from its threshold that Jane Shore was led to undergo her penance at Paul's Cross.

In the reign of Edward the First, St. Paul's Cathedral, with the bishop's palace and the other ecclesiastical buildings, were surrounded by a wall, the gates of which were always carefully closed at night. Many of the neighbouring thoroughfares, such as Ave-Maria Lane, Paternoster Row, Creed Lane, Canon Alley, Holyday Court, and Amen Corner, derive their names from their contiguity to, and their connection with, the old cathedral.

Another interesting building connected with old St. Paul's was the Lollards' Tower at the west front, which was long used as a prison for heretics, and is said to have witnessed many fearful scenes of suffering and distress. The tale of Richard Hunne, who was committed a prisoner to the Lollards' Tower, in 1514, is one of the darkest in the annals of human misery. This person, a merchant-tailor of London, had become involved in a dispute with his rector, who summoned him before the spiritual court. Hunne retorted by taking out a writ of *premunire* against the rector, an act of defiance which gave such offence to the Roman Catholic clergy that the formidable charge of heresy was brought against him, and he was thrown into the Lollards' Tower. A few days afterward his lifeless body was found suspended from a hook in the ceiling, when, the presumption being that he had committed suicide, the usual process was commenced against the corpse, which was condemned to be burned at Smithfield. In the meantime, however, suspicions of foul play had got abroad, and, consequently, a coroner's inquest was appointed to sit on the body. According to Burnet: "They found his neck had been broken, as they judged, with an iron chain, for the skin was all fretted and cut. They saw some streams of blood about his body, besides several other evidences, which made it clear that he had not murdered himself; whereupon, they did acquit the dead body, and laid the murder on the officers that had the charge of that prison. By other proofs, they found the bishop's summoner and the bell-ringer guilty of it; and, by the deposition of the summoner himself, it did appear that the chancellor and he and the bell-ringer did murder him, and then hung him up." The criminals, however, had a powerful champion in Fitzjames, Bishop of London, and accordingly, although the crime was clearly brought home to Horsey, the chancellor of the diocese, not only did the perpetrators of the crime receive the king's pardon, but the ashes of Hunne were ignominiously committed to a suicide's grave. The king, indeed, so far interfered on the side of justice as to obtain the reversion of Hunne's property to his children. "The last person confined here," writes Pennant, "was Peter Burchet, of the Temple, who, in 1573, desperately wounded our famous seaman, Sir Richard Hawkins, in the open street, whom he had mistaken for Sir Christopher Hatton. He was committed to this prison, and afterward removed ·to the Tower. He there barbarously murdered one of his keepers ; was tried, convicted, had his right hand struck off, and then hanged. He was found to be a violent enthusiast, and thought it lawful to kill such who opposed the truth of the gospel."

It was in St. Paul's Cathedral, in May, 1213, that King John — overawed by the disaffection of his subjects, by the secret combination of his barons, and the dreaded approach of the mighty armament with which Philip of France was preparing to invade England — consented to submit himself to the judgment of the Pope, at the same time formally acknowledging the supremacy of the Apostolic See. Here, too, it was, in 1401, that William Sautre, the parish priest of St. Osithes in London, conspicuous as the first English martyr, underwent the imposing ceremony of being stripped of his priestly vestments, and being degraded from his priestly office, preparatory to his being led forth to a death of agony in the flames.

With the tale of the illustrious Wickliffe, the father of the Reformation in England, St. Paul's is also intimately associated. Here it was, on the 19th of February, 1377, that this extraordinary man took his stand before a solemn conclave of the Church of Rome, the members of which were prepared to crush him with all the weight of their formidable authority. Instead, however, of presenting the humbled look of a criminal or a suppliant, he appeared before the haughty synod, supported on one side by the great John of Gaunt, Duke of Lancaster, and by Lord Percy, the earl marshal, on the other. Moreover, these great lords were severally accompanied by a formidable train composed of their armed retainers. " With whatever intent," writes Southey, " these powerful barons accompanied him, their conduct was such as discredited the cause. Before the proceedings could begin, they engaged in an angry altercation with Bishop Courtenay, who appears to have preserved both his temper and his dignity, when Lancaster had lost all sense of both. Here, however, the feeling of the people was against Wickliffe, probably because he was supported by an unpopular government ; and when the citizens who were present heard Lancaster mutter a threat of dragging their bishop out of the church by the hair of his head, they took fire ; a tumult ensued ; the synod was broken up, and the barons were glad to effect their escape as they could."

After the mysterious death of the ill-fated Richard the Second in Pomfret Castle, it was to St. Paul's Cathedral, on a bier drawn by four black horses, and followed by four knights habited in black, that his body was conveyed. Here it was exposed to public view for three days, during which period, as Froissart writes, "There came in and out twenty thousand persons, men and women, to see him where he lay, his head upon a black cushion, and his visage open. Some had pity on him, and some had none, but said he had long ago deserved death." From St. Paul's the royal corpse was conveyed to Langley, " and there this Kyng Richard was buried — God have mercy on his soule!" According to Stow, among those who were present at the performance of the preliminary funeral obsequies over King Richard's body, in St. Paul's, was his rival and successor, Henry the Fourth.

In 1470, when the revolution effected by the great king-maker, Earl of Warwick, drove Edward the Fourth into temporary exile, we find Henry the Sixth obsequiously led from his prison-rooms in the Tower, whence, on horseback, — clad in a robe of blue velvet, and with the crown upon his head, — he was conducted by the Duke of Clarence, the Earls of Warwick and Shrewsbury, and other noblemen, to St. Paul's, where he returned thanks for his unexpected deliverance. From this period, till Henry was led back a prisoner to the Tower the following year, he appears to have principally held his court in the Bishop of London's palace at St. Paul's. The sequel of his melancholy history is well known. On the very morning after the triumphal entry of Edward the Fourth into London, the meek usurper was found dead in the Tower. From the Tower his body was brought by torchlight to St. Paul's, whence, after it had lain for some days on a bier exposed to the view of the multitude, it was carried by torchlight to the riverside, where it was placed on board a barge, and thence conveyed to Chertsey for interment.

From the reign of Queen Elizabeth to that of Charles the First, the body or middle aisle of St. Paul's Cathedral was the common and fashionable resort of the gay and the idle; of the politician, the adventurer, the newsmonger, and the man of fashion. The time of day at which it was principally resorted to was between the hours of eleven and twelve in the morning, and between three and six in the afternoon. Those who frequented it were called Paul's Walkers, and occasionally Paul's Men, in the same way that the fashionable promenaders of Bond Street were in our own time styled Bond Street Loungers. For instance, among the *dramatis personæ* in Jonson's "Every Man in His Humour," we find "Captain Bobadil, a Paul's Man." Dekker has left us a very graphic and amusing account of the strange medley of persons who were daily to be seen assembled in Paul's Walk. "At one time, in one and the same rank, yea, foot by foot, and elbow by elbow, shall you see walking the knight, the gull, the gallant, the upstart, the gentleman, the clown, the captain, the apple-squire, the lawyer, the usurer, the citizen, the rankrout, the scholar, the beggar, the doctor, the idiot, the ruffian, the cheater, the Puritan, the cutthroat, the high-man, the low-man, the true-man, and the thief. Of all trades and professions some; of all countries some. Thus, whilst Devotion kneels at her prayers, doth Profanation walk under her nose in contempt of religion." Massinger, in his " City Madam," also alludes to the disreputable characters who frequented " Paul's Walk."

" I'll hang you both, I can but ride
You for the purse, you cut in sermon time at Paul's."

" I bought him in Paul's," is Falstaff's expression, in speaking of Bardolph. Thus, too, the witty Doctor Corbett, Bishop of Norwich, speaks of the manner in which, in his time, the old cathedral was desecrated:

" When I pass Paul's, and travel in that walk,
Where all our British sinners swear and talk;
Old Harry ruffians, bankrupts, soothsayers,
And youth whose cozenage is old as theirs;
And then behold the body of my lord
Trod under foot by vice, which he abhorr'd,
It woundeth me."

The once popular phrase of "dining with Duke Humphrey" was, as we have already remarked, applied to persons who, not having the means of providing themselves with a dinner, whiled away in the aisles of Saint Paul's the hours at

which others were enjoying their comfortable
meal. "Duke Humphrey's Walk," as the middle aisle of St. Paul's was occasionally designated,
was so called from its containing a conspicuous
monument, supposed to be that of Humphrey
Plantagenet, Duke of Gloucester, but which there
seems to be little doubt was the tomb of Sir John
Beauchamp, the royal standard-bearer at the battle of Cressy, and one of the original Knights of
the Garter.

> "'Tis Ruffio: trow'st thou where he dined to-day?
> In sooth I saw him sit with Duke Humfray."
> — *Bishop Hall's Satires.*

On the destruction of St. Paul's Cathedral, the
nave of Westminster Abbey became the fashionable walk of London.

In old St. Paul's were interred two of our old
Saxon kings, — Sebba, King of the East Saxons,
who was converted to Christianity by Erkenwald
in 667; and Ethelred the Second, who died in
1016. Here, too, were interred a number of
eminent persons, whose tombs — many of them
of great beauty — perished with the cathedral in
the great fire of London. Of those persons,
Henry de Lacy, Earl of Lincoln, the distinguished
statesman and warrior of the reign of Edward the
First, died "at his mansion-house called Lincoln's
Inn, in the suburbs of London," in 1312. His
effigy in old St. Paul's represented him lying

down, clad in complete armour, his body being covered with a short mantle, and his legs crossed. Another ancient and conspicuous monument was that of Sir John Beauchamp, Constable of Dover Castle, to which we have just referred; his effigy also representing him in full armour, and in a recumbent posture. Sir John, who was summoned to Parliament in the reign of Edward the Third as "Johannes de Bello-Campo de Warrewyk," died in 1358, when the barony became extinct.

Under a beautiful Gothic arch lay the armed effigy of the unfortunate Sir Simon Burleigh, perhaps the most accomplished man of his age. Living on affectionate terms with Edward the Third, and the chosen companion of the Black Prince, he was selected by the latter to be the tutor of his son, afterward Richard the Second. Having become involved in the ruined fortunes of his royal master, he was ordered by the inexorable Thomas, Duke of Gloucester, to the block; the queen, Anne of Bohemia, in vain throwing herself at Gloucester's feet, and imploring him to spare the life of one so accomplished and so esteemed. By the sentence passed on him he was to be hanged, drawn, and quartered; but in consideration of his being a Knight of the Garter, and of the services which he had rendered to the late king, the sentence was changed to decapitation, which was duly carried into effect on Tower Hill. "To write of his shameful death," writes

Froissart, "right sore displeases me; for when I was young I found him a noble knight, sage and wise: yet no excuse could be heard; and on a day he was brought out of the Tower and beheaded like a traitor: God have mercy on his soul."

Perhaps the most magnificent, and certainly not the least interesting, tomb in old St. Paul's, was that of the great John of Gaunt, Duke of Lancaster. Under an exquisitely carved Gothic canopy lay his effigy, side by side with that of his first wife, Blanche, the heiress of the Plantagenets, Dukes of Gloucester. Over his monument hung his ducal cap of state, as well as his shield and spear, which had served him so often and so well in the tournament and on the battlefield. He was alike the son, the uncle, and the father of kings; yet, as has been justly observed of him, he had a far stronger title to nobility as the supporter of Wickliffe and as the friend and patron of Chaucer.

The next monument which we shall notice was to the memory of a man of very different fortunes, the learned John Colet, Dean of St. Paul's, the friend of Erasmus and Budæus, and the founder of St. Paul's School. Surmounting his monument was his bust in terra-cotta; while underneath was represented a skeleton lying on a mat, the upper part of which was rolled up in the form of a pillow under its head.

Another sumptuous monument in the old cathedral was that of the crafty but magnificent favourite, William, first Earl of Pembroke, who died in 1570. Having married Anne, sister of Queen Katherine Parr, he was consequently brother-in-law to Henry the Eighth. The effigies of the earl and his countess lay beneath a beautiful arched canopy; their daughter Anne, Lady Talbot, kneeling at their head, and their sons, Henry, Earl of Pembroke, and Sir Edward Herbert, kneeling at their feet. According to Stow, such was the magnificence of Earl William's funeral, that the mourning presents alone cost £2,000.

Another monument of no slight pretensions was that of Sir Nicholas Bacon, father of the great Lord Bacon. Although a civilian, his effigy represented him in complete armour. Sir Nicholas, who was the first lord keeper who ranked as lord chancellor, died in 1578, having caught his death by sleeping in a chair at an open window.

Perhaps the most insignificant monument in old St. Paul's — for it was merely a board containing eight indifferent lines in verse [1] — was that of

[1] England, Netherland, the heavens, and the arts,
The soldiers, and the world have made six parts
Of the noble Sydney; for none will suppose
That a small heap of stones can Sydney enclose.
His body hath England, for she it bred;
Netherland his blood, in her defence shed;
The heavens have his soul; the arts have his fame;
All soldiers the grief, the world his good name.

the chivalrous Sir Philip Sydney. After having received his death-wound on the field of Zutphen, his remains were placed on board a vessel at Flushing, and having been landed at the Tower wharf, lay in state for a considerable time in the Minories. At length, every preparation having been made for his funeral, his body was brought from the Minories to St. Paul's, where, on the 16th of January, 1586–87, it was lowered into the earth. Such was the sensation created by the death of this illustrious man, that not only did the public mourn for him as for a near relative, but, for many months after his death, "it was accounted indecent," we are told, "for any gentleman of quality to appear at court or in the city in any light or gaudy apparel."

In the dead of night, on the 6th of April, 1590, was lowered into the grave in old St. Paul's, in silence and stealth, the body of the wily, the eloquent, and insinuating Sir Francis Walsingham, he who, with equal grace and versatility of talent, had breathed soft nothings into the ear of Queen Elizabeth, had bandied wit with Henry the Fourth of France, and had discussed the philosophy of Plato and the graces of Euripides with James the First. So far was he from having enriched himself while employed in the service of his country, that his friends, apprehensive that his body might be seized by his creditors, buried him at their own expense in the stealthy manner to which we have alluded.

Another magnificent monument was to the memory of Sir Christopher Hatton, the gallant Lord Chancellor of England, whose graceful dancing at a masque is said to have first attracted the notice of Queen Elizabeth.

The last monument which we shall mention is that of Doctor Donne, to which a curious history attaches itself. In order to have near him a constant memento of the uncertainty of life, he caused himself to be wrapped up in a winding-sheet, in the same manner as if he had been dead. Being thus shrouded, with so much of the sheet put aside as served to discover his attenuated form and deathlike countenance, he caused a skilful painter to take his picture, his face being purposely turned toward the east, whence he expected the second coming of our Saviour. This painful picture he kept constantly by his bedside, and it afterward served as a pattern for his tomb. In the last hours of his life he summoned several of his most intimate friends to his sick-chamber. Having taken an affectionate farewell of them, he prepared himself to die with the utmost cheerfulness and resignation ; pronouncing with his last breath the words, " Thy kingdom come, thy will be done." Of all the monuments in old St. Paul's Cathedral, it is remarkable that Doctor Donne's was the only one which remained uninjured by the great fire. It is still to be seen in the crypt beneath the present edifice, together with the mutilated effigies of Sir Nicholas Bacon, of Dean Colet, and one or two others.

In old St. Paul's was buried the great painter Vandyke, but no monument seems to have been erected to his memory.

At the northeast of St. Paul's Cathedral stood the famous Paul's Cross. "In the midst of the churchyard," writes Stow, "is a pulpit-cross of timber, mounted upon steps of stone, and covered with lead, in which are sermons preached by learned divines every Sunday in the forenoon; the very antiquity of which cross is to me unknown. I read that in the year 1259, King Henry III. commanded a general assembly to be made at this cross, where he in proper person commanded the mayor that on the next day following he should cause to be sworn before the aldermen every stripling of twelve years of age, or upward, to be true to the king and his heirs, Kings of England. Also, in the year 1262, the same king caused to be read at Paul's Cross a bull, obtained from Pope Urban IV., as an absolution for him, and for all that were sworn to maintain the articles made in Parliament at Oxford. Also, in the year 1299, the Dean of Paul's cursed, at Paul's Cross, all those which had searched in the church of St. Martin-in-the-Field for a hoard of gold. This pulpit-cross was, by tempest of lightning and thunder, defaced. Thomas Kempe, Bishop of London, new built it in form as it now standeth."

Anciently, on the occasion of sermons being preached at Paul's Cross, seats were set apart in covered galleries for the king, the lord mayor, and the principal citizens, while the remaining part of the congregation sat in the open air. At Paul's Cross the Church of Rome was accustomed for centuries to thunder forth its anathemas on transgressors against its will and power. Here it was the custom to announce to the assembled citizens the will and pleasure of the sovereign and the bulls of the Pope. Hither the Kings of England were accustomed to repair, whether to listen to some eminent preacher or to return thanks for the success of their arms. Here royal marriages were proclaimed, and rebellious subjects denounced; and lastly, here it was that the wanton were made to perform penance, and the apostate to recant his religious errors with the emblematical faggot in his arms.

It was at Paul's Cross, in 1457, that the well-known Reginald Peacocke, Bishop of Chichester, submitted to the degrading ceremony of publicly recanting the religious opinions which he had advanced in his writings. " Let no one," writes Southey, " reproach his memory because martyrdom was not his choice ! Considering the extreme humiliation to which he submitted, it can hardly be doubted but that death would have been the preferable alternative, had he not acted under a sense of duty. He was brought in his episcopal habit to

St. Paul's Cross, in the presence of twenty thousand people, and placed at the archbishop's feet, while fourteen of his books were presented to the Bishops of London, Rochester, and Dunholm, as judges. These books he was ordered to deliver with his own hands to the person by whom they were to be thrown into the fire, there ready for that purpose. Then standing up at the cross, he read his abjuration in English, confessing that, presuming upon his own natural wit, and preferring the natural judgment of reason before the Scriptures, and the determination of the Church, he had published many perilous and pernicious books, containing heresies and errors, which he then specified as they had been charged against him." As many copies of his books as could be collected were then thrown into the flames.

It was at Paul's Cross, as has been already intimated, that Jane Shore, the beloved mistress of Edward the Fourth, was compelled to perform penance and to confess her transgression before the assembled multitude. "In her penance," writes Holinshed, "she went in countenance and pace demure ; so womanly, that albeit she was out of all array, save her kirtle only, yet went she so fair and lovely, while the wondering of the people cast a comely red in her cheeks (of which she before had most want) that her great shame was her most praise amongst those that were more amorous of her body than curious of her soul."

When Richard the Third, then Duke of Gloucester, had matured his designs of taking the crown
from the head of his nephew and placing it on his
own, it was from the pulpit at Paul's Cross that
he caused his intentions to be announced to the
astonished multitude. The preacher appointed
for the occasion was Dr. John Shaw, brother of
the lord mayor.

In 1501, we find the marriage of Margaret,
daughter of Henry the Seventh, with James the
Fourth of Scotland, proclaimed with great ceremony at Paul's Cross. The Te Deum was sung;
and at night bonfires blazed in the streets, and
twelve hogsheads of wine were distributed among
the citizens.

Paul's Cross is intimately associated with the
progress of the Reformation in England. Henry
the Eighth engaged the most eminent divines here
to preach against the Pope's supremacy, and here,
in the reign of Edward the Sixth, Bishop Latimer
upheld the doctrines for which he afterward suffered martyrdom in the flames. Another illustrious
martyr, Bishop Ridley, was also a frequent preacher
at Paul's Cross. Perhaps the most memorable
occasion on which he officiated was on the 1st of
November, 1552, when, writes Stow, "Being the
feast of All Saints, the new service book, called of
Common Prayer, began in Paul's Church, and the
like through the whole city. The Bishop of London, Doctor Ridley, executing the service in Paul's

Church in the forenoon, in his rochet only, without cope or vestment, preached in the choir; and at afternoon he preached at Paul's Cross, the lord mayor, aldermen, and crafts in their best liveries being present; which sermon, tending to the setting forth the said late-made "Book of Common Prayer," continued till almost five of the clock at night, so that the mayor, aldermen, and companies entered not into Paul's Church, as had been accustomed, but departed home by torchlight."

Another interesting occasion on which Ridley preached at Paul's Cross, was on the 9th of July, 1553, three days after the death of Edward the Sixth, when he advocated the claims of the Lady Jane Grey, and congratulated his audience on having escaped the dangers which would have attended the accession of Queen Mary.

But the fate of both the Lady Jane and of Ridley was sealed. Queen Mary had no sooner established herself on the throne, than the champions of the Reformation were compelled to succumb to the Roman Catholic priesthood, who once more thundered forth their anathemas from Paul's Cross. Strype, for instance, mentions a remarkable sermon delivered at Paul's Cross, about five weeks after the queen's accession, before the lord mayor and aldermen, the preacher being Doctor Bourn, incumbent of High Ongar, in Essex. "This man," he writes, "did, according to his instructions, fiercely lay about him in accusing the doings of the former reign, with such reflections upon things that were dear to the people, that it set them all into a burly-burly; and such an uproar began, such a shouting at the sermon, and casting up of caps, as that one who lived in those times, and kept a journal of matters that then fell out, writ it was as if the people were mad; and that there might have been great mischief done, had not the people been awed somewhat by the presence of the mayor and Lord Courtenay." A dagger was actually hurled at the preacher, and it was only by the timely interference of two influential Protestant clergymen — John Bradford and John Rogers, both of whom subsequently suffered martyrdom at the stake — that Bourn was conveyed in safety to a house in the neighbourhood. On the following Sunday it was thought necessary to surround Paul's Cross with two hundred of the queen's guards, in order to ensure the safety of the preacher.

During the reign of Queen Mary, and the consequent predominance of the old worship, we discover the notorious Stephen Gardiner, Bishop of Winchester, more than once preaching at Paul's Cross. Thus, Strype mentions his delivering a sermon here on Sunday, the 30th of October, 1553, "which he did with much applause before an audience as great as ever was known, and among the rest all the council that were then at court. Again, on the 2d of December following, we find him preaching before King Philip of Spain. One of the audience on this occasion was Cardinal Pole, who, we are told, proceeded by water from Lambeth Palace to Paul's wharf, where he landed, and " from thence to Paul's Church with a cross, two pillars, and two pole-axes of silver, borne before him."

On the accession of Elizabeth, the doctrines in defence of which Latimer and Ridley had yielded up their lives in the flames were again proclaimed from Paul's Cross, to the great joy and satisfaction of the citizens of London.   Hither, on the 24th of November, 1588, we find Elizabeth proceeding, attended by the Earl of Essex and a gorgeous array of lords and ladies, to return thanks for the destruction of the " Invincible Armada."   The sermon was preached by Doctor Pierce, Bishop of Salisbury, the queen being seated in a closet that had been prepared for her against the north wall of the church.   The coach in which she came to Paul's Cross is said to have been the first which had been used in England.

On the 26th of March, 1620, we find James the First proceeding on horseback in great state to Paul's Cross to hear a sermon preached by Dr. John King, Bishop of London.   The last time that a sermon at Paul's Cross was preached before one of our sovereigns appears to have been on the 30th of May, 1630, when Charles the First proceeded in state to St. Paul's to return thanks for the birth of his son, afterward Charles the Second.

In September, 1643, the Long Parliament voted

the destruction of the different crosses in London and Westminster, as offensive relics of popery, and accordingly, the following year, Paul's Cross was razed to the ground.

The gradual decay and final destruction of the venerable cathedral may be briefly related. Like many other religious structures which for centuries had been the glory of the land, St. Paul's suffered considerably at the Reformation. Not only were its ancient monuments and brasses either defaced or destroyed, but, as has already been mentioned, its beautiful cloisters were sacrificed to furnish materials for the Protector Somerset's new palace in the Strand. Again, in 1561, we find the noble steeple entirely destroyed by fire, besides other parts of the edifice being at the same time greatly injured. In this state of semi-dilapidation it appears to have remained till 1633, when, chiefly by the instrumentality of Archbishop Laud, large sums of money were subscribed for the purpose of restoring it to its ancient magnificence. Laud laid the first stone, and Inigo Jones the fourth. Charles the First, at his own expense, erected the portico at the west front, while Sir Paul Pindar not only restored the beautiful screen at the entrance into the choir, but also gave £4,000 toward the repair of the south transept. At length, with the exception of the steeple, the whole was completed, at an expense of nearly £100,000, in 1643, when the breaking out of the civil wars again doomed St.

Paul's to havoc and desecration. The beautiful carved ornaments were recklessly demolished by the Puritans with axes and hammers, and the body of the church converted into stalls for troopers' horses. Lord Brooke was even heard to observe that he hoped to see the day when not one stone of St. Paul's should be left upon another. Charles the Second commenced repairing it in 1663, but three years afterward it was entirely destroyed by the great fire.

The present St. Paul's Cathedral — less interesting, perhaps, but still a scarcely less magnificent structure than its predecessor — was commenced in 1675, and, with the exception of some of the decorations, was completed in 1710. Not only is it unquestionably the greatest architectural work ever designed and erected by a single individual, but the fact is a singular one, that, notwithstanding it occupied thirty-five years in building, it was begun and completed by one architect, Sir Christopher Wren ; under one Bishop of London, Dr. Henry Compton ; and under one master-mason, Mr. Thomas Strong ; whereas St. Peter's at Rome occupied 155 years in building, under the rule of nineteen Popes, and under the superintendence of twelve successive architects. The height of St. Peter's to the top of the cross is 437½ feet ; its length 729 feet ; and its greatest breadth 510 feet. The dimensions of St. Paul's are 365 in length, and 282 at its extreme breadth. The total orig-

inal cost of the present St. Paul's Cathedral was
£747,954 2s. 9d.

As a remuneration for his labours in superintend-
ing the progress of his great work, Sir Christopher
Wren is said to have received no more than two
hundred a year. The celebrated Duchess of Marlborough was once squabbling with an architect
whom she employed in the works at Blenheim;
the latter insisting that a charge which he had
made was not an exorbitant one, " Why," said the
duchess, " Sir Christopher Wren was content to
be dragged up to the top of St. Paul's three times
a week in a basket, and at a great hazard, for £200
a year." But the true reward of Wren was the
prospect of undying fame. When compelled to
add the side aisles, which unfortunately injure the
effect of his noble cathedral, he is said to have actually shed tears. The addition of these aisles is
stated to have been owing to the influence of the
Duke of York, who, contemplating the day when
high mass might again be performed in St. Paul's,
proposed to convert them into auxiliary chapels.

The greatest satisfaction of Sir Christopher
Wren at the close of his life is said to have been
derived from the occasional visits which he paid to
London for the purpose of contemplating the magnificent structure which his genius had created.
His remains lie interred in the crypt of the cathedral, beneath the great dome.

" Si monumentum requiris circumspice."

Among many other celebrated men whose remains lie interred in the present cathedral may be
mentioned the names of Bishop Newton, Sir Joshua
Reynolds, Benjamin West, James Barry, John Opie,
Lord Nelson, Lord Collingwood, Sir Thomas Lawrence, Henry Fuseli; John Rennie, the architect
of Waterloo Bridge ; and the Duke of Wellington.

In the crypt of the cathedral the resting-place
of Nelson is probably that which excites the most
general interest.   The sarcophagus which encloses
his coffin was originally made at the expense of
Cardinal Wolsey, and was intended to contain
the remains of his royal master, Henry the
Eighth.   The coffin itself was manufactured out
of the mainmast of the French ship, *L'Orient*,
blown up at the battle of the Nile.   It was sent
as a present to Nelson by one of his gallant followers, Captain Hallowell, of the *Swiftsure*.   "I
have taken the liberty," he wrote to the hero, "of
presenting you a coffin made from the mainmast
of *L'Orient*, that, when you have finished your
military career in this world, you may be buried
in one of your trophies."   Nelson accepted the
melancholy offering in the same spirit in which it
had been sent.   He even ordered it to be placed
upright in his cabin, as if to serve him as a *memento mori* in the hour of victory and triumph ;
and it was only at the entreaties of an old and
favourite servant that he at length consented to its
removal.

CHAPTER X.

THE OLD BAILEY, NEWGATE, CHRIST'S HOSPITAL, ST. SEPULCHRE'S CHURCH.

Derivation of Name Old Bailey — Great Antiquity of Court of Justice There — The Press Yard — "*Peine Forte et Dure*" — Major Strangeways — Gaol fever — Newgate Prison — Ivy Lane — Pannier Alley — Old Christ Church, Newgate — Persons Interred There — Modern Christ Church, Newgate — Christ's Hospital — St. Sepulchre's Church — Curious Ceremony at Executions — Pie Corner — Green Arbour Court.

THE street which bears the name of the Old Bailey runs parallel with the site of that part of the city wall which anciently connected Lud Gate with New Gate. Here stood Sidney House, the residence of the Sidneys, Earls of Leicester, previously to their removal to Leicester Square; and here, at the house of his father, in May, 1551, was born the celebrated antiquary, William Camden. No. 68, close to Ship Court, was the residence of the notorious Jonathan Wild, and in Ship Court Hogarth's father kept a school.

The word Old Bailey has been supposed to be derived from the ballium, or outer walled court, attached to the ancient fortifications. According

to other accounts, the word is corrupted from Bail
Hill, the place where offenders were tried by the
bailiff, — a derivation which appears to be the
more reasonable, from the circumstances of that
part of the court in which prisoners are confined
previously to their trial still retaining the name of
the bail-dock.

This famous court of justice, which is of great
antiquity, is associated with the fate of many
celebrated and many notorious persons. Could
its gray and gloomy walls speak, what fearful
chronicles of crime, what tales of human suffering
could they not unfold! Within its area how many
virtuous patriots and martyrs, how many murderers and desperate malefactors, have stood from
time to time at the bar of justice! How many
hearts have palpitated in that awful moment, when
the ear of the prisoner is stretched forth to catch
the verdict, on which depends either his restoration to all that life holds most dear, or his being
condemned to perish by an ignominious death at
the hands of the hangman! Here, on the 9th
of October, 1660, commenced the famous trial of
the regicides, many of whom were subsequently
dragged on hurdles to Charing Cross to expiate
their offences, attended by the most terrifying
circumstances that barbarity could invent. Here
stood at the bar of justice the sturdy enthusiast,
General Harrison ; the witty atheist, Henry Mar-
ten ; the fanatic preacher, Hugh Peters ; Cook,

who had conducted the prosecution on the part of the Commons of England at the trial of Charles the First; and Colonel Hacker, who had guarded the king on the scaffold.   Here, in 1683, the high-minded and virtuous William, Lord Russell, was arraigned for high treason.   Here Jack Sheppard was sentenced to be hanged in 1724, and Jonathan Wild in 1725; here the ill-fated poet, Richard Savage, underwent his trial for killing a fellow creature in a drunken brawl at Charing Cross in 1727; here Doctor Dodd was condemned to death for forgery in 1777; Bellingham, for assassinating Mr. Percival in the lobby of the House of Commons in 1812; and Thistlewood, and the other Cato Street conspirators, in 1820.

Another spot in the Old Bailey which still retains its ancient name, and recalls to our memory many a scene of horror, is the Press Yard. Not unfrequently we read of cases in the olden times, when a criminal, in order to avoid conviction, has refused to plead at the bar, and thus, though his own life has been sacrificed, has preserved his property to his family, instead of its falling into the hands of the Crown.   In order to overcome this difficulty, a new law was passed, which provided that in future cases of contumacy the prisoner should be removed from the bar, and, having been stretched on his back, a large weight of iron should be placed on his chest and stomach, to be gradually increased either till the culprit consented to plead, or till death should release him from his agony. Of this terrible kind of torture, styled *" Peine forte et dure,"* the Press Yard in the Old Bailey is said to have been but too frequently the scene. At a later period, apparently from motives of humanity, a preliminary and milder form of torture was introduced, namely, that of forcibly compressing the thumb with whipcord, in order, if possible, to force the prisoner to plead, without having recourse to the more intolerable infliction of *" Peine forte et dure."* Incredible as it may appear, these barbarous expedients were actually resorted to as late as the reign of George the Second. For instance, in 1721 we find one Mary Andrews undergoing the agony of the compression, till three whipcords had been severally broken ; nor was it till a fourth had been applied that she consented to plead. A still more remarkable instance occurred the same year, in the case of Nathaniel Hawes. The application of the cord failing to produce any effect, he was subjected to the severer torture, which he endured for seven minutes under a weight of two hundred and fifty pounds, when human nature could hold out no longer, and he consented to plead. The latest occasion of the Old Bailey having been the scene of these horrors appears to have been in 1734.

As a striking example of the application of the *" Peine forte et dure,"* we may mention the painful story of Major Strangeways, who died under its tortures in 1659. The father of Strangeways had left him in possession of a farm, in which he lived happily with an elder sister till she happened to form an intimate acquaintance with one Fussell, a lawyer of respectability, but so obnoxious to Strangeways that he was heard to swear, "if ever she married Fussell, to be the death of him either in his study or elsewhere." Nevertheless the marriage took place, and was followed by Fussell prosecuting certain suits against his brother-in-law. One day, as the former was sitting in his lodgings in London, whither he had repaired on business, he was struck by two bullets, which deprived him of life. Suspicion falling on Strangeways, he was taken into custody and carried before the coroner's jury, where, we are told, "he was commanded to take his dead brother-in-law by the hand, and to touch his wounds," an expedient, however, which seems to have entirely failed in producing the intended effect.

On the 24th of February, Strangeways was brought up for trial at the Old Bailey, but it was in vain that he was exhorted to plead. By not doing so, he said, "he would both preserve an estate to bestow on such friends for whom he had most affection, and withal free himself from the ignominious death of a public gibbet." Lord Chief Justice Glynn then passed on him the terrible sentence, that he "be put into a mean house, stopped from any light, and be laid upon his back

with his body bare; that his arms be stretched
forth with a cord, the one to one side, the other
to the other side of the prison, and in like manner his legs be used; and that upon his body be
laid as much iron and stone as he can bear, and
more; and the first day shall he have three morsels of barley bread, and the next shall he drink
thrice of the water in the next channel to the
prison door, but of no spring or fountain, and this
shall be his punishment till he die!" Accordingly, on the Monday following, clothed in white
from head to foot, and wearing a mourning-cloak,
he was "by the sheriffs conducted to a dungeon,
where, after prayers, his friends placed themselves
at the corner of the press, whom he desired, when
he gave the word, to lay on the weights. This
they did at the signal of 'Lord Jesus, receive my
soul;' but, finding the weight too light for sudden
execution, many of those standing by added their
burthens to disburthen him of his pain." Eight
or ten minutes are said to have elapsed before he
expired.

Before quitting our notices of the Old Bailey,
let us not omit to mention the frightful gaol-fever,
which raged in its precincts in the month of May,
1750, and especially in the neighbouring gaol of
Newgate. Notwithstanding every precaution had
been taken to prevent it, the malaria made its way
into court, hurrying to the grave, among other victims, the Judge of the Common Pleas, Sir Thomas

Abney; Baron Clark; the lord mayor, Sir Samuel Pennant; and several members of the bar and of the jury.

Adjoining the Old Bailey is the prison of New-gate, deriving its name from one of the old city gates, which as late as 1778 was still standing, and formed a portion of the prison. The original gate appears to have been built about the time of Henry the First, from which early period till centuries afterward it continued to be used as a place of confinement. Here, in the reign of Edward the Third, the chancellor, Robert Baldock, ended his days in prison, and here, in 1457, was imprisoned Sir Thomas Percy, Lord Egremont, who afterward fell at the battle of Northampton.

In the course of the strange and romantic career of Owen Tudor, grandfather of Henry the Seventh, it was twice his good fortune to effect his escape from Newgate. At a later period we find William Penn, the founder of Pennsylvania, confined here for preaching in Gracechurch Street against the Established Church; and again, in 1702, not only was Daniel Defoe a prisoner here, but within its walls he wrote his " Review," which is said to have afforded Steele his first idea of the *Tatler*. For a long lapse of years it bore the name of Chamberlain's-gate, but in the reign of Henry the Fifth it was rebuilt and its name changed to New-gate. Having been considerably injured by the great fire of London, it was again rebuilt in 1672. In 1778 the latter building was demolished to make room for the present Newgate Prison. This massive building was scarcely completed, when, in 1780, broke out the famous riots which bear the name of their instigator, Lord George Gordon. In their fury, the mob tore away the stones, two or three tons in weight, to which the doors of the cells were fastened ; the prisoners were released ; the building was fired in several places, and in a short time became a mass of ruins. Within the walls of the restored prison Lord George died on the 1st November, 1793. The first execution which took place at Newgate was on the 9th December, 1783.

In the neighbourhood of Newgate Street are many places and objects of interest. From the south side, in the direction of St. Paul's Cathedral, runs Ivy Lane, a narrow, gloomy street, in which, for about eight years, Doctor Johnson presided over a convivial and literary club of which he was himself the founder. "The club," writes Sir John Hawkins, "met weekly at the King's Head, a famous beefsteak house in Ivy Lane, every Tuesday evening. Thither Johnson constantly resorted, and, with a disposition to please and be pleased, would pass those hours in a free and unrestrained interchange of sentiments, which otherwise had been spent at home in painful reflection." Speaking of some years later, Sir John Hawkins again writes : "About the year 1756,

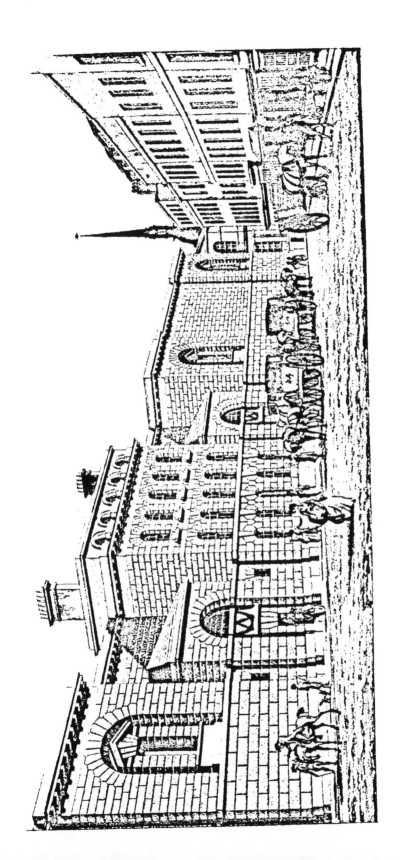

time had produced a change in the situation of many of Johnson's friends who were used to meet him in Ivy Lane. Death had taken from them M'Ghie; Barker went to settle as a practising physician at Trowbridge; Dyer went abroad; Hawkesworth was busied in forming new connections;[1] and I had lately made one that removed me from all temptations to pass my evenings from home. The consequence was that our symposiums at the King's Head broke up, and he who had first formed it into a society was left with fewer around him than were able to support it." According to Stow, Ivy Lane derives its name from the ivy which anciently grew on the walls of the prebend houses of St. Paul's, overlooking the lane.

In front of No. 78 in Newgate Street, a house standing on the site of Bull Head Court, is a small sculpture in stone, representing the redoubtable Sir Jeffery Hudson, the favourite dwarf of Queen Henrietta Maria, standing by the side of William Evans, the gigantic porter of Charles the First. The story of Sir Jeffery's having been served up to the king and queen in a cold pie; the anecdote of the big porter drawing him forth from his capacious pocket at a masque at Whitehall; the story

---

[1] M'Ghie and Barker were physicians; Samuel Dyer was the eminent scholar to whom the authorship of the "Letters of Junius" has sometimes been absurdly attributed; and Hawkesworth is still better known as the translator of " Telemachus," and one of the principal writers in the *Adventurer*.

of his bloody duel with Mr. Crofts, and of his imprisonment and death in the Gatehouse at Westminster, we have already related.   Glancing, therefore, for a moment at this curious relic of the past, let us turn down Bagnio Court, now called Bath Street, which derives its name from a once fashionable bagnio, the first that was established in London.   Strype speaks of it as a "neatly contrived building, after the Turkish fashion, for the purposes of sweating and hot-bathing; and much approved by the physicians of the time."   According to Aubrey, it was built and first opened by some Turkish merchants in December, 1679.

The Queen's Arms Tavern in Newgate Street, the site of which is now covered by new buildings for the general post-office, was a favourite resort of Tom d'Urfey, the poet; and at No. 17, at the sign of the Salutation and Cat, Coleridge used to seek a retreat in his youthful and moody days.   Here it was that Southey found him out, and remonstrated with him on his culpable supineness, and here Charles Lamb used to share his more social hours.

At the east end of Newgate Street is Pannier Alley, against one of the houses in which is a curious stone, representing a naked boy sitting upon a pannier or basket.   On the lower part is inscribed the following doggerel couplet:

"When ye have sought the city round,
    Yet still this is the highest ground.
                        August the 27, 1688."

Of the ancient churches of London there is perhaps not one whose destruction is more deeply to be lamented than that of Christ Church, Newgate. Its magnificent monuments, erected to the memory of heroes, princes, and prelates, fell sacrifices to the blind zeal of the Reformation, the church itself being subsequently destroyed by the great fire of 1666. The present edifice, the work of Sir Christopher Wren, dates no farther back than 1687.

Christ Church stands on the north side of Newgate Street, on the site of a priory of Gray, or Mendicant Friars, of the order of St. Francis, founded about the year 1225 by John Ewen, mercer, who himself entered the order as a lay-brother. The habits of self-denial practised by the friars, as well as their charities and blameless lives, soon brought them into such high repute and respect that in 1306, at the private expense of some of the most illustrious persons in the realm, the old church was taken down, and a far more magnificent edifice erected on its site. Margaret, the second wife of Edward the First, began the choir. Isabella, queen of Edward the Second, gave a considerable sum of money toward the completion of the building. Philippa, the beautiful wife of Edward the Third, followed their pious example. The body of the church was built at the expense of John de Bretagne, Duke of Richmond, who, moreover, furnished the hangings, the vestments for the priests, and a rich chalice for the altar.

Lastly, Gilbert de Clare, Earl of Gloucester, supplied the beams from his forest at Tunbridge.
"And so," writes Stow, "the work was done
within the space of twenty-one years, 1337."

Of the vast size of the Gray Friars' Church we
are enabled to form a tolerable conception, from
the fact of the present spacious church covering
less than half the ground occupied by its predecessor. Moreover, the old church, with its stained
glass, its decorated chancel, and stately tombs, was
unquestionably one of the most magnificent places
of worship in the metropolis. "This abbey-
church," writes Weever, in his "Funeral Monuments," "hath been honoured with the sepulture
of four queens, four duchesses, four countesses,
one duke, two earls, eight barons, and some thirty-
five knights; in all, from the first foundation unto
the dissolution, six hundred and sixty-three persons of quality were here interred." Here, with
the heart of her murdered husband resting on her
breast, was interred Isabella of France, queen of
Edward the Second; and here, under the same
roof with the remains of the ruthless queen, were
interred those of her haughty paramour, Roger,
Lord Mortimer. He was carried to London, and,
after a hurried trial, was hanged. It was not,
however, till his body had remained for two days
and two nights suspended on the common gallows
at Smithfield, that it was allowed sepulture among
the royal and illustrious dead.

Besides Isabella of France, here were laid the remains of Margaret, daughter of Philip the Hardy and queen of Edward the First; of Joan, daughter of Edward the Second and wife of David Bruce, King of Scotland; of Isabella, wife of William, Baron Fitzwarren, sometime Queen of the Isle of Man; of Beatrix, daughter of Henry the Third and Duchess of Bretagne; and of Isabella, daughter of Edward the Third and wife of Ingelram de Courcy, Earl of Bedford. Here, too, were interred the young and chivalrous John Hastings, Earl of Pembroke, who was killed in Woodstock Park during some Christmas rejoicings in 1389; John, Duke of Bourbon, who was taken prisoner at the battle of Agincourt, and who wore out a melancholy captivity in England of eighteen years; Walter Blunt, Lord Mountjoy, Lord Treasurer of England in the reign of Edward the Fourth; Sir Robert Tressilian and Sir Nicholas Brember, both of whom were executed for high treason; Sir John Mortimer, beheaded in 1423 for his attachment to the house of York; Thomas Burdett, beheaded in 1477, and the Lady Alice Hungerford, who was executed for the murder of her husband in 1523. The latter lady, having been conducted from the Tower to Holborn, was there placed in a cart with one of her servants, and thence carried to the place of execution at Tyburn. The fate of Burdett was also a remarkable one. Having a favourite white buck, which the king, Edward the Fourth, happened to kill, he was imprudent enough to make use of some intemperate expressions, to the effect that he wished its horns had been in the body of the man who had induced the king to shoot his favourite. These words having been repeated to the king, Burdett was not only committed to take his trial, but was subsequently executed in pursuance of the sentence passed upon him by the judge.

One of the most sumptuous monuments in the old church appears to have been that of the beautiful Venetia Digby, erected to her memory by her eccentric husband, Sir Kenelm Digby. It was believed at the time that he made use of the most singular expedients to increase the lustre of her charms; that he invented cosmetics with this especial object, and that, among other fantastic experiments, he supplied her with the flesh of capons which had been fed with vipers. After her death, only a small portion of brains having been found in her head, Sir Kenelm attributed it to her drinking viper-wine; but, says Aubrey, "spiteful women would say it was a viper husband who was jealous of her." According to Pennant, in his "Journey from Chester to London," the woods in the neighbourhood of Gothurst, once the seat of Sir Kenelm, are the most northern haunt of the great snail, or *pomatia*, which is of exotic origin; and he adds, "Tradition says it was introduced by Sir Kenelm, as a medicine for the use of his lady." Digby's well-known jealousy of his beautiful wife, and the application of these strange medicaments, gave rise to a report, doubtless an idle one, that he had administered poison to her. Her monument in Christ Church, which was of black marble surmounted by her bust in copper gilt, was demolished by the great fire, and the vault in which she lay was partially broken open. The bust, however, Aubrey tells us he some years afterward saw exposed for sale in a brazier's stall. Unfortunately he neglected to purchase it at the time, and when subsequently he made inquiries respecting it, he discovered that it had been melted down. By his will Sir Kenelm desired that he should be buried in the same vault with his wife, but that no inscription should be engraved on the tomb.

Of the modern church but little remains to be said. Its interior is not without merit, and the tower has been deservedly admired. Beyond its historical associations, however, it boasts no particular interest; nor, with the exception of the celebrated non-conformist divine, Richard Baxter, author of the "Saints' Everlasting Rest," does any very eminent person appear to have been interred within its walls.

In the "green churchyard" of Christ Church, it may be mentioned, was buried the Marquis de Guiscard, famous for having stabbed the lord high treasurer, Robert Harley, Earl of Oxford, in the council-chamber at Whitehall. The scene was a remarkable one.   Guiscard was about to be removed in custody, when he suddenly drew a knife from his bosom, and plunged it into the breast of the minister.   The blade broke at the first thrust, but the assassin, ignorant of the fact, continued desperately to repeat the stroke.   The members of the council were for a moment stupefied, till Lord Bolingbroke, then Mr. St. John, recovered his self-possession, and rushed toward Guiscard. Other members of the council followed his example ; some of them drawing their swords and stabbing at the assassin, and others striking at him with chairs, while Guiscard, on his part, rushed desperately against his assailants, as if his only object was to encounter death at their hands.   He was at length secured and conveyed to Newgate, where he refused all aid from medicine, and in a few days died of a mortification which had resulted from the wounds he had received in the council-chamber.

The ground on which the priory of the Gray Friars stood was conferred in the first instance by Henry the Eighth on his chancellor, Sir Thomas Audley, and afterward on the Lord Mayor and Corporation of London, who caused the church to be reopened for the performance of divine service. Subsequently, Edward the Sixth, in the sixth year of his reign, caused the old priory to be properly repaired, and, encouraged by Bishop Ridley, founded within it that noble establishment called

Christ's Hospital, or the Bluecoat School, for the education and maintenance of orphans and the children of indigent persons. "Ridley," writes Southey, in his "Book of the Church," "had preached before him, and, with that faithfulness which his preachers were encouraged to use, dwelt upon the pitiable condition of the poor, and the duty of those who were in authority to provide effectual means for their relief. As soon as the service was over, the king sent him a message, desiring him not to depart till he had spoken with him; and calling for him into a gallery where no other person was present, made him there sit down, and be covered, and gave him hearty thanks for his sermon and his exhortation concerning the poor. 'My lord,' said he, 'ye willed such as are in authority to be careful thereof; and to devise some good order for their relief; wherein I think you mean me, for I am in highest place, and therefore am the first that must make answer unto God for my negligence, if I should not be careful therein.' Declaring then that he was before all things most willing to travel that way, he asked Ridley to direct him as to what measures might best be taken. Ridley, though well acquainted with the king's virtuous disposition, was nevertheless surprised, as well as affected, by the earnestness and sincere desire of doing his duty which he now expressed. He advised him to direct letters to the lord mayor, requiring him, with such assistance as he should think meet, to consult upon the matter. Edward would not let him depart till the letter was written, and then charged him to deliver it himself, and signify his special request and commandment, that no time might be lost in proposing what was convenient, and apprising him of their proceedings. The work was zealously undertaken, Ridley himself engaging in it, and the result was that by their advice he founded Christ's Hospital, for the education of poor children ; St. Thomas's and St. Bartholomew's, for the relief of the sick; and Bridewell, for the correction and amendment of the vagabond and lewd ; provision also being made that the decayed housekeeper should receive weekly parochial relief. The king endowed these hospitals, and, moreover, granted a license, that they might take in mortmain lands, to the yearly value of four thousand marks, fixing that sum himself, and inserting it with his own hand when he signed the patent, at a time when he had scarcely strength to guide the pen. 'Lord God,' said he, 'I yield thee most hearty thanks that thou hast given me life thus long, to finish this work to the glory of thy name!' That innocent and most exemplary life was drawing rapidly to its close, and in a few days he rendered up his spirit to his Creator, praying God to defend the realm from papistry."

A portion of the cloisters of the old priory of the Gray Friars still exists. The magnificent hall, too, though a modern building, and defective in some of its details, is nevertheless well worthy of a visit; more especially as it contains some pictures of considerable historical interest. The most striking one, attributed to Holbein, represents Edward the Sixth granting the charter to the lord mayor and governors of the hospital, who are represented in their scarlet gowns in a kneeling posture; the boys and girls being arranged in double rows on each side of the throne. The young king, robed in scarlet and ermine, is seated, with his sceptre in his hand; the chancellor, holding the seals, standing by his side, and Bishop Ridley kneeling before him in the attitude of prayer, as if in the act of invoking a blessing on the new foundation.

The next picture in importance is by Verrio, and is perhaps one of the largest ever painted. It represents James the Second, who is seated on a throne of crimson damask in the midst of his courtiers, receiving the lord mayor, governors, and children of the hospital, who are severally painted in a kneeling attitude. By the king's side stands the lord chancellor, while in one corner Verrio has introduced himself in a long wig, apparently inquiring of the bystanders their opinion of his performance.

Besides these pictures, there are in the hall a portrait of Charles the Second, by Sir Peter Lely, and a very curious picture representing Brooke

Watson, afterward Lord Mayor of London, attacked while bathing, by a shark, which actually carried off his leg. In the counting-house also is a very fine portrait of Edward the Sixth, said to be the work of Holbein.

Christ's Hospital has produced many eminent men. Among these may be named Camden, the historian, preparatory to his being removed to St. Paul's School; Bishop Stillingfleet; Joshua Barnes, the scholar and historian; Thomas Middleton, the first Bishop of Calcutta; Jeremiah Markland, the eminent critic and scholar; Richardson, the novelist; Thomas Mitchell, the translator of Aristophanes; Charles Lamb; and Coleridge, the poet. "Samuel Taylor Coleridge!" writes Charles Lamb, in his "Essays of Elia;" "Logician, metaphysician, bard! How have I seen the casual passer through the cloisters stand still, entranced with admiration, while he weighed the disproportion between the speech and the garb of the young Mirandula; to hear thee unfold, in thy deep and sweet intonations, the mysteries of Jamblichus, or Plotinus, — for even in those years thou waxedst not pale at such philosophic draughts, — reciting Homer in his Greek, or Pindar; while the walls of the old Gray Friars reëchoed to the accents of the inspired charity boy!"

With another interesting extract from the "Essays of Elia," we conclude our notices of Christ's Hospital. After alluding to the repug-

nance of the school to gags, as the fat and uneat-
able scraps of meat were styled, Lamb thus relates
the singular story of one of his schoolfellows, who
was held in especial abhorrence as a gag-eater.
" He was observed after dinner carefully to gather
up the remnants left at his table, — not many, nor
very choice remnants, you may credit me, — and
these disreputable morsels he would convey away,
and secretly stow in the settle that stood at his
bedside.   None saw when he ate them.   It was
rumoured that he privately devoured them in the
night.   He was watched, but no traces of such
midnight practices were discoverable.   Some re-
ported that on leave-days he had been seen to
carry out of the bounds a large blue check hand-
kerchief full of something.   This, then, must be
the accursed thing.   Conjecture next was at work
to imagine how he could dispose of it.   Some said
he sold it to the beggars.   This belief generally
prevailed.   He went about moping.   None spake
to him.   No one would play with him.   He was
excommunicated ; put out of the pale of the school.
He was too powerful a boy to be beaten, but he
underwent every mode of that negative punishment which is more grievous than many stripes.
Still he persevered.   At length he was observed
by two of his schoolfellows — who were determined to get at the secret, and had traced him one
leave-day for that purpose — to enter a large worn-
out building, such as there exist specimens of in

Chancery Lane, which are let out to various scales
of pauperism, with open door and common staircase.   After him they silently slunk in, and followed by stealth up four flights, and saw him tap
at a poor wicket, which was opened by an aged
woman, meanly clad.   Suspicion was now ripened
into certainty.   The informers had secured their
victim.   They had him in their toils.   Accusation
was formally preferred, and Hathaway, the then
steward, with that patient sagacity which tempered
all his conduct, determined to investigate the matter before he proceeded to sentence.   The result
was, that the supposed mendicants, the receivers
or purchasers of the mysterious scraps, turned out
to be the parents of the culprit, — an honest couple
come to decay, — whom this seasonable supply had
in all probability saved from mendicancy ; and that
this young stork, at the expense of his own good
name, had all this while been only feeding the old
birds!   The governors on this occasion, much to
their honour, voted a present relief to the family,
and presented him with a gold medal.   I had left
school then, but I well remember him.   He was a
tall, shambling youth, with a cast in his eye, not
at all calculated to conciliate hostile prejudices.
I have since seen him carrying a baker's basket.
I think I heard that he did not do quite so well by
himself as he had done by the old folks."

At the north end of the Old Bailey is St. Sepulchre's Church, dedicated to the Holy Sepulchre,

supposed to have been originally built about the
year 1100. It was either entirely or partially
rebuilt in the reign of Henry the Sixth, when
Popham, Chancellor of Normandy and treasurer
of the king's household, erected a handsome chapel
on the south side of the choir, as well as the
beautiful porch, which still exists at the northwest corner of the edifice. The striking and venerable tower was probably built at the same period.
The church was severely damaged by the great
fire in 1666, nothing but the walls and the tower
being left. It was restored, after designs by Sir
Christopher Wren, in 1670, and again underwent
considerable alterations and repairs in 1790. The
organ, built in 1677, is said to be the oldest, and
one of the finest, in London.

In St. Sepulchre's Church lies buried — though
without any memorial of his resting-place — the
elegant scholar, Roger Ascham, whose love for
the classic writings of Greece and Rome was ex-
ceeded only by his fondness for cock-fighting. He
is now, perhaps, chiefly remembered from having
been the tutor of Queen Elizabeth. Here, too, lies
buried one whose romantic adventures and daring
exploits have rarely been surpassed, Capt. John
Smith, a conspicuous soldier of fortune in the
reigns of Elizabeth and James the First. In
the early part of his career he served for some
time under the banner of the emperor against the
Grand Signior, and during the war in Hungary

distinguished himself by cutting off the heads of three Turks of quality, whom he had challenged to single combat. For this exploit Sigismund, Duke of Transylvania, gave him his picture set in gold, besides settling on him a pension of three hundred ducats, and permitting him to bear three Turks' heads between a chevron in his armorial bearings. He afterward went to America, where he was taken prisoner by the Indians, but contrived to make his escape from them after a short captivity. On numerous occasions he hazarded his life in naval engagements with pirates, with Spanish men-of-war, and in every kind of adventure; but the most important act of his life was the share which he had in civilising the natives of New England, and reducing that province to obedience to Great Britain. On his monument, which formerly existed in St. Sepulchre's Church, were inscribed the following quaint lines:

"Here lies one conquered, that hath conquered Kings,
Subdued large territories, and done things,
Which to the world impossible would seem,
But that the truth is held in more esteem.
Shall I report his former service done,
In honour of his God, and Christendom?
How that he did divide, from pagans three,
Their heads and lives, types of his chivalry?—
For which great service, in that climate done,
Brave Sigismundus, King of Hungarion,
Did give him, as a coat of arms, to wear
Three conquered heads, got by his sword and spear;—

Or shall I tell of his adventures since,
Done in Virginia, that large Continent?
How that he subdued Kings unto his yoke,
And made those heathens flee, as wind doth smoke;
And made their land, being of so large a station,
An habitation for our Christian nation;
Where God is glorified, their wants supplied;
Which else, for necessaries, must have died.
But what avails his conquests, now he lies
Interred in earth, a prey to worms and flies?
Oh! may his soul in sweet Elysium sleep,
Until the Keeper, that all souls doth keep,
Return to judgment; and that after thence,
With angels he may have his recompense."

By the will of one Robert Dow, citizen and mer-chant-tailor, who died in 1612, the annual sum of 26s. 8d. was bequeathed for the delivery of a solemn exhortation to the condemned criminals in Newgate on the night previous to their execution. According to Stow, it was provided that the offi-ciating clergyman of St. Sepulchre's " should come in the night-time, and likewise early in the morn-ing, to the window of the prison where they lie, and there ringing certain tolls with a hand-bell, appointed for the purpose, should put them in mind of their present condition and ensuing exe-cution, desiring them to be prepared therefore, as they ought to be. When they are in the cart, and brought before the wall of the church [on their way to Tyburn], there he shall stand ready with the same bell, and after certain tolls, rehearse an appointed prayer, desiring all the people there present to pray for them." [1]

According to the "Annals of Newgate," it was for many years a custom for the bellman of St. Sepulchre's, on the eve of an execution, to proceed under the walls of Newgate, and to repeat the following verses in the hearing of the criminals in the condemmed cell ::

" All you that in the condemn'd cell do lie,
    Prepare you, for to-morrow you shall die.
    Watch all and pray, the hour is drawing near,
    When you before th' Almighty must appear.
    Examine yourselves, in time repent,
    That you may not t' eternal flames be sent;
    And when St. 'Pulcre's bell to-morrow tolls,
    The Lord have mercy on your souls!

                        Past twelve o'clock ! "

[1] The affecting admonitions here referred to were as follows:

" Admonition to the Prisoners in Newgate, on the Night before Execution.

        " You prisoners that are within,
        Who for wickedness and sin,

after many mercies shown, are now appointed to die to-morrow, in the forenoon; give ear, and understand, that to-morrow morning, the greatest bell of St. Sepulchre's shall toll for you, in form and manner of a passing-bell, as used to be tolled for those that are at the point of death: to the end that all godly people, hearing that bell, and knowing it is for your going to your deaths, may be stirred up heartily to pray to God to bestow his grace and mercy upon you, whilst you live. I beseech you, for Jesus Christ's sake, to keep this night in watching and prayer, to the salvation of your own souls, while there is yet time and place for mercy; as knowing to-morrow you must appear before

Till within the last seventy years there existed another singular custom, of presenting, from the steps of St. Sepulchre's Church, a nosegay to every criminal passing on his way to Tyburn.

In the churchyard of St. Sepulchre's, Sarah Malcolm, the murderess, was buried in 1733.

We have already mentioned that the first person who, in the reign of Queen Mary, suffered at the stake on account of his religious principles, was the Rev. John Rogers, Vicar of St. Sepulchre's.

Running from Newgate Street into West Smith-

the judgment seat of your Creator, there to give an account of all things done in this life, and to suffer eternal torments for your sins committed against Him, unless, upon your hearty and unfeigned repentance, you find mercy through the merits, death, and passion of your only Mediator and Advocate Jesus Christ, who now sits at the right hand of God, to make intercession for as many of you as penitently return to him."

" Admonition to the Condemned Criminals as they are passing by St. Sepulchre's Church-wall, to Execution.

"All good people, pray heartily unto God for these poor sinners, who are now going to their death, for whom this great bell doth toll.

"You that are condemned to die, repent with lamentable tears; ask mercy of the Lord, for the salvation of your own souls, through the merits, death, and passion of Jesus Christ, who now sits at the right hand of God, to make intercession for as many of you as penitently return unto Him.

"Lord have mercy upon you.
Christ have mercy upon you.
Lord have mercy upon you.
Christ have mercy upon you."

field is Giltspur Street, — anciently called Knightrider Street, — which derives its names from the
knights with their gilt spurs having been accustomed to ride this way from the Tower, to the
jousts and tournaments which in the olden time
were held in Smithfield. We have already mentioned that Knightrider Street, in the neighbourhood of Doctors' Commons, derives its name from
a similar circumstance.

In Giltspur Street, at the end of Cock Lane, is
Pie Corner, so called, according to Stow, from the
sign of a well-frequented hostelry which anciently
stood on the spot. Strype speaks of Pie Corner
as "noted chiefly for cooks' shops, and pigs dressed
there during Bartholomew Fair." In our old writers there are many references to its cooks' stalls
and dressed pork. Shadwell, for instance, in
"The Woman Captain" (1680), speaks of "meat
dressed at Pie Corner by greasy scullions," and
Ben Jonson writes, in the "Alchemist" (1610):

" I shall put you in mind, sir, at Pie Corner,
    Taking your meal of steam in, from cooks' stalls."

The principal interest, however, attached to Pie
Corner, is from its having been the spot where the
great fire terminated in 1666. It commenced, as
is well-known, in Pudding Lane, and consequently
that it should have ended at Pie Corner, was certainly a curious coincidence. At the corner of
Cock Lane may be seen the figure of a fat naked

boy with his hands across his stomach, to which the following inscription was formerly attached: "This boy is in memory put up of the late fire of London, occasioned by the sin of gluttony, 1666."

An especial interest is attached to Green Arbour Court, running west of the Old Bailey. Here, on the site of No. 12, in the first-floor rooms, resided, in 1758, the gifted and warm-hearted Oliver Goldsmith, and here, if any faith is to be placed in tradition, he composed his " Traveller," and other works. In this miserable abode he was visited by Bishop Percy, the collector of the " Reliques of English Poetry," who was accustomed to relate an interesting account of their interview. In a " wretchedly dirty room," in which there was but one chair, he found the poet engaged in writing his " Enquiry into Polite Learning." " While they were engaged in conversation," said the bishop, " some one gently rapped at the door, and on being desired to come in, a poor little ragged girl, of very decent behaviour, entered, who, dropping a curtsey, said, ' My mamma sends her compliments, and begs the favour of your lending her a potful of coals.' " In consequence of its threatening to fall from age and dilapidation, the miserable abode of Goldsmith in Green Arbour Court, together with the adjoining houses, was a few years since razed to the ground. From Green Arbour Court Goldsmith removed, in 1760, to Wine-office Court, Fleet Street.

In **Sea** Coal Lane, close by, have at **various** times been discovered considerable remains of massive stone walls, leading to the supposition that here stood some of the important outworks connected with the ancient fortifications.

CHAPTER XI.

FLEET STREET.

DESCENDING Ludgate Hill, we enter Fleet Street, one of the most interesting thoroughfares in London. As we wend our way along this famous street, let us pause for a few moments to gaze on the graceful steeple of St. Bride's Church, which, with the exception of that of Bow Church, is unquestionably the most beautiful in London. St. Bride's, moreover, in addition to its architectural merits, recalls many interesting memories of the past. Here was interred Wynkyn de Worde, the famous printer in the reign of Henry the Seventh, whose father kept the Falcon Inn in Fleet Street. He himself lived in the street, as appears by his "Fruyte of Tymes," printed in

1515, which purports to be issued from his establishment at the "sygne of the Sonne," in Fleet
Street. At the west end of St. Bride's Church
was interred the ill-fated poet, Richard Lovelace,
and here, also, rests another bard, whose hopes
were once as ambitious, John Ogilby, the translator
of Homer. Half hidden by one of the pews on
the south side, is the gravestone of Richardson,
the novelist; and here also lies buried Sir Richard
Baker, author of the "Chronicle of the Kings of
England," the story of whose melancholy end
belongs to our notices of the Fleet Prison.

Nor are Ogilby, Lovelace, and Sir Richard Baker
the only unfortunate authors who are interred in
St. Bride's Church. Here also are buried Francis
Sandford, author of the "Genealogical History,"
who died in the Fleet in 1693, and Robert Lloyd,
the poet, who, in 1764, also died in that prison.
Ogilby, Sandford, Richardson, and Lloyd were
buried in the present edifice; as were also Thomas
Flatman, the poet, who died in 1688, and Dr.
Charles Davenant, the celebrated political writer
of the reign of Queen Anne. In the churchyard
of St. Bride's lie the remains of Dr. Robert Levet,
the intimate friend of Doctor Johnson.

It may be worth mentioning that in St. Bride's
Church was buried the abandoned Mary Frith,
known as Moll Cutpurse, who, from the days of
James the First to those of the Commonwealth,
carried on the united professions of procuress,

fortune-teller, pickpocket, thief, and receiver of stolen goods. Her most famous exploit was robbing General Fairfax upon Hounslow Heath. Butler has immortalised her in his " Hudibras: "

> " He Trulla loved, Trulla more bright,
>   Than burnished armour of her knight;
>   A bold virago, stout and tall,
>   A Joan of France, or English Mall."

Swift likewise alludes to her in his " Baucis and Philemon : "

> " The ballads pasted on the wall,
>   Of Joan of France, and English Mall."

Moll Cutpurse died of the dropsy in the seventy-fifth year of her age, and was buried in St. Bride's on the 10th of August, 1659.

St. Bride's, or rather St. Bridget's Church, is unquestionably of very ancient foundation. Originally a structure of moderate dimensions, it was in the year 1480 considerably enlarged and beautified by William Venor, a pious warden of the Fleet Prison, who erected a spacious fabric at the west end, consisting of a middle and two side aisles, to which the ancient church served as the choir. The patronage of the living was for centuries vested in the Abbot and Convent of Westminster, till, at the dissolution of the monasteries, on Westminster being elevated into a bishopric, Henry the Eighth granted the preferment to the new diocesan. On the reinstatement of the Abbot and

monks of Westminster in the reign of Queen
Mary, the patronage was restored to them, but it
was afterward again made over to the Dean and
Chapter of Westminster, by whom it is still enjoyed. The old church having been destroyed by
the great fire of London, the present noble edifice
was erected on its site by Sir Christopher Wren,
at the expense of £11,430.

It was in St. Bride's Churchyard that Milton
took up his residence after his return from Italy
in 1642. Here it was that he superintended the
education of his two nephews, John and Edward
Philips, as well as that of a few other youths whose
parents had prevailed upon him to take their children under his charge. It was also during the
period of his residence in St. Bride's Churchyard
that he formed his ill-assorted marriage with his
first wife, Mary Powell. "His first wife," writes
Aubrey, "was brought up and lived where there
was a great deal of company, merriment, and
dancing; and when she came to live with her
husband at Mr. Russell's, in St. Bride's Churchyard, she found it very solitary; no company
coming to her, and oftentimes hearing his nephews
beaten and cry. This life was irksome to her
so she went to her parents at Forest Hill. He
sent for her after some time, and I think his servant was evilly treated; but, as for wronging his
bed, I never heard the least suspicions, nor had he
of that any jealousy."

On the same side of Fleet Street as St. Bride's
Church is Salisbury Court, so called from the
London residence of the Bishops of Salisbury,
which anciently stood on its site.   Here the great
Lord Clarendon was residing for a short time after
the Restoration.   To the literary student the principal interest attached to Salisbury Square is from
its having been the residence of Richardson, the
author of " Pamela " and of " Sir Charles Grandison."   Here he was visited by the most eminent
literary men of the last century and here he was
constantly surrounded by a bevy of ardent admirers, to whom he delighted in reading aloud the
last effusions of his pen.   " My first recollection
of Richardson," writes a lady who knew him well,
" was in the house in the centre of Salisbury Square,
or Salisbury Court as it was then called ; and of
being admitted as a playful child into his study,
where I have often seen Doctor Young and others,
and where I was generally caressed and rewarded
with biscuits, or bonbons, of some kind or other,
and sometimes with books, for which he, and some
more of my friends, kindly encouraged a taste,
even at that early age, which has adhered to me
all my long life, and continues to be the solace of
many a painful hour.   I recollect that he used to
drop in at my father's, for we lived nearly opposite,
late in the evening, to supper ; when, as he would
say, he had worked as long as his eyes and
nerves would let him, and was come to relax with

a little friendly and domestic chat." Again, the same lady writes : " Besides those I have already named, I well remember a Mrs. Donellan, a venerable old lady, with sharp, piercing eyes; Miss Mulso, afterward Mrs. Chapone, etc.; Secker, Archbishop of Canterbury ; Sir Thomas Robinson (Lord Grantham), etc., who were frequent visitors at his house in town and country. The ladies I have named were often staying at North End, at the period of his highest glory and reputation, and in their company and conversation his genius was matured. His benevolence was unbounded, as his manner of diffusing it was delicate and refined."

Richardson, with all his excellent qualities, appears to have been entirely spoiled by his female coterie, who pampered him with an amount of fulsome flattery from which most men would have turned with disgust. By Doctor Johnson it was said of him, that he had little "conversation, except about his own works ; " while another of his intimate acquaintances, Sir Joshua Reynolds, observed that he was always willing to talk of his writings, and "glad to have them introduced." When Doctor Johnson took Bennet Langton to introduce him to Richardson, he boasted of his skill in "drawing out" the novelist in conversation : " Sir," he said, " I can make him rear." All that Langton, however, could remember of the interview worth repeating, was the circumstance of Richardson drawing their attention to the fact

of his novel, " Clarissa," having had the honour of
being translated into German, of which the German
copy lay in the room.

John Dryden and Thomas Shadwell, the dramatic
poet, lived at different periods in Salisbury Court.
Here also, shortly after the Restoration of Charles
the Second, were residing the celebrated actors,
Thomas Betterton and Joseph Harris.

The Salisbury Court Theatre, so often the scene
of Betterton's triumphs, was first established in
1629, in the granary of Salisbury House. In
March, 1649, it was destroyed by the Puritan
authorities, but was subsequently rebuilt and reopened by William Beeston, an actor, in 1660.
Here the duke's company acted till their removal
to the Lincoln's Inn Theatre, in the spring of
1662, four years after which it was destroyed by
the great fire. This theatre must not be confounded with the Dorset Gardens Theatre, which
stood in the immediate neighbourhood, but nearer
to the Thames.

In Dorset Court, the great philosopher, John
Locke, was residing in 1689, and hence he dates
the dedication to his "Essay on Human Understanding."

Gough Square, Fleet Street, a small paved
court, or square, consisting of old houses of a
lofty size, was for ten years the residence of
Doctor Johnson. The entrance to it is by a narrow passage, called Hind Court, on the north side

of Fleet Street, opposite to Whitefriars Street. The residence of Doctor Johnson was No. 4. His fine poem, the " Vanity of Human Wishes," published in 1749, was written partly in Gough Square, but principally during his occasional visits to Hampstead, where Mrs. Johnson had taken lodgings for the benefit of country air. In Gough Square he wrote the " Rambler," and here also he composed a considerable portion of his dictionary. " While the dictionary was going forward," writes Boswell, " Johnson lived part of the time in Holborn, part in Gough Square, Fleet Street ; and he had an upper room fitted up like a counting-house for the purpose, in which he gave to the copyists their several tasks."

Doctor Johnson was residing in Gough Square at the time when he lost his wife, his beloved " Tetty." " The dreadful shock of separation," writes Boswell, " took place in the night, and he immediately despatched a letter to his friend, the Rev. Doctor Taylor, which, as Taylor told me, expressed grief in the strongest manner he had ever read ; so that it is much to be regretted it has not been preserved. The letter was brought to Doctor Taylor, at his house in the cloisters, Westminster, about three in the morning, and as it signified an earnest desire to see him, he got up, and went to Johnson as soon as he was dressed, and found him in tears and in extreme agitation. After being a little while together,

Johnson requested him to join with him in prayer. He then prayed extempore, as did Doctor Taylor, and thus by means of that piety which was ever his primary object, his troubled mind was in some degree soothed and composed."

The ten years passed by Doctor Johnson in Gough Square were perhaps the most melancholy of his life. Hypochondriacism embittered his social hours, and want stared him in the face. Sad, indeed, must have been the distress which compelled him to address the following appeal to Richardson, the novelist:

"GOUGH SQUARE, 16th March, 1756.

"SIR:— I am obliged to entreat your assistance. I am now under arrest for five pounds, eighteen shillings. Mr. Strahan, from whom I should have received the necessary help in this case, is not at home, and I am afraid of not finding Mr. Millar. If you will be so good as to send me this sum, I will very gratefully repay you, and add it to all former obligations. I am, sir, your most obedient and most humble servant,

"SAM. JOHNSON."

"Sent six guineas,

"Witness, William Richardson."

Johnson, speaking of Richardson's invariable kindness to him, once observed: "I remember writing to him from a sponging-house; and was

so sure of my deliverance through his kindness
and liberality, that, before his reply was brought, I
knew I could afford to joke with the rascal who
had me in custody, and did so, over a pint of
adulterated wine, for which, at that instant, I had
no money to pay."

In Gough Square, on the 3d of February, 1777,
died Hugh Kelly, the dramatic writer, in his thirty-
eighth year. Doctor Johnson, who ridiculed the
vanity of the "poetical staymaker" in his lifetime,
wrote a prologue for the benefit of his wife and
children when he was no more.

Johnson's Court and Bolt Court, both of them
on the north side of Fleet Street, within a short
distance of Fetter Lane, are severally and equally
interesting to us from their association with Doctor
Johnson. At No. 7 in Johnson's Court, he resided
from 1765 to 1777, and at No. 8 in Bolt Court,
from 1777 till his death on the 13th of December,
1784. Of Johnson's Court Boswell writes: "On
Tuesday, April 27 [1773], Mr. Beauclerk and I
called on him in the morning. As we walked up
Johnson's Court, I said, 'I have a veneration for
this court,' and was glad to find that Beauclerk
had the same reverential enthusiasm." At the
time when Johnson accompanied Boswell into
Scotland, the London residence of the former
was in this court. Alluding to this circumstance,
and also to a local term by which the Scottish
lairds were in the habit of designating them-

selves, he humourously styled himself "Johnson of that ilk."

It has occasionally, we believe, been supposed that Johnson's Court, Fleet Street, derives its name from the great lexicographer, and Boswell Court from his biographer, James Boswell. In neither instance, however, is this the case. As regards Boswell Court, it was so called from having been the site of Boswell House, the residence of a Mr. Boswell in the reign of Queen Elizabeth. The charming Lady Fanshawe and her husband were for some time residents in Boswell Court.

In Bolt Court Doctor Johnson breathed his last. From the author of the " Pleasures of Memory " we learn that, having an ardent desire, when a boy, to behold and converse with one so illustrious in English literature, he determined on introducing himself to the great lexicographer in Bolt Court, in the hope that his youth and inexperience might plead his excuse. Accordingly, thither he proceeded, and after much hesitation, had actually his hand on the knocker, when his heart failed him, and he went away. The late Mr. D'Israeli used to relate in conversation a similar anecdote. Anxious to obtain the acquaintance and the countenance of so illustrious a name, and smitten with the literary enthusiasm of youth, he enclosed some verses of his own composition to Doctor Johnson, and in a modest appeal solicited the opinion of the great critic as to their merits. Having waited for some time without receiving any acknowledgment of his communication, he proceeded to Bolt Court, where he laid his hand upon the knocker of the doctor's door, with the same feelings of shyness and hesitation which had influenced his youthful contemporary, Mr. Rogers. His feelings may be readily imagined when, on making the necessary inquiries of the servant who opened the door, he was informed that, only a few hours before, the great lexicographer had breathed his last.

These incidents not only throw an additional interest over Bolt Court, but also prove how extraordinary was the reputation enjoyed by Doctor Johnson in his lifetime. Moreover, they were probably far from having been the only instances of similar literary pilgrimages being paid to Bolt Court. For instance, the late Mrs. Rose, to whose reminiscences of Doctor Johnson, Cowper, and Hayley, the author has often listened with delight, supplied Mr. Croker with the following anecdote to illustrate his edition of "Boswell's Life of Johnson."

"It was near the close of his life, that two young ladies, who were warm admirers of his works, but had never seen himself, went to Bolt Court, and, asking if he was at home, were shown up-stairs, where he was writing. He laid down his pen on their entrance, and as they stood before him, one of the females repeated a speech of some length, previously prepared for the occasion. It was an enthusiastic effusion, to which, when the speaker had finished, she panted for her idol's reply.   What was her mortification, when all he said was, 'Fiddle-de-dee, my dear!'"   The house in Bolt Court, in which Johnson lived and died, is unfortunately no longer standing.

In Bolt Court, in November, 1776, died James Fergusson, the eminent mechanist and astronomer, and here at one time resided the political writer, William Cobbett.

Running parallel with Bolt Court, within a short distance of Shoe Lane, is Wine-office Court, another spot rendered interesting from its connection with the genius and the misfortunes of Oliver Goldsmith.   Here he appears to have resided from 1760 to 1762, during which period he earned a precarious livelihood by writing for the booksellers. It was while he was residing in Wine-office Court that Goldsmith formed the acquaintance of Doctor Johnson ; and here, apparently, the famous scene took place, in which the unfortunate poet, having sent for Johnson to assist him in his difficulties, placed the MS. of the "Vicar of Wakefield" in his hands, as the only hope he had of obtaining pecuniary relief.   "I received," said Johnson, "one morning, a message from poor Goldsmith that he was in great distress, and, as it was not in his power to come to me, begging that I would come to him as soon as possible.   I sent him a guinea, and promised to come to him directly.   I accordingly went as soon as I was dressed, and found that his landlady had arrested him for his rent, at which he was in a violent passion. I perceived that he had already changed my guinea, and had got a bottle of Madeira and a glass before him. I put the cork into the bottle, desired he would be calm, and began to talk to him of the means by which he might be extricated. He then told me that he had a novel ready for the press, which he produced to me. I looked into it, and saw its merit; told the landlady I should soon return; and, having gone to a bookseller, sold it for sixty pounds. I brought Goldsmith the money, and he discharged his rent, not without rating his landlady in a high tone for having used him so ill." From Wine-office Court, Goldsmith removed to the house of a Mrs. Elizabeth Fleming, at Islington, where he continued to reside till 1764.

Opposite to Shoe Lane, which runs from Fleet Street into Holborn, stood one of those noble conduits for which the city of London was anciently famous. It appears to have been originally completed in 1471, but was rebuilt with a larger cistern in 1589. On the occasion of Queen Anne Boleyn proceeding in state from the Tower to her coronation at Westminster, the neighbourhood of the Conduit in Fleet Street must have presented a striking scene. Here, we are told, stood a tower having four turrets, on each of which stood a child, representing a cardinal virtue, who, on the procession halting, in turn addressed the royal bride in appropriate speeches. "In the midst of the tower," writes Stow, "was such several solemn instruments, that it seemed to be an heavenly noise, and was much regarded and praised; and besides this, the conduit ran wine, claret and white, all the afternoon; so she, with all her company and the mayor, rode forth to Temple Bar, which was newly painted and repaired, where stood also diverse singing-men and children, till she came to Westminster Hall, which was richly hanged with cloth of arras." Preceding the beautiful queen on this occasion rode bishops and mitred abbots; the judges in their scarlet robes; the Knights of the Bath in their "violet gowns, with hoods purfelled with minever;" and the barons, earls, and marquises of the realm, attired for the most part in crimson velvet. After these came the Lord Mayor of London, in his robes; Garter king-at-arms, in his herald's attire; and the Earl Marshal and Lord High Constable of England, bearing the ensigns of their offices. Next, under a canopy of cloth of gold supported by knights carrying silver staves, appeared Anne herself, seated in an open chariot drawn by two palfreys. Her dress was a garment of white cloth of tissue, with a mantle of the same furred with ermine, while on her head she wore a circlet of precious stones, from underneath which her long tresses flowed over her shoulders. Other chariots followed, containing her ladies of honour; and lastly, the procession closed with a long train of guards and attendants, clad in scarlet dresses.

In 1659 we find General Monk, afterward Duke of Albemarle, lodged near the Conduit in Fleet Street.

In Shoe Lane, on the site of Bangor Court, stood, as early as the year 1378, the London residence of the Bishops of Bangor. Bishop Dolben, who died in 1633, was the last Bishop of Bangor who resided here. From Brayley we learn that a part of the garden, with lime-trees and a rookery, existed in 1759; indeed, as late as the year 1828 a portion of the old mansion still remained. The Bishops of Peterborough also had anciently their London residence in this neighbourhood; the site being still pointed out by Peterborough Court, on the north side of Fleet Street.

In Shoe Lane, John Florio — tutor to Henry, Prince of Wales, and compiler of the well-known Italian and English Dictionary — resided till the breaking out of the plague in 1625, when he retired for safety to Fulham, where he died. In Harp Alley, Shoe Lane, at the shop of one Charles Kerbye, we find Izaak Walton in the habit of purchasing his fish-hooks.

On the south side of Fleet Street, nearly opposite Fetter Lane, stood, till 1788, the famous Mitre Tavern.

"Meet me strait
At the Mitre door in Fleet Street"

occurs in a comedy by Lodovick Barrey published in 1611 ; and in 1640 William Lilly, the astrologer, mentions his dining there with some choice associates.   In the reign of Charles the Second we find it frequented by Pepys ; and in the reign of William the Third it was the favourite resort of the witty and eccentric physician, Doctor Radcliffe. At the Mitre Tavern, Doctor Johnson was for years accustomed to pass many of his social hours. " I had learnt," writes Boswell, " that his place of frequent resort was the Mitre Tavern in Fleet Street, where he loved to sit up late, and I begged I might be allowed to pass an evening with him there soon, which he promised I should.   A few days afterward I met him near Temple Bar, above one o'clock in the morning, and asked if he would then go to the Mitre. ' Sir,' said he, ' it is too late ; they won't let us in, but I'll go with you another night with all my heart.' "   Subsequently Boswell had numerous opportunities of enjoying the conversation of the great philosopher at his favourite tavern.   A short time afterward he writes : " Johnson agreed to meet me in the evening at the Mitre.   I called upon him, and we went thither at nine.   We had a good supper and port wine, of which he then sometimes drank a bottle.   The orthodox high-church sound of the Mitre, the figure and manner of the celebrated Samuel Johnson, the extraordinary power and precision of his conversation, and the pride arising from my finding myself admitted as his companion, produced a variety of sensations and a pleasing elevation of mind beyond what I had ever before experienced." At a later period some of the most agreeable conversations recorded by Boswell took place at their late suppers at the Mitre, at more than one of which Goldsmith is stated to have been present.

Opposite Mitre Court, in March, 1733, was executed Sarah Malcolm, a charwoman twenty-five years of age, for the murder of three persons in the Temple. Hogarth has immortalised her with his pencil, and there is a print of her in the *Gentleman's Magazine* for 1733. Mitre Court and Ram Alley formed part of the famous Alsatia.

On the north side of Fleet Street, near Fetter Lane, is Crane Court, where the Royal Society held their meetings from 1710 to 1782, when they removed to Somerset House.

The Rainbow Tavern, close to Inner Temple Lane, occupies the site of another tavern of the same name, famous as a place of recreation for more than two centuries. In 1667 it was kept by one James à Barke; at which period, curiously enough, we find the proprietor threatened with an indictment by the ward of St. Dunstan's in the West, "for making and selling a sort of liquor called coffee, as a great nuisance and prejudice to the neighbourhood." Doubtless the tavern-keepers of the day were not a little incensed against the introducers and advocates of the new drink, which shortly grew to be so far popular as to interfere seriously with their profits.   Howell, speaking in 1659 of the curious and eccentric traveller, Sir Henry Blount, observes, "This coffee drink hath caused a great sobriety among all nations. Formerly apprentices, clerks, etc., used to take their morning draughts in ale, beer, or wine, which often made them unfit for business.   Now they play the good fellows in this wakeful and civil drink.   The worthy gentleman, Sir James Muddiford, who introduced the practice hereof first in London, deserves much respect of the whole nation."   Sir Henry himself appears to have been a constant frequenter of the Rainbow.   Aubrey, in his brief memoir of him, observes, "When coffee first came in, he was a great upholder of it, and hath ever since been a constant frequenter of coffee-houses ; especially Mr. Farres, at the Rainbow, by Inner Temple Gate ; and lately John's Coffee-house, in Fuller's Rents."   Sir Henry, notwithstanding his sober habits, appears to have delighted in practical jokes, of which the following is recorded by Aubrey as having been practised by him at the Rainbow.   Two young gentlemen who happened to be in his company, having related some anecdotes which bordered closely upon the marvellous, Sir Henry took upon himself to relate a circumstance even more extraordinary.   There was an inn, he said, at St. Albans, — at the same time mentioning the name, — the landlord of which having sacrilegiously converted a freestone coffin into a hog's trough, "the pigs after grew lean, and, dancing and skipping, would run up on the tops of the houses like goats. The two young gentlemen that heard Sir Henry tell this sham so gravely, rode the next day to St. Albans to inquire. Coming there, nobody had heard of any such thing. 'Twas altogether false. The next night, as soon as they alighted, they came to the Rainbow, and found Sir Henry. Looking leeringly on him, they told him they wondered he was not ashamed to tell such stories, etc. 'Why, gentlemen,' said Sir Henry, 'have you been there to make inquiry?' 'Yea,' said they. 'Why, truly, gentlemen,' said Sir Henry, 'I heard you tell strange things that I knew to be false. I would not have gone over the threshold of the door to have found you out in a lie.' At which all the company laughed at the two young gentlemen."

But a still more celebrated house of entertainment than either the Mitre or the Rainbow was the Devil Tavern, which stood next door to Child's banking-house, deriving its name and its sign from the legend of St. Dunstan seizing the evil spirit by the nose with a pair of hot tongs; St. Dunstan being the saint to whom the neighbouring church is dedicated. The Devil Tavern is famous as having been the favourite resort of Ben Jonson, who presided here, — in an apartment called the "Apollo," — over the celebrated club of which he was the founder. Over the door of the Apollo remained inscribed, as late as the year 1787, the following verses of Jonson's own composition :

> "Welcome all who lead or follow,
>   To the Oracle of Apollo;
>   Here he speaks out of his pottle,
>   Or the tripos, his tower bottle;
>   All his answers are divine,
>   Truth itself doth flow in wine.
>   Hang up all the poor hop drinkers,
>   Cries old Sim, the king of skinkers;
>   He the half of life abuses,
>   That sits watering with the Muses.
>   Those dull girls no good can mean us;
>   Wine it is the milk of Venus,
>   And the poet's horse accounted:
>   Ply it, and you all are mounted.
>   'Tis the true Phœbian liquor,
>   Cheers the brain, makes wit the quicker,
>   Pays all debts, cures all diseases,
>   And at once three senses pleases.
>   Welcome all who lead or follow,
>   To the Oracle of Apollo."

It should be mentioned that "old Sim, the king of skinkers," alluded to in the foregoing verses, was Simon Wadloe, the landlord of the Devil Tavern in the days of Ben Jonson. As late as the period of the Restoration, the Devil was still kept by one Wadloe, probably a descendant of "Old Sim." On the 22d April, 1661, Pepys — alluding to the progress of Charles the Second

from the Tower to Whitehall — writes : " My Lord
Monk rode bare after the king, and led in his hand
a spare horse, as being master of the horse.   The
king, in a most rich embroidered suit and cloak,
looked most noble.   Wadloe, the vintner at the
Devil in Fleet Street, did lead a fine company of
soldiers, all young comely men, in white doublets."
It was old Simon Wadloe who was the original of
the favourite air of Squire Weston, in "Tom Jones,"
" Old Sir Simon the King."   On being some time
since conducted over Messrs. Child's banking-house,
it was an unexpected pleasure to the author to find,
in one of the apartments, not only a bust of Apollo,
but also a tablet, on which were inscribed, in gilt
letters, the celebrated verses we have just quoted,
with the familiar words beneath them, — " O rare
Ben Jonson ! "

Over the chimneypiece of the Apollo were also
inscribed, on marble, Jonson's well-known *leges
conviviales*, which have been thus paraphrased in
English :

1. " As the fund of our pleasure let each pay his shot,
      Except some chance friend, whom a member brings
      in.
2. Far hence be the sad, the lewd fop, and the sot,
      For such have the plague of good company been.

3. " Let the learned and witty, the jovial and gay,
      The generous and honest, compose our free state ;
4. And the more to exalt our delight whilst we stay,
      Let none be debarred from his choice female mate.

5. " Let no scent offensive the chamber infest;
6.   Let fancy, not cost, prepare all our dishes.
7. Let the caterer mind the taste of each guest;
    Let the cook, in his dressing, comply with their
        wishes.

8. " Let's have no disturbance about taking places,
    To show your nice breeding, or out of vain pride.
9. Let the drawers be ready with wine and fresh glasses,
    Let the waiters have eyes, though their tongues must
        be tied.

10. " Let our wines, without mixture or stum, be all fine,
    Or call up the master, and break his dull noddle.
11. Let no sober bigot here think it a sin,
    To push on the chirping and moderate bottle.

12. " Let the contests be rather of books than of wine;
13.   Let the company neither be noisy, nor mute;
14. Let none of things serious, much less of divine,
    When belly and head's full, profanely dispute.

15. " Let no saucy fiddler presume to intrude,
    Unless he is sent for to vary our bliss;
16. With mirth, wit and dancing, and singing conclude,
    To regale every sense, with delight in excess.

17. " Let raillery be without malice or heat;
18.   Dull poems to read let none privilege take;
19. Let no poetaster command or entreat
    Another extempore verses to make.

20. " Let argument bear no unmusical sound,
    No jars interpose, sacred friendship to grieve;
21. For generous lovers let a corner be found,
    Where they in soft sighs may their passions relieve.

22. " Like the old Lapithites, with the goblets to fight,
    Our own 'mongst offences unpardon'd will rank,
Or breaking of windows, or glasses, for spite,
    And spoiling the goods for a rakehelly prank.

23. "Whoever shall publish what's said, or what's done,
    Be he banished for ever our assembly divine.
24. Let the freedom we take be perverted by none,
    To make any guilty by drinking good wine."

These verses, though far from conveying a
proper notion of the epigrammatic neatness and
elegance of the original rules, nevertheless afford
some idea of the spirit of conviviality and wit
which pervaded the club. Jonson — in one of
his memoranda, the MSS. of which are preserved
at Dulwich — observes, " The first speech in my
Catiline, spoken to Scylla's ghost, was writ after
I had parted with my friends at the Devil
Tavern: I had drunk well that night, and had
brave notions."

The next notice which we find of the Devil
Tavern is in a curious memoir of Mull Sack,
alias John Cottington, a famous highwayman in
the days of the Commonwealth. The fact is
a rather singular one, that this person not only
had the honour of picking the pocket of Oliver
Cromwell, when Lord Protector, but that he subsequently robbed Charles the Second, then living
in exile at Cologne, of plate valued at £1,500.
Another of his feats was his robbing the wife of
the Lord General Fairfax at a fashionable chapel

on Ludgate Hill. "This lady," we are told, "used to go to a lecture on a week-day, to Ludgate Church, where one Mr. Jacomb preached, being much followed by the Precisians. Mull Sack observing this, and that she constantly wore her watch hanging by a chain from her waist, against the next time she came there dressed himself like an officer in the army; and having his comrades attending him like troopers, one of them takes off the pin of a coach-wheel that was going upward through the gate, by which means it falling off, the passage was obstructed, so that the lady could not alight at the church door, but was forced to leave her coach without. Mull Sack, taking advantage of this, readily presented himself to her ladyship, and having the impudence to take her from her gentleman usher who attended her alighting, led her by the arm into the church; and by the way, with a pair of keen or sharp scissors for the purpose, cut the chain in two, and got the watch clear away, she not missing it till sermon was done, when she was going to see the time of the day."

The visits paid by Mull Sack to the Devil Tavern were in his occasional character of a man of fashion; a character probably assumed by him partly out of vanity, and partly from the opportunities which it must from time to time have afforded him of relieving the company of their watches and purses. There is extant a very rare

print of him, in which he is represented partly in
the garb of a chimney-sweep, his original avoca-
tion, and partly in the fashionable costume of the
period. Underneath are inscribed the following
lines :

> " I walk the Strand and Westminster, and scorn
> To march i' the City, though I bear the horn.
> My feather and my yellow band accord
> To prove me courtier ; my boot, spur, and sword,
> My smoking-pipe, scarf, garter, rose on shoe,
> Show my brave mind t' affect what gallants do.
> I sing, dance, drink, and merrily pass the day,
> And, like a chimney, sweep all care away."

Mull Sack was hanged at Smithfield in April,
1659, in his fifty-sixth year, for the murder of one
John Bridges, with whose wife he had long been
on terms of too great intimacy. After his con-
demnation, in hope of saving his life, he intimated
that at the time he robbed Charles the Second of
his plate, he had also carried off some important
papers containing state intelligence ; but the information he possessed was not of sufficient
importance to save him from the gallows. His
peculiar cognomen is said to have been derived
from his extraordinary addiction to mulled sack,
a favourite liquor of the period.

The Devil Tavern was the frequent resort of
Thomas Shadwell, the dramatic writer and poet-
laureate, the hero of whose worship was Ben
Jonson, and to whom consequently the Devil

Tavern was classic ground. Whatever may be our estimate of Shadwell's abilities as a dramatic writer, we have the testimony of his contemporaries that his conversational powers rendered him worthy of being the chosen associate even of Jonson himself. By Lord Rochester it was said of him, that had he burnt all he had written, and printed all he had spoken, his character for wit and humour would have been unrivalled. At the Devil, Killigrew has laid one of his scenes in the " Parson's Wedding ; " and here,—in the Apollo, — in the last century, the poets-laureat were in the habit of rehearsing their Birthday Odes.

From the days of " Rare Ben Jonson " to those of Dr. Samuel Johnson, this celebrated tavern continued to be the favourite resort of men of letters. "I dined to-day," writes Swift to Stella, on the 12th of October, 1710, "with Doctor Garth and Mr. Addison at the Devil Tavern, by Temple Bar, and Garth treated." Here too it was, in 1751, that Doctor Johnson assembled a jovial party to celebrate the production of Mrs. Charlotte Lenox's first novel, — " The Life of Harriot Stuart." " One evening, at the Ivy Lane Club," writes Sir John Hawkins, " Johnson proposed to us the celebrating the birth of Mrs. Lenox's first literary child, as he called her book, by a whole night spent in festivity. Upon his mentioning it to me, I told him I had never sat up a whole night in my life, but he continuing to press me, and saying that I should find great delight in it, I, as did all the rest of our company, consented. The place appointed was the Devil Tavern; and there, about the hour of eight, Mrs. Lenox and her husband, and a lady of her acquaintance still [1785] living, as also the club, and friends to the number of near twenty, assembled. The supper was elegant, and Johnson had directed that a magnificent hot apple-pie should make a part of it, and this he would have stuck with bay-leaves; because, forsooth, Mrs. Lenox was an authoress, and had written verses; and further, he had prepared for her a crown of laurel, with which — but not till he had invoked the Muses by some ceremonies of his own invention — he encircled her brows. The night passed, as must be imagined, in pleasant conversation and harmless mirth, intermingled, at different periods, with the refreshments of coffee and tea. About five, Johnson's face shone with meridian splendour, though his drink had been only lemonade; but the far greater part of the company had deserted the colours of Bacchus, and were with difficulty rallied to partake of a second refreshment of coffee, which was scarcely ended when the day began to dawn. This phenomenon began to put us in mind of our reckoning; but the waiters were all so overcome with sleep that it was two hours before a bill could be had, and it was not till near eight that the creaking of the street door gave the signal for our departure."

It was at the Devil Tavern, in 1774, that Doctor
Kenrick used to read his lectures under the title
of "The School of Shakespeare." Goldsmith has
an allusion to them in his happy poem, "Retalia-
tion."

The last notice of any interest which we have
to record of the Devil Tavern is in connection
with an amusing practical joke played by John,
second Duke of Montague, on Heidegger, the
"Swiss Count" of the *Tatler*, and conductor of
the fashionable operas and masquerades in the
reign of George the Second. A few days previous
to one of the latter entertainments, at which the
king had promised to be present, the duke invited
Heidegger to sup with him at the Devil Tavern,
where he plied him with wine till he fell into a
state of insensibility. While in this condition Mrs.
Salmon, a well-known modeller in wax, was introduced, who took a cast of his face, which was
afterward painted to the very image of life. The
duke next procured a suit of clothes exactly resembling those ordinarily worn by Heidegger, and
having secured the services of a person whose
voice and figure closely resembled those of the
German, he contrived to manufacture an admirable
counterfeit of his unfortunate butt. The night of
the masquerade having arrived, Heidegger, so soon
as the king made his appearance, gave the signal
to the band to strike up the national anthem;
while, at the same moment, to his intense anger

and vexation, the counterfeit Heidegger stepped forward and commanded them to play the then disloyal Jacobite tune of " Over the Water to Charley." The king, as well as the musicians, was evidently in the secret of the joke. As for Heidegger, he was exhibiting all the gestures of a madman, when the Duke of Montague, with every appearance of serious formality, intimated to him that the king was highly incensed at his conduct; recommending him at the same time to repair at once to the royal box, and there afford the best explanation in his power. Accordingly he had just commenced a warm vindication of his conduct, when his counterfeit, who appears to have followed him to the box, began a no less indignant defence, insisting that he was the real Heidegger and the other an impudent impostor. The king allowed the joke to continue till he perceived his countryman was suffering real pain, when he terminated it by ordering the fictitious Heidegger to pull off his mask.

The Devil Tavern was pulled down in 1788, when the present Child's Buildings, or Child's Place, were erected on its site. In the immediate neighbourhood stood at one time Apollo Court, deriving its name from Ben Jonson's famous club.

Fleet Street, and more especially that portion of it near Temple Bar, is associated with many celebrated names beside those we have already recorded. In Fleet Street, in 1605, the eminent lawyer, Bulstrode Whitelock, was born; and in this street, in June, 1664, died Katherine Philips, the " matchless Orinda," to whom Bishop Taylor addressed his "Measures and Offices of Friendship," and on whose early death Cowley composed an elegiac ode. At the time of the great fire of London, James Shirley, the dramatic poet, was residing in Fleet Street, near the Inner Temple Gate.

Cowley, Michael Drayton, and Izaak Walton appear to have resided within a short distance of each other in Fleet Street. The house in which Cowley was born, and in which he afterward resided with his mother, was, as Aubrey informs us, "in Fleet Street, London, near the end of Chancery Lane." Here, apparently, it was that the perusal of the " Faerie Queene " made him " irrecoverably a poet." "I believe," he writes, "I can tell the particular little chance that filled my head first with such chimes of verses, as have never since left ringing there; for I remember, when I began to read, and take some pleasure in it, there was wont to lie in my mother's parlour — I know not by what accident, for she herself never in her life read any book but of devotion — but there was wont to lie Spenser's works. This I happened to fall upon, and was infinitely delighted with the stories of the knights, and giants, and monsters, and brave houses, which I found everywhere — though my understanding had little to do with all this — and by degrees with the tinkling of the rhyme, and dance of the numbers; so that I think I had read him all over before I was twelve years old, and was thus made a poet."

The residence of Michael Drayton was situated, according to Aubrey, "at the bay-window house next the east end of St. Dunstan's Church in Fleet Street." The site of Izaak Walton's residence, where he carried on the trade of a linen-draper, has also been distinctly pointed out. "He dwelt," writes Sir John Hawkins, "on the north side of Fleet Street, in a house two doors west of the end of Chancery Lane, and abutting on a messuage known by the sign of the Harrow." The shop of Edmund Curll, the bookseller, the sign of which was the "Dial and Bible," stood against St. Dunstan's church; as did that of another well-known bookseller, Smethwick, who describes his shop as "in St. Dunstan's Churchyard, in Fleet Street, under the Dial." This particular locality would seem to have been a very favourite one with the publishers of the seventeenth and eighteenth centuries.

On the south side of Fleet Street, between the Temple Gates, are some ancient houses, one of which was once occupied by the no less celebrated bookseller, Bernard Lintot. The sign of his shop was the "Cross Keys."

"Hence miscellanies spring, the weekly boast
Of Curll's chaste press, and Lintot's rubric post."
— *Dunciad.*

And Gay writes in his "Trivia:"

"Oh Lintot! let my labours obvious lie,
    Ranged on thy stall for every curious eye;
    So shall the poor these precepts gratis know,
    And to my verse their future safeties owe."

Pope's expression of the "rubric post" is said to have reference to the red-lettered title-pages of the books which were exposed for sale on Lintot's stall. The old houses to which we have alluded were probably, at one period, the residence of royalty; the ceiling of one of the rooms being still elaborately ornamented with the Prince of Wales's feather, and the initials P. H., having reference apparently to Henry, Prince of Wales, son of James the First.

Next door to Lintot's was "Nando's," once a much-frequented coffee-house, and the favourite place of resort of Lord Chancellor Thurloe when a young man.

In Fleur-de-Luce Court, Fetter Lane, the notorious Elizabeth Brownrigg practised those fearful cruelties on her female apprentices which have rendered her name so infamous. When accidentally discovered by the neighbours, one of them, Mary Clifford, was found concealed in a cupboard, in a dying state, presenting one of the most shocking objects that the imagination can conceive. According to a contemporary narrative: "Her head was swelled to almost double the natural size, and her neck so much that she could neither speak nor swallow; her mouth stood open, and the surgeon who examined her deposed that she was all one wound from her head to her toes; that her shift stuck to her body; that she was in a fever, and the wounds beginning to mortify from neglect." To another apprentice, Mary Mitchell, the conduct of Brownrigg was found to have been equally inhuman. Her trial and conviction for the murder of Mary Clifford took place on the 12th of September, 1767, two days after which she was executed, amidst the execrations of the assembled multitude. "Her house," writes Leigh Hunt, "with the cellar in which she used to confine her starved and tortured victims, and from the grating of which their cries of distress were heard, was one of those on the east side of the lane, looking into the long and narrow alley behind, called Fleur-de-Luce Court."

Chancery Lane, corrupted from Chancellor Lane, and anciently called New Street, is represented in the reign of Edward the First as having been so full of ruts and holes as to be rendered dangerous, if not entirely impassable. It appears to have been built in the reign of Henry the Third. In this street, at the house of his maternal grandfather, was born, on the 13th of April, 1593, Thomas Wentworth, the great Earl of Strafford. It was in Chancery Lane, also, on the wall of the garden of Lincoln's Inn, that Ben Jonson is stated to have been employed as a bricklayer, with a trowel in one hand and a Horace in the other.

On the west side of Chancery Lane, about seven doors from Fleet Street, Izaak Walton resided from 1627 to 1644. In Chancery Lane, also, near Sergeants' Inn, was the residence of Lord Keeper Guildford. "When his lordship lived in this house," writes his biographer, Roger North, "before his lady began to want her health, he was in the height of all the felicity his nature was capable of. He had a seat in St. Dunstan's Church appropriated to him. His house was to his mind, and having, with leave, a door into Sergeants' Inn garden, he passed daily with ease to his chambers dedicated to business and study. His friends he enjoyed at home, but formal visitants and polite ones often found him out at his chambers."

The shop of the famous bookseller, Jacob Tonson, previously to his removal, in 1696 or 1697, to Gray's Inn Gate, stood at the Fleet Street end of Chancery Lane. Lord Eldon, in the early part of his career, lived in Cursitor Street, Chancery Lane. "Here was my first perch," he said; "how often have I run down to Fleet Market, with sixpence in my hand, to buy sprats for supper!"

In Chancery Lane are situated Sergeants' Inn and Clifford's Inn; the former having been the residence of the sergeants at law at least as early as the reign of Henry the Fourth, when it was styled Faryndon Inne; and the latter deriving its name from having been the inne or mansion of the great family of the Cliffords, afterward Earls of Cumberland. This latter spot is especially interesting as presenting, apparently, the only existing remains of the London residence of an English baron in the Middle Ages. The old mansion was the gift of Edward the Second to Robert, Lord Clifford, whose widow, Isabel, daughter of Maurice, Lord Berkeley, let it to the students of the law, since which time it has continued to be an Inn of Chancery. In the eighth year of Edward the Fourth we find it designated: "Messuag. cum gardino adjacen' vocat' Clifford's Inne, in vico vocat' Fleet Streete, London', nuper Johannis Domini Clifford." The arms of the Cliffords — checky Or and Azure of fesse Gules within a bordure of the third, charged with a Bezanet — are still the arms of this inn or society, and may be seen ornamenting the interesting old hall.

In Clifford's Inn the unbending republican, Major-General Harrison — one of the ten regicides who were executed in October, 1666 — was bred an attorney's clerk.

Close to Clifford's Inn is situated the Rolls' House and Chapel, erected on the site of a college, or asylum, founded by Henry the Third, for converted Jews. On the expulsion of that persecuted people from England, in the reign of Edward the Third, the candidates for admission into the establishment became so few, that in 1377 the king conferred it on the first master in chancery for the time being, as a place for the preservation of the rolls in chancery. The chapel, the work of Inigo Jones, is, in consequence of the interesting monuments which it contains, well worthy of inspection. Among these may be mentioned the fine monument of Dr. John Yonge, said to be the work of Torregiano; the recumbent effigy of Sir Edward Bruce, created Baron of Kinloss by James the First; and a handsome monument to the memory of Sir Richard Allington, of Horseheath, in Cambridgeshire. Among other masters in chancery who lie buried here is Sir John Strange, whose name perhaps may be familiar to the reader by the following well-known quibbling line:

"Here lies an honest lawyer; that is Strange."

Bishop Burnet; Atterbury, Bishop of Rochester; and Bishop Butler, author of the "Analogy of Religion," were severally preachers at the Rolls' Chapel.

One would like to be able to point out the identical house in Chancery Lane, on the steps of which the author of "Christabel" and the "Ancient Mariner" sat down in a "reverie of tumultuous feelings," on the night of his arrival in London after his sudden and ill-advised departure from Cambridge. "Walking along Chancery Lane," writes Mr. Gilman, "Coleridge noticed a bill posted on the wall, — 'Wanted, a few smart

lads for the 15th, Elliot's Light Dragoons.' He
paused a moment, and said to himself: 'Well, I
have had all my life a violent antipathy to soldiers
and horses; the sooner I can cure myself of these
absurd prejudices, the better, and I will enlist in
this regiment.' Forthwith he went, as directed,
to the place of enlistment. On his arrival he was
accosted by an old sergeant, with a remarkably
benevolent countenance, to whom he stated his
wish. The old man, looking at him attentively,
asked him if he had been in bed. On being
answered in the negative, he desired him to take
his, made him breakfast, and bade him rest himself awhile, which he did. This feeling sergeant,
finding him refreshed in his body, but still suffering apparently from melancholy, in kind words
begged him to be of good cheer and consider well
the step he was about to take; gave him half a
guinea, which he was to repay at his convenience,
with a desire at the same time that he would go
to the play and shake off his melancholy, and not
return to him. The first part of the advice Coleridge attended to, but returned after the play to
the quarters he had left. At the sight of him
this kind-hearted man burst into tears. 'Then it
must be so,' said he. This sudden and unexpected
sympathy from an entire stranger deeply affected
Coleridge, and nearly shook his resolution. Still,
considering that the die was cast, and that he
could not in honour even to the sergeant, without

implicating him, retreat, he preserved his secret, and after a short chat they retired to rest. In the morning, the sergeant, not unmindful of his duty to his sovereign, mustered his recruits, and Coleridge with his new comrades was marched to Reading. On his arrival at the quarters of the regiment, the general of the district inspected the recruits, and looking hard at Coleridge with a military air, inquired: 'What's your name, sir?' 'Comberbach,'—the name he had assumed. 'What do you come here for, sir?' as if doubting he had any business there. 'Sir,' said Coleridge, 'for what most other people come, to be made a soldier.' 'Do you think,' said the general, 'you can run a Frenchman through the body?' 'I do not know,' replied Coleridge, 'as I never tried; but I'll let a Frenchman run me through the body before I run away!' 'That will do,' said the general, and Coleridge was turned into the ranks."

Running parallel with Chancery Lane, close to Temple Bar, was till recently Shire or Sheer Lane, so called, according to Stow, because the city of London is here divided from the city of Westminster. In this lane, of late years a wretched thoroughfare, resided Elias Ashmole, the antiquary. Anthony Wood writes, on the 1st of May, 1670: "Dined with Mr. Ashmole, at his house in Sheer Lane, near Temple Bar, and John Davis, of Kidwelly, was there. After dinner, he conducted A. W. to his lodgings in the Middle Temple, where he showed him all his rarities, viz., ancient coins, medals, pictures, old MSS., etc., which took them up near two hours' time."

In Shire Lane the celebrated " Kit-Cat Club," founded in the reign of James the Second, originally held their meetings. According to Defoe, the club obtained its name from one Christopher Catt, or Katt, the maker of certain mutton pies, which formed a favourite and standing dish of the club.

" Immortal made as Kit Kat by his pies."

The *Spectator*, however (No. 9), is of opinion that the club derived its designation from the pies themselves, which were called " Kit-Cats," and not from the name of the maker. For instance, in a Tory pasquinade of the period we find :

" Here did the Assembly's title first arise,
    And Kit-Cat wits first sprung from Kit-Cat pies."

And again, in the prologue to Burnaby's comedy, " The Reformed Wife "(1700) :

" . . . Though the town all delicates afford,
    A Kit-Cat is a supper for a lord."

In the reign of Queen Anne, we find the Kit-Cat Club consisted of thirty-nine noblemen and gentlemen, all of them zealously attached to Protestant ascendency and the house of Hanover. At a later period the Kit-Cat Club held their meetings at the Fountain Tavern in the Strand, whence they

removed to the house of their secretary, the celebrated Jacob Tonson, at Barn Elms, previously the
residence of Cowley, the poet. The portraits of
the most distinguished members were painted by
Sir Godfrey Kneller, of one uniform size, which
is still known among artists as the Kit-Cat size.
At one period we find the club holding their summer meetings at "the Upper Flask," on Hampstead Heath.

> " Or when, Apollo-like, thou'rt pleased to lead
> Thy sons to feast on Hampstead's airy head —
> Hampstead that, towering in superior sky,
> Now with Parnassus does in honour vie."
> — *The Kit-Cats, by Sir R. Blackmore.*

In connection with the Kit-Cat Club, Lady
Mary Wortley Montagu used to relate the following lively anecdote. Her father, Evelyn, Duke
of Kingston, as a man of high rank and a stanch
Whig, was a prominent member of the club.
"One day," said Lady Mary, "at a meeting to
choose toasts for the year, a whim seized him to
nominate her, then not eight years old, a candidate,
alleging that she was far prettier than any lady on
their list. The other members demurred, because
the rules of the club forbade them to elect a beauty
whom they had never seen. 'Then you shall see
her,' cries he; and in the gaiety of the moment,
sent orders home to have her finely dressed, and
brought to him at the tavern, where she was re-

ceived with acclamations, her claim unanimously allowed, her health drunk by every one present, and her name engraved in due form upon a drinking-glass. The company consisting of some of the most eminent men in England, she went from the lap of one poet, or patriot, or statesman, to the arms of another; was feasted with sweetmeats, overwhelmed with caresses, and, what perhaps already pleased her better than either, heard her wit and beauty loudly extolled on every side. Pleasure, she said, was too poor a word to express her sensations; they amounted to ecstasy: never again, throughout her whole future life, did she pass so happy a day."

At a public-house in Shire Lane (No. 86), called the Trumpet (afterward the Duke of York), old Isaac Bickerstaff, the "Tatler," is described as meeting his club. The "Tatler" himself is described as residing at "the upper end" of Shire Lane, whence many of his papers are dated.

Before taking leave of Fleet Street, it remains to us to introduce a brief notice of St. Dunstan's Church, near Temple Bar. St. Dunstan, to whom this church is dedicated, appears to have been one of those gifted beings, who, had he been born in the nineteenth instead of in the tenth century, would have achieved the highest eminence as a man of learning and science, but whose accomplishments, in the dark age in which he flourished, led to his being persecuted as a magician. He was born of noble parentage, at Glastonbury, in Somersetshire, about the year 925. As a sculptor, a chemist, a painter, a musician, and a "worker in iron and brass," he appears to have far outstripped his contemporaries. Thus gifted, he repaired to the court of King Athelstan, in hopes of attaining to the highest honours in the state, but unfortunately, however, genius proved his bane. Among other sorceries of which he was accused, it was represented to the king that his harp — doubtless the Æolian harp of modern days — played of its own accord, without the touch of mortal fingers, and accordingly he was driven from the court, and compelled to return to Glastonbury.

> " St. Dunstan's harp, fast by the wall,
>   Upon a pin did hang a',
> The harp itself, with ly and all,
>   Untouched by hand did twang a'."

On his return to his native place, St. Dunstan became a Benedictine monk in the abbey of Glastonbury, of which he subsequently rose to be abbot. It was while employed in his cell at this place, in forging iron trinkets, that the devil is said to have appeared to him in the shape of a beautiful woman. St. Dunstan, however, it is added, fortunately recognised the foul fiend, and accordingly seizing him by the nose with his red-hot tongs, he made him utter such terrific shrieks as to be heard by the whole neighbourhood. After

the death of Athelstan, he was recalled to court by
King Edmund, and in the reign of King Edred
rose successively to be Bishop of Worcester and
London, and Archbishop of Canterbury. He died
at Canterbury in 987, and was buried under the
high altar of its cathedral.

Although St. Dunstan's Church, Fleet Street,
appears to have been of very ancient foundation,
we discover no direct mention of it till 1237, in
which year the Abbot and Convent of Westminster
transferred it to King Henry the Third, "toward
the maintenance of the house called the Rolls, for
the reception of converted Jews." The present
church was built between the years 1829 and
1833, after designs of the late John Shaw.

Old St. Dunstan's Church appears to have contained the remains of a greater number of lord
mayors, sheriffs, and aldermen, than perhaps any
other church in London. The great Lord Strafford, and Bulstrode Whitelocke, the author of the
well-known "Memorials," were baptised in this
church, and in 1620 Doctor Donne was appointed
to the vicarage.

Many of our readers will doubless recollect the
quaint dial-piece of old St. Dunstan's clock, as it
formerly projected into Fleet Street. In an alcove
above it stood two figures of savages of the size
of life, each holding a knotted club in his right
hand, with which they struck the hours and the
quarters on two bells suspended between them.

We are told that it was "a whimsical conceit, calculated only for the amusement of countrymen
and children," and so in fact it was; and yet,
among the childish recollections of thousands, it
has probably not been the least vivid.

> "When labour and when dulness, club in hand,
>   Like the two figures at St. Dunstan's stand;
>   Beating alternately, in measured time,
>   The clockwork tintinnabulum of rhyme:
>   Exact and regular the sounds will be,
>   But such mere quarter-strokes are not for me."
>   — *Cowper's Table Talk.*

The statue of Queen Elizabeth, a conspicuous
object on the exterior of St. Dunstan's Church,
anciently ornamented the front of old Lud Gate.

The fire of London was arrested within three
doors of St. Dunstan's Church, on one side of
Fleet Street; and, on the other side, within a
short distance from the Inner Temple Gate.

CHAPTER XII.

THE FLEET PRISON.

The Fleet Used as a State Prison at an Early Date — Persons Incarcerated There: Bishops Gardiner and Hooper, Doctor Donne, Martin Keys, Prynne, Lilburne, James Howell, Lords Surrey and Falkland, Sir Richard Baker, Oldys, Wycherley, Sandford — Tyranny and Tortures Practised in the Prison — General Oglethorpe — Prison Burnt at the Great Fire — Fleet Marriages — Keith, the Notorious Fleet Parson.

COULD the walls of the old Fleet Prison have spoken, what fearful tales of vice, misery, and misfortune might they not have unfolded! This interesting pile, with its host of melancholy and historical associations, has passed away for ever. It was very soon after its demolition had commenced that the author wandered through its dingy apartments and narrow corridors, which then offered a striking contrast, by their utter stillness and desolation, to what they must have presented but a short time before, when they were the scenes of reckless riot and crowded wretchedness.

The Fleet — *prisona de la Fleet* — was used as a state prison at least as early as the twelfth century. In the first year of the reign of Richard

the First we find that monarch conferring the custody of it on Osbert, brother to Longchamp, Chancellor of England, and on his heirs for ever; twelve years after which, however, we find King John installing the Archbishop of Wells in its care and custody. From this time till it was burned by the followers of Wat Tyler, in 1381, we discover no important incident connected with its history.

During the reigns of Edward the Sixth and Queens Mary and Elizabeth, the Fleet appears to have been constantly the prison of conscientious sufferers in the cause of religion, many of whom, in the reign of the former queen, suffered martyrdom in the flames.

Hither, shortly after the accession of Edward the Sixth, was committed the learned but unfeeling Stephen Gardiner, Bishop of Winchester, who was doomed to experience within its walls, and subsequently in the dungeons of the Tower, those rigours which he had formerly so unrelentingly practised against the unfortunate Protestants. Hither, also, was committed, on the 1st of September, 1547, the infamous Edmund Bonner, Bishop of London, for refusing to take the oath of supremacy to the young king. Neither of these unworthy prelates appear to have been long inmates of the Fleet. Gardiner was removed to the Tower, and Bonner, after suffering an imprisonment of six weeks, obtained the freedom which he so little deserved.

But the most illustrious prisoner about this period was Bishop Hooper, who has left us a very interesting account of his sufferings in the Fleet, as preserved by Fox in his "Book of Martyrs." "On the 1st of September, 1553," he writes, "I was committed unto the Fleet from Richmond, to have the liberty of the prison; and within five days after I paid for my liberty five pounds sterling to the warden for fees, who immediately upon the payment thereof complained unto Stephen Gardiner, Bishop of Winchester, and so I was committed to close prison one quarter of a year, in the lower chamber of the Fleet, and used very extremely. Then, by the means of a good gentlewoman, I had liberty to come down to dinner and supper; not suffered to speak with any of my friends, but as soon as dinner and supper were done to repair to my chamber again. Notwithstanding, while I came down thus to dinner and supper, the warden and his wife picked quarrels with me, and complained untruly of me to their great friend, the Bishop of Winchester. After one quarter of a year, and somewhat more, Babington, the warden, and his wife, fell out with me for the wicked mass; and thereupon the warden resorted to the Bishop of Winchester, and obtained an order to put me into the ward, where I have continued a long time, having nothing appointed to me for my bed but a little pad of straw, and a rotten covering with a tick and a few feathers therein, the chamber being vile and stinking, until by God's means good people sent me bedding to lie in. On the one side of which prison is the sink and filth of the house, and on the other side the town ditch, so that the stench of the house hath infected me with sundry diseases. During which time I have been sick, and the doors, hasps, and chains being all closed, and made fast upon me, I have mourned, called, and cried for help; but the warden, when he hath known me many times ready to die, and when the poor men of the wards have called to help me, hath commanded the doors to be kept fast, and charged that none of his men should come at me, saying, 'Let him alone, it were a good riddance of him.' And amongst many other times he did thus the 18th of October, 1553, as many are witness. I paid always like a baron to the said warden, as well in fees as for my board, which was twenty shillings a week, besides my man's table, until I was wrongfully deprived of my bishoprick, and since that time I have paid him as the best gentleman doth in his house; yet hath he used me worse, and more vilely than the veriest slave that ever came to the hall commons. The said warden hath also imprisoned my man, William Downton, and stripped him out of his clothes to search for letters, and could find none, but only a little remembrance of good people's names that gave me their alms to relieve me in prison; and to undo them also, the warden delivered the same bill unto the said Stephen Gardiner, God's enemy and mine. I have suffered imprisonment almost eighteen months; my goods, living, friends, and comfort taken from me; the queen owing me by just account eighty pounds or more; she hath put me in prison, and giveth nothing to find me; neither is there any suffered to come at me, whereby I might have relief. I am with a wicked man and woman, so that I see no remedy (saving God's help), but I shall be cast away in prison before I come to judgment. But I commit my just cause to God, whose will be done, whether it be life or death." In the Fleet this exemplary prelate remained a prisoner till his removal to Gloucester, the principal town of his diocese, where he suffered martyrdom by being burnt in a slow fire, on the 9th of February, 1554–55.

Under somewhat romantic circumstances, the pious poet and divine, Doctor Donne, was for a time a prisoner in the Fleet. After having accompanied the Earl of Essex in his expeditions against Cadiz and the Azores, and having travelled for some time in Italy and Spain, he obtained, on his return to England, the appointment of secretary to Lord Chancellor Ellesmere, in whose family he lived contentedly for five years. As it happened, under the roof of his patron he constantly met a beautiful girl, the daughter of Sir George More, chancellor of the Order of the Garter, and lieutenant of the Tower. Between this young lady, who was a niece of Lady Ellesmere, and the secretary there sprung up a mutual attachment, of which Sir George More having obtained some intimation, he removed his daughter in all haste to his own house at Lothesley, in the county of Surrey. The lovers, however, who had already solemnly plighted their troth, not only found means to correspond with each other, but the Rev. Samuel Brooke, an intimate friend of Donne, and formerly his fellow student at Cambridge, was prevailed upon to unite them in a secret marriage.

The virtues and talents of Donne had endeared him to Henry Percy, the "stout old Earl of Northumberland," — himself eminent as a philosopher and a mathematician, — to whom the lovers confided their secret, and who readily undertook the task of breaking the intelligence to, and softening the anger of, Sir George More. Not only, however, did Sir George prove inexorable, but his sister, Lady Ellesmere, being no less incensed than himself, insisted upon the chancellor at once dismissing Donne from his post of secretary, a demand which with the greatest reluctance he complied with. " I part," he said, "with a friend, and with such a secretary as is fitter to serve a king than a subject." Neither was Sir George's anger satisfied till he had obtained the committal of his son-in-law to the Fleet Prison. Fortunately Donne obtained his release after a short durance, when by the kindness and friendship of Sir Francis Wooley, he was enabled to support his wife and young children till the dawn of brighter days.

A still more romantic clandestine marriage, connected with the Fleet, was that of the Lady Mary Grey, the youngest daughter of Henry, Duke of Suffolk. This young lady, being great-granddaughter of Henry the Seventh, by the marriage of her grandfather, Charles Brandon, Duke of Suffolk, to Mary, Queen Dowager of France, daughter of King Henry, was consequently first cousin to Queen Elizabeth. Before she had reached the age of womanhood, the Lady Mary's existence had been far more checkered than commonly falls to the lot of humanity. As a child, she had stood by the altar at Durham House, in the Strand, when her sister, Lady Jane Grey, gave her hand to Lord Guildford Dudley. Within less than two years from that time not only had that sister and that brother-in-law died by the hands of the executioner, but eleven days afterward her father suffered the same fate on Tower Hill. Moreover, she could hardly have attained her fifteenth year, when she suffered a fresh misfortune by the death of her mother. Providence had given her no brother, and, as has been already mentioned, her only surviving sister, Lady Katherine, had been committed to the Tower, where she died, by Queen Elizabeth, for uniting herself to Edward Seymour, Earl of Hertford. Thus, finding herself alone in the world, and exposed to constant peril, from the

jealousy of Elizabeth, who hated her for her affinity
to the throne, the Lady Mary was induced to give
her hand secretly to a private gentleman, Martin
Keys, sergeant-porter to the queen. Keys was
immediately arrested and sent to the Fleet, from
which, after a brief imprisonment, he was set free.
Lady Mary, however, survived his release but a
short time. She died on the 20th of April, 1578,
and was buried near her mother in Westminster
Abbey.

The Fleet Prison is intimately associated with
the misfortunes and mutilation of the learned
Puritan, William Prynne. For his libel on Queen
Henrietta Maria in his famous " Histrio Mastix,"
he was condemned by the star chamber to pay a
fine of £5,000; to stand in the pillory; to be
branded on both his cheeks; to have his nose mutilated; to lose both his ears; and to be kept a prisoner for life. Prynne endured his punishment
with extraordinary constancy and courage. When,
shortly after his mutilation, Sir Symonds d'Ewes
paid him a visit in the Fleet, he found in him " the
rare effects of an upright heart and a good conscience, by his serenity of spirit and cheerful
patience."

Another eminent Puritan who was imprisoned
in the Fleet in the seventeenth century was the
sturdy clothier, John Lilburne, who subsequently
wielded his sword with no less intrepidity at the
battles of Edgehill, Brentford, and Marston Moor

than he had formerly exercised his pen in his furious attacks on the bishops and the Church of England. In consequence of the publication of his seditious works, the " Merry Liturgy " and the " News from Ipswich," he was committed to the Fleet Prison, where he remained till summoned before the star chamber, when he was sentenced by that infamous tribunal to imprisonment, the pillory, and flagellation at the cart's tail. " To the end," runs the sentence, "that others may be the more deterred from daring to offend in the like manner hereafter, the court hath further ordered and decreed that the said John Lilburne shall be whipped through the street from the prison of the Fleet unto the pillory, to be erected at such time and in such place as this court shall hold fit ; and he shall be set in the said pillory, and from thence returned to the Fleet." Accordingly, after having been whipped " smartly " from the Fleet Prison to New Palace Yard, he was there exposed on a pillory set up between the entrance to Westminster Hall and the star chamber. The intrepidity with which he endured his painful and degrading punishment led, of course, to his admirers regarding him as a martyr. " Whilst he was whipped at the cart, and stood in the pillory," writes Rushworth, " he uttered many bold speeches against the tyranny of bishops, etc. ; and when his head was in the hole of the pillory, he scattered sundry copies of pamphlets, said to be seditious,

and tossed them among the people, taking them
out of his pocket." This bold and contumacious
conduct having reached the ears of the members
of the star chamber, who were sitting at the
time, directions were promptly issued by them to
gag him during the remainder of his punishment;
in addition to which orders were sent to the Fleet
to load his hands and feet with irons on his return
thither, and to place him among the meanest and
most degraded prisoners.

The circumstance which led to Lilburne's release
from the close and painful restraint to which he
was subjected was somewhat remarkable. "Having," says Rushworth, "for some time endured
close imprisonment, lying with double irons on his
feet and hands, and laid in the inner wards of the
prison there happened a fire in the prison, of
the Fleet, near to the place where he was prisoner,
which gave a jealousy that Lilburne, in his fury
and anguish, was desperate, and had set the Fleet
Prison on fire, not regarding himself to be burnt
with it. Whereupon, the inhabitants without the
Fleet (the street then not being five or six yards
over from the prison door), and the prisoners, all
cried, 'Release Lilburne, or we shall all be burnt!'
and thereupon they ran headlong, and made the
warden remove him out of his hold; and the fire
was quenched, and he remained a prisoner in a
place where he had some more air." Lilburne
was finally released from the Fleet at the com-

mencement of the Long Parliament, in November, 1640, when the sum of £2,000 was voted for him out of the estates of the royalists.

After perusing these and similar instances of bigotry and brutality on the part of the advisers of Charles the First, can we wonder that when the Puritans obtained the mastery they should in their turn have wreaked vengeance on their oppressors? If retribution was ever made manifest in human affairs, it certainly overtook that haughty conclave whose mildest sentences amounted to mutilation, impoverishment, the pillory, and the gaol. Of those who from time to time sat at the council-table of Charles, in the memorable star chamber at Westminster, how many there were whose fate was destined to be a violent and a bloody one. Charles himself; the chivalrous James, Duke of Hamilton; the severe Strafford; the bigot Laud; and the gay and graceful Holland, perished severally on the scaffold. The haughty Buckingham fell by the hand of an assassin, and the virtuous Falkland on the battle-field.

It was not long after the release of Lilburne that the Fleet opened its gates to receive more than one of the devoted adherents of Charles the First.

> "The arbiters of others' fate
> Were suppliants for their own."

Among these was James Howell, the author of the delightful letters which bear his name. The circumstances of his arrest are related by himself in a letter dated, " The Fleet, November 20, 1643 : " " There rushed into my chamber," he writes, " five armed men, with swords, pistols, and bills, who told me they had a warrant from the Parliament for me. I desired to see their warrant ; they denied it. I desired to see the date of it ; they denied it. I desired to see my name in the warrant ; they denied all. At last one of them pulled a greasy paper out of his pocket, and showed me only three or four names subscribed, and no more. So they rushed presently into my closet, and seized on all my papers and letters, and anything that was manuscript ; and many printed books they took also, and hurled all into a great trunk, which they carried away with them. I had taken a little physic that morning, and with very much ado they suffered me to stay in my chamber, with two guards upon me, till the evening." Howell appears to have borne his misfortune with becoming philosophy. Nine months after his committal, he writes to Sir Bevis Thelwall : " If you would know what cordial I use against it [melancholy], in this my sad condition, I will tell you. I pore sometimes on a book, and so I make the dead my companion ; and that is one of my chiefest solaces. If the humour work upon me stronger, I rouse my spirits, and raise them up toward heaven, my future country ; and one may be on his journey thither, though shut up in prison, and happily go a straighter way than if he were abroad. I consider that my soul, while she is cooped within these walls of flesh, is but in a perpetual kind of prison; and now my body corresponds with her in the same condition. My body is the prison of the one, and these brick walls the prison of the other." Howell remained a prisoner in the Fleet till some time after the execution of his royal master. During his imprisonment, he employed himself in composing many of his celebrated letters, and in other literary labours.

Several other persons whose names are eminent in the literature of our country have at different times been prisoners in the Fleet. Among these may be mentioned the "darling of the Muses," Henry Howard, Earl of Surrey, who about the year 1542, when in the zenith of his fame as a poet and a soldier, was at two different times committed to this prison. On the first of these occasions it was on account of a private quarrel; on the second, for eating flesh in Lent and breaking the windows of the citizens of London with stones from his crossbow; the latter, as Mr. Campbell observes, "a strange misdemeanour, indeed, for a hero and a man of letters." His own excuse was that he acted from religious motives. "He perceived," he said, "that the citizens were sinking into papacy and corrupt manners, and he was desirous, by an unexpected chastisement, to demonstrate to them that divine retribution was about to overtake them."

Lord Surrey describes the Fleet as "a noisome place with a pestilent atmosphere."

Another individual, scarcely less distinguished in the paths of literature, — whose youthful indiscretions led to his being immured within the walls of the Fleet, — was Lucius Cary, Lord Falkland, the future statesman, moralist, and hero. "My lord, in his youth," writes Aubrey, "was very wild, and also mischievous, as being apt to stab and do bloody mischiefs; but it was not long before he took up to be serious, and then grew to be an extraordinary hard student." It was for one of his juvenile misdemeanours that he was committed to the Fleet, as shown by a moving petition addressed to the king by his father, Henry, Lord Falkland, in which he prays for the pardon of his offending son. Shortly after the release of the latter from the Fleet, we find him setting on his travels accompanied by a suitable tutor; from which period we hear nothing more of the profligacy or wildness of the future patriot.

In the Fleet Prison expired one of our most indefatigable students, Sir Richard Baker, the author of the "Chronicle of the Kings of England." Possessed of the manor of Middle-Aston, in Oxfordshire, and at one time high sheriff of that county, he appears till middle age to have lived not only in easy but in affluent circumstances with his wife, Margaret, daughter of Sir George Mainwaring, of Ightfield, in Shropshire. Unfortunately he was induced to involve himself in the pecuniary embarrassments of his wife's family, the result being that he found himself a ruined man and a prisoner in the Fleet. Here he composed several works, among which was a memoir of his own life, which was unhappily destroyed by his son-in-law. At length, "after a life full of troubles and cares," he expired in the Fleet on the 18th of February, 1645, and the next day was buried in the south aisle of St. Bride's Church, Fleet Street.

Another literary inmate of the Fleet Prison was William Oldys, the author of "The British Librarian." So congenial to his tastes and convivial habits was the society which he here met with, that to the close of his life he continued to pass his evenings at a tavern within the rules, which was frequented by his former associates. A short time after his release from the Fleet he published his "Life of Sir Walter Raleigh,' which so delighted the Duke of Norfolk that he conferred upon him the appointment of Norroy king-at-arms. His love of the bottle, added probably to his incessant literary labours, is said to have shortened his life. He died in 1761. Among his MSS. was found the following ingenious anagram, which may probably be new to the reader :

" In word and WILL I am a friend to you,
And one friend OLD is worth a hundred new."

In the Fleet Prison languished for seven years William Wycherley, the dramatist. James the Second happening to attend the theatre one night when Wycherley's " Plain Dealer" was being performed, the play recalled to his mind its gifted author, and he made some inquiries respecting him. Being informed that he was a prisoner in the Fleet, James not only gave orders for the payment of his debts, but settled on him a pension of two hundred a year.

In the Fleet Prison died, in 1693, Francis Sandford, the author of the "Genealogical History." Here also expired, in 1764, Robert Lloyd, the poet, —the friend and schoolfellow of Churchill. The Fleet Prison is doubtless associated with the misfortunes of many more of the sons of genius, Pope speaking ironically of it as the "haunt of the Muses:"

" Others timely to the neighbouring Fleet,
Haunt of the Muses, made their safe retreat."

In 1773, Noorthouck thus describes the Fleet Prison: "The body of this prison is a lofty brick building, of considerable length, with galleries in every story, which reach from one end of the house to the other; on the sides of which galleries are rooms for the prisoners. All sorts of provisions are brought into this prison every day, and cried as in the public streets. A public coffee-house, with an eating-house, are kept in it; and all sorts of games and diversions are carried on in a

large open area, enclosed with a high wall. This
is properly the prison belonging to the Common
Pleas; the keeper is called warden of the Fleet,
which is a place of very great benefit, as well as
trust. Prisoners for debt in any part of England
may be removed by habeas corpus to the Fleet;
and enjoy the rules, or liberty to walk abroad, and
to keep a house within the liberties of this prison,
provided he can find security to the warden for his
forthcoming. The rules comprehend all Ludgate
Hill, from the Ditch to the Old Bailey on the
north side of the hill, and to Cock Alley on the
south side of the hill; both sides of the Old Bailey,
from Ludgate Hill eastward to Fleet Lane; all
Fleet Lane, and the east side of the Ditch or market, from Fleet Lane to Ludgate Hill."

As late as the year 1739 the Fleet Prison continued to be the scene of the most frightful atroc-
ities exercised by those who had authority over its
unfortunate inmates. The person to whose humanity was owing the exposure and mitigation of this
fearful state of things, was Gen. James Oglethorpe,
the fellow soldier of Prince Eugene in his cam-
paigns against the Turks, and the friend of Pope
and Doctor Johnson.

> " Driven by strong benevolence of soul,
> Shall fly, like Oglethorpe, from pole to pole."

General Oglethorpe, whose philanthropic exertions
in founding the colony of Georgia had already ob-

tained immortality for him in the verse of Pope, happened to pay a visit to the Fleet, to a friend of the name of Castell, — an architect, and author of a translation of Vitruvius, — who was a prisoner within its walls. From the lips of this person the general learned quite sufficient of the system of cruelty and oppression which was practised by the warden and his myrmidons, to induce him, in his place in the House of Commons, to move for, and obtain the appointment of a committee to investigate the state of the prisons throughout the kingdom, he himself being appointed its chairman. The first gaol which the committee visited was the Fleet; the names of its warden and deputy warden being John Huggins and Thomas Bainbridge, persons apparently of respectable birth and education. Here, in due time, they satisfied themselves that the most infamous extortions, and the most cruel and arbitrary punishments, notorious breaches of trust, cases in which debtors had been permitted to escape, and others in which they had been unlawfully loaded with irons and thrust into dungeons, were of frequent occurrence.

One of the most striking features in this affair was the contempt with which the committee, in the early stages of their inquiry, appear to have been treated by the functionaries of the prison. For instance, on the occasion of their first visit, on the 27th of February, 1729, among other prisoners whom they examined, was Sir William Rich, a baronet, whom they had found immured in one of the dungeons, loaded with irons. It might have been imagined that the baronet for the future would have been exempted from similar cruel coercion, but no sooner had the committee quitted the prison, than Bainbridge, the deputy warden, sent him back to his miserable quarters. But a still more remarkable instance in point was the warden's treatment of Castell, notwithstanding he was the personal friend of the chairman, General Ogle-thorpe. Being unable to meet an extortionate demand which had been made on him in the shape of a fee, he was ordered to be removed from his apartment, which happened to be in an airy part of the prison, to a quarter in which the small-pox was frightfully raging. Having a nervous horror of this distemper, he passionately entreated, although to no purpose, to be allowed to remain in his present apartments, insisting that, in the event of his removal, he was satisfied he would catch the distemper and die. His words proved prophetic. He was removed, was locked up in his miserable apartment, sickened, and died.

The tyranny and tortures, indeed, practised in the Fleet Prison not a century and a half ago, almost exceed belief. The sufferings which an unfortunate Portuguese, named Jacob Mendez Solas, endured at the hands of the inhuman Bainbridge are especially dwelt upon by the committee. "The said Bainbridge," run the words of the report, "one day called him into the gate-house of the prison, called the Lodge, where he caused him to be seized, fettered, and carried to Corbell's, the sponging-house, and there kept for upward of a week. When brought back into the prison, Bainbridge caused him to be turned into the dungeon, called the Strong Room, on the master's side. This place is a vault like those in which the dead are interred, and wherein the bodies of persons dying in the same prison are usually deposited till the coroner's inquest is passed upon them. It has no chimney or fire-place, nor any light but what comes over the door or through a hole of about eight inches square. It is neither paved nor boarded, and the rough bricks appear both on the sides and top, being neither wainscoted nor plastered. What adds to the damp-ness and stench of the place is its being built over the common sewer, and adjoining to the sink and dunghill where all the filth of the prison is cast. In this miserable place the poor wretch was kept by Bainbridge, manacled and shackled, for near two months." We have the authority of the committee, that, after the release of Solas from his dungeon, when the probability of Bainbridge returning as warden of the Fleet was incidentally mentioned to him, he not only fainted away, but the blood started out of his nose and mouth.

In this case, as in the parallel one of a Capt. John McPhedris, the only offence committed appears to have been an inability to meet the extortionate demands, in the shape of fees, which were made by the authorities of the Fleet. The case of McPhedris was even more cruel than that of Solas. Having been dragged from the apartment of another prisoner, in which he had sought refuge, he was thrust, in spite of his entreaties, into a miserable dungeon, in which there was not even a bed. In vain he implored to be carried before a magistrate, insisting that if he had committed any offence he was willing to be judged and punished by the laws. In vain, too, he complained that his fetters were not only too small for him, but that they caused him intolerable torture. Bainbridge coolly replied that they had been selected with that express intention. Again, when the unfortunate man remonstrated, that torture was forbidden by the laws of England, "Never mind," said Bainbridge, "I will do it first, and answer for it afterward." Such, in fact, was the treatment he experienced, that before long his legs became so severely lacerated by the irons, that symptoms of mortification actually presented themselves. When, at the expiration of three weeks, he was liberated from his miserable dungeon, he was not only incurably lame, but, according to the report of the committee, his eyesight was so much impaired that he was in danger of losing it altogether.

Another instance of the exercise of unlawful and despotic power inquired into by the committee was the case of one Thomas Hogg. This person, who had formerly been a prisoner in the Fleet, but who had since been regularly discharged, was some time afterward passing by the Fleet, when he stopped at the grating to bestow a small sum in charity on his former fellow prisoners. Whatever may have been the reasons, this simple act of kindness appears to have given extraordinary offence to the authorities. Accordingly Hogg was immediately seized by a turnkey named Barnes, and, having been forced into the building, was by Bainbridge ordered to be detained a prisoner. At the time when the committee visited the Fleet, this person had actually continued in confinement upward of nine months without any ostensible excuse or legal authority whatever.

In perusing these extraordinary facts, let us bear in mind that they are derived, not from the common hearsay or gossip of the period, but from a grave official report presented to the House of Commons by their own committee. The House was unanimous in the resolution at which it arrived. It was voted, not only that the charges of extortion and breach of trust had been clearly brought home to the officers of the prison, but that they had barbarously, cruelly, and illegally ill-treated those committed to their charge, in gross violation and contempt of the laws of the land. Huggins, the late warden, and Bainbridge, the deputy warden, were committed close prisoners to Newgate, to-

gether with four of the turkneys, Barnes, Pindar,
Everett, and King, against all of whom the attor-
ney-general received orders to commence a prosecution. Of the guilt of these inhuman wretches
there cannot exist a doubt. Nevertheless, although
the death of more than one fellow creature had
been clearly brought home to them, such was the
state of the laws that they escaped the punishment
which they so richly merited. Twenty years after
his acquittal, Bainbridge is said to have cut his
throat. His cruelties have been immortalised by
the pencil of Hogarth.

"And here can I forget the generous band,
　Who, touched with human woe, redressive searched
　Into the horrors of the gloomy gaol,
　Unpitied and unheard where misery moans?
　Where sickness pines, where thirst and hunger burn,
　And poor misfortune feels the lash of vice?
　While in the land of liberty, — the land
　Whose every street and public meeting glow
　With open freedom, — little tyrants raged;
　Snatched the lean morsel from the starving mouth,
　Tore from cold wintry limbs the tattered weed,
　E'en robbed them of the last of comforts, sleep;
　The free-born Briton to the dungeon chained,
　Or, as the lust of cruelty prevailed,
　At pleasure marked him with inglorious stripes,
　And crushed out lives by secret barbarous ways,
　That for their country would have toiled or bled.
　O great design, if executed well,
　With patient care and wisdom —, tempered zeal!
　Ye sons of mercy! yet resume the search:

Drag forth the legal monsters into light;
Wrench from their hands oppression's iron rod;
And bid the cruel feel the pains they give."
— *Thomson's Winter.*

The Fleet Prison was burned to the ground in the great fire of London, and was again destroyed by fire during the Gordon Riots in 1780, when an infuriated rabble broke into it and set the prisoners at liberty.

One of the most singular features connected with the old Fleet Prison was the celebration of the notorious "Fleet marriages," which, for many years, were performed there by a set of profligate clergymen, who, being already prisoners for debt, stood little in awe of the fine of a hundred pounds, which was formerly the penalty inflicted by the law on those who solemnised irregular marriages. "In walking along the street in my youth," says Pennant, "on the side next to this prison, I have often been tempted by the question, 'Sir, will you please to walk in and be married?' Along this most lawless space was hung the frequent sign of a male and female hand conjoined, with 'Marriages performed within,' written beneath. A dirty fellow invited you in. The parson was seen walking before his shop, a squalid, profligate figure, clad in a tattered plaid nightgown, with a fiery face, and ready to couple you for a dram of gin or roll of tobacco." This account is corroborated by the *Gentleman's Magazine* for 1745, where a corre-

spondent, in lamenting the number of ruinous marriages which then daily took place in the Fleet,
represents them as having been performed by "a
set of drunken, swearing parsons, with their myrmidons, that wear black cloaks, and pretend to be
clerks and registers to the Fleet; plying about
Ludgate Hill, pulling and forcing people to some
peddling ale-house or brandy-shop to be married,
and, even on Sundays, stopping them as they go
to church." Evidence was produced before Parliament, that between the 19th of October, 1704,
and the 12th of February, 1705, no fewer than
2,954 marriages had been solemnised in the Fleet
without either license or the publication of banns.
In many cases, in consideration of the payment of
a small sum of money, the entry of the marriage
was either altogether omitted in the Fleet registers,
or else the names were merely denoted by particular marks.

The vast amount of human misery occasioned
by these easy and hasty marriages, as well as the
number of romantic incidents connected with the
celebration of many of them, may be readily imagined. In Knight's "London" may be found a
full and interesting account of this nefarious traffic,
as well as some very curious extracts from the
marriage registers of the Fleet, from which the
following are taken:

"*Nov. 21, 1742.* Akerman, Richard, turner, of
Christ Church, Bat, to Lydia Collet; brought by

Mrs. Crooks. N. B. They behaved very vilely, and attempted to run away with Mrs. Crooks's gold ring."

"*1744, Aug. 20.* John Newsam, labourer, of St. James, West^r, and Ann Laycock, do. wid^r and wid^w. They ran away with the Scertifycate, and left a pint of wine to pay for. They are a vile sort of people, and I will remember them of their vile usage."

"*1st Oct., 1747.* John Ferren, gent. sen., of St. Andrew's, Holborn, b^r., and Deborah Nolan, ditto, sp^r. The supposed John Ferren was discovered after the ceremony was over to be in person a woman."

"*26th June, 1744.* Nathaniel Gilbert, gent., of St. Andrew's, Holborn, and Mary Lupton ——, at Oddy's. N. B. There were five or six in company. One amongst them seemed to me by his dress and behaviour to be an Irishman. He pretended to be some grand officer in the army. He, ye said Irish gent., told me, before I saw the woman that was to be married, y^t it was a poor girl going to be married to a common soldier; but when I came to marry them, I found myself imposed upon; and, having a mistrust of some Irish roguery, I took upon me to ask what the gentleman's name was, his age, etc., and likewise the lady's name and age. Answer was made me — what was that to me? — d—n me! If I did not immediately marry them, he would use me ill. In short, apprehending it to be a conspiracy, I found myself obliged to marry them *in terrorem*."

Many cases appear to have occurred in which at least one of the parties married by proxy; others, where marriages were most iniquitously antedated, and several cases where certificates were given without the ceremony having been performed at all. For instance:

"November 5th, 1742, was married Benjamin Richards, of the parish of St. Martin's in the Fields, b., and Judith Lance, spin., at the Bull and Garter, and gave g., etc., for an antedate to March the 11th in the same year, which Lilley complied with, and put 'm in his book accordingly, there being a vacancy in the book suitable to the time."

The following are instances of secrecy having been attained by the omission of the surnames of the persons united in marriage:

"*Sept. y⁴ 11th, 1745.* Edwᵈ —— and Elizbeth —— were married, and would not let me know their names; the man said he was a weaver, and lived in Bandyleg Walk, in the Borough."

"*March y⁴ 4th, 1740.* William —— and Sarah ——, he dressed in a gold waistcoat, like an officer, she, a beautiful young lady, with two fine diamond rings, and a black high crown hat, and very well dressed — at Boyce's."

On one occasion, in 1719, we find a young lady, of the name of Ann Leigh, — possessed of an

income of two hundred a year, besides £6,000 in ready money, — not only inveigled away from her friends, and forcibly married in the Fleet Chapel, but also in other respects treated with so much brutality that her life was placed in danger. But a still more remarkable instance of abduction is related in Knight's "London," on the authority of a correspondent to the *Grub Street Journal*, in September, 1732. A lady, it appears, "had appointed to meet a gentlewoman at the old playhouse in Drury Lane, but extraordinary business prevented her coming. Being alone when the play was done, she bade a boy call a coach for the city. One dressed like a gentleman helped her into it, and jumped in after her. 'Madam,' said he, 'this coach was called for me, but since the weather is so bad, and there is no other, I beg leave to bear you company. I am going into the city, and will set you down wherever you please.' The lady begged to be excused, but he bade the coachman to drive on. Being come to Ludgate Hill, he told her his sister, who waited his coming but five doors up the court, would go with her in two minutes. He went and returned with his pretended sister, who asked her to step in one minute, and she would wait upon her in the coach. Deluded with the assurance of having his sister's company, the poor lady foolishly followed her into the house, when instantly the sister vanished, and a tawny fellow, in a black coat and black wig, appeared. 'Madam, you are come in good time; the doctor was just a-going.' 'The doctor!' said she, horribly frightened, fearing it was a madhouse, 'what has the doctor to do with me?' 'To marry you to that gentleman: the doctor has waited for you three hours, and will be paid by you, or that gentleman, before you go.' 'That gentleman,' said she, recovering herself, 'is worthy a better fortune than mine,' and begged hard to be gone. But Doctor Wryneck swore she should be married, or, if she would not, he would still have his fee, and register the marriage for that night. The lady, finding she could not escape without money or a pledge, told them she liked the gentleman so well, she would certainly meet him to-morrow night, and gave them a ring as a pledge, 'which,' said she, 'was my mother's gift on her death-bed, enjoining that, if ever I married, it should be my wedding-ring;' by which cunning contrivance she was delivered from the black doctor and his tawny crew." The conspirators, satisfied with the booty they had obtained, allowed her to depart, and, as may be readily conceived, she never returned to redeem her pledge.

Among the most notorious of the Fleet parsons was the well-known Alexander Keith, who about the year 1730 opened a chapel in May Fair for the performance of clandestine marriages. Having been excommunicated in 1742, and committed to the Fleet Prison, he opened a small chapel within its walls, which appears to have proved a scarcely less profitable speculation to him than his former one in the more fashionable locality of May Fair. At length, however, the Marriage Act, which came into operation on the 25th of March, 1753, effectually put a stop to his discreditable vocation. It was doubtless a bitter pill for Keith to swallow, and accordingly he entered his protest against it in an amusing publication, entitled "Observations on the Act for Preventing Clandestine Marriages," by the Rev. Mr. Keith, D. D., with his portrait prefixed. To George Montagu, Walpole writes, on the 11th of June, 1753: "I shall only tell you a bon mot of Keith's, the marriage broker, and conclude. 'D—n the bishops!' said he, — I beg Miss Montagu's pardon, — 'so they will hinder my marrying! Well, let them; but I'll be revenged! I'll buy two or three acres of ground, and by G— I'll under-bury them all.'"

As the day approached on which the Marriage Act was to become the law of the land, the number of individuals of the lower orders who hastened to take advantage of the intervening period was remarkable. On the last day especially, the 24th of March, no fewer than 217 couples were united, of whom a hundred couple were married by Keith. Keith himself, it may be mentioned, died in the Fleet Prison in 1758.

It was in the Fleet that the libertine and improvident poet, Charles Churchill, formed his juvenile and imprudent marriage. According to Southey, in his " Life of Cowper," the marriage took place in the interval between Churchill leaving Westminster School and his graduating at Trinity College, Cambridge.

END OF VOLUME II.